Lawn
Keeping

ROBERT W. SCHERY

A SPECTRUM BOOK

PRENTICE-HALL, INC., Englewood Cliffs, New Jersey

Library of Congress Cataloging in Publication Data

Schery, Robert W
  Lawn keeping.

  (A Spectrum Book)
  Includes index.
  1. Lawns.   I. Title.
SB433.S36   635.9′64′0973   76–4565
ISBN 0–13–526889–3
ISBN 0–13–526863–X pbk.

ROBERT W. SCHERY is Director of The Lawn Institute
and the author of *A Perfect Lawn.*

A Spectrum Book

10 9 8 7 6 5 4 3 2 1

Printed in the United States of America

Prentice-Hall International, Inc., *London*
Prentice-Hall of Australia Pty. Limited, *Sydney*
Prentice-Hall of Canada, Ltd., *Toronto*
Prentice-Hall of India Private Limited, *New Delhi*
Prentice-Hall of Japan, Inc., *Tokyo*
Prentice-Hall of Southeast Asia Pte. Ltd., *Singapore*

Contents

Preface

Lawn Keeping is obviously about lawns and their care. I have tried to word it simply and forthrightly, avoiding terminology peculiar to the professionals. But it would be a disservice not to acknowledge the "reasons why" that call for the suggested procedures. Many measures can be undertaken to spruce up the lawn a bit in one way or another. However, *Lawn Keeping* emphasizes the relatively few that are of paramount importance, such as choice of grass, mowing, fertilization, and weed control. The reader must decide for himself how far beyond these basics he wants to go. Obviously, where one lives has a bearing upon what is important. Lawns can be grown in the eastern United States without irrigation, but in the Southwest only on the mountaintops unless watered. In a humid climate the lawn will have a great assortment of weeds with which to contend, while in drylands (at least with new lawns) such weeds do not occur naturally. Thus peculiarities of climate and environment much influence the kind of care you will give your turf.

America seems bent upon reassessing old values. A dichotomy

shows up with respect to lawns: (1) Most of us like a "nice" lawn, traditional since America moved to the suburbs; but (2) an increasing minority wonders if this represents true value in times that call for increased conservation and husbanding of energy. I sympathize with the latter viewpoint and, indeed, am inclined to let "nature take over" in those rare situations where the size of the property and the appropriateness of its surroundings permit it. But I very much fear that an attitude credited to the English—of "what's in the lawn doesn't make much difference; anything green is good, and the less the maintenance the better"—will not find much of a following in America. For one thing, few parts of America are graced with the benign, maritime climate that England enjoys, where the land seems to support some kind of cover no matter how abused it is (as from heavy rolling). Nor are American homeowners and custodians of commercial properties accustomed to overlooking a pocked and weedy sward in favor of landscaping features in the flower beds beyond. Few are likely to sit idly by watching an expensive lawn investment deteriorate into a weed-patch.

America is fond of technology; new devices or new products are quickly offered to "correct" every ill and any inconvenience, real or imagined. Without common sense, one can become so overloaded with temperamental gadgetry and special programs that tending lawn does indeed become a burden. Sports fields and golf courses often employ artificial "soils" compounded to prescription and provide elaborate "automatic" water regulation that almost requires a Ph.D. to design and an engineer to supervise! For average homeowners most such systems would be a constant worry and a handicap. The promised results hardly merit the expense and effort. Most of the time elaborate programs don't make that much difference in lawn quality, either; unwisely used they can even spawn disaster.

We all like the convenience technology brings. But some of the side effects are worrisome. The official preoccupation these days with "safety" is a case in point. Consumers are presumed to have next to no intelligence and to exercise no responsibility for proper use of a product. To spare from harm a few dunderheads who refuse to follow directions, everyone must endure increased cost and inconvenience. Some of the "protective" features proposed for lawnmowers, for example, would make them so cumbersome as to negate their usefulness, so expensive that few would avail themselves of newer models, so involved to service that they'd be cheaper to discard than to repair. All this because some theorist, probably little acquainted with lawn keeping himself, equates marginal features, no matter how difficult to engineer, with the social good. Complicated devices, frustrating to maintain, are not conducive to lawn-keeping tranquility.

Accomplishing things in the simplest, most practical way and avoiding unnecessary measures are part of the philosophy of this book. This means adapting as well as is possible to local conditions. Of course, as we will see, a lawn is by definition "unnatural," since it is a regulated crop rather than nature's way for clothing the land; thus it can never be completely adapted. Owner expectations, too, vary from constant concern to carefree disregard. So plenty of room for choice exists, not only as to what kind of lawn, but as to the dedication with which it will be tended. Whatever that decision, I believe the reader will find food for thought, if not stern admonitions, in *Lawn Keeping*. No magic formula guarantees success; the more demanding the expectation, the greater will be the effort needed. With sufficient effort an elegant monoculture (such as are the greens on most golf courses) can be had; most of us, however, prefer to settle for a bit less elegance in exchange for greater convenience and less expensive maintenance. May the remainder of this book help you decide upon the lawn most suitable to your needs and guide you towards the most practical maintenance for it.

1 Rules of the Game: Ecology

All living things interrelate with their environment, and that's all ecology really is. Don't be scared by the formal name; ecology stems from the simplest of principles, that an organism will respond to its environment. It may thrive and increase, linger on fitfully, or run down and be lost to the community. Yet, ecology is also exceedingly complex and comprehensive. We are not capable of understanding all the complexities of a "web of life." We see and measure apparent cause and effect, but we are usually quite unaware of the myriad of subtle side effects involving microorganisms, the chemical milieu, and the internal condition of the organism (does it "feel good" or have a "hangover"?). Scientists can observe, let us say, the response of grass to a particular temperature. A creeping bentgrass, for example, when grown at artificially high temperatures adopts a completely different form; its leaves become short, erect, and stiff until it is hardly recognizable as a bentgrass. But we don't know how the temperature incites such drastic response, whether through hormonal changes, chemical imbalances, or even indirectly through influence of microorganisms that fraternize with the grass.

Similarly, we see a progression of events when the lawn is mowed too short: Grass roots grow less deeply, matching topgrowth; sunlight reaches the soil more fully, warming it appreciably; and root growth is further reduced because of the higher temperature. The grass then suffers from drought, because more moisture is lost from the warmer, more exposed ground, and weakened grass roots cannot range so profusely in search of water. A chain reaction has been set in motion that feeds upon itself to the detriment of the lawn. But this is only the obvious skein of events. What happens in the thatch, to the organisms which build soil fertility, with water-air relationships that may favor one fungus over another (perhaps allowing disease to erupt), and so on? We really don't know, but for certain all these things (and many more) are interrelated. Or take a simple pH reading, which tells us whether a soil is acid or alkaline. But why does a low pH confer advantage on a fescue grass compared to a bluegrass or a ryegrass? We know it happens, but not why (although under certain kinds of stress, such as deep shade, fescues do several things "better" than does bluegrass, such as "breathing" more efficiently and not using up food reserves so much).

Fig. 1-1 The same ecosystem, summer and winter, presents extremes to which organisms must adapt. This bluegrass turf actually gets along very well under a protective snow cover; it has a harder time with the heat of summer (see Chapter Two).

Fig. 1-2

Unfortunately, man has disturbed nature's balance so much that we are confronted today mostly with "unnatural" conditions compared to those found in the world only a few tens of thousands of years ago. Floras have been wiped out (forests are felled, prairies are plowed), destruction of soil proceeds apace (it is bulldozed, lost through erosion, exposed to various deteriorating influences), and civilization spews its pollution upon the land and into the waterways (an insult that could be absorbed were human occupation not so voluminous). Certainly your lawn's "climate" is drastically changed from what it would have been prior to civilization. Some believe that large-scale world climatic patterns have been altered as well. We grope for answers, while still furthering change through use of pesticides, heavy use, and unnatural demands, only belatedly recognizing that in this finite world we had better begin appreciating ecological consequences more than has been customary.

THE LAWN

So much for the "big picture"; let's zero in on a lawn, or a would-be lawn, instead. Do you imagine that it's simply a thin stratum of green grass atop a solid soil? No, indeed; it's a complex world of its own. Grass may dominate visually, and a closer look will almost surely reveal more than one kind of grass. If your lawn is like most, there are many nongrass plants as well, those we call weeds. The lawn supports quite a variable population. Habitat varies, too. For example, in some places the lawn is shaded, elsewhere not; tiny creatures deep in the sod, as well as macroscopic forms, respond to such contrasting habitats. Did you ever notice that crabgrass won't grow in the shade? It's a lawn problem only in the sun!

Trees vary, too, and their roots do curious things to the soil environment. Of course tree roots can grab much of the fertility and most of the moisture from a lawn, but there is more to it. Tree roots (indeed almost all species and plant parts) secrete distinctive compounds which influence the growth of other organisms. Thus silver maple roots have been proven to repress bluegrasses, not only competitively (by competing for resources such as nutrients and water), but chemically as well. Some grasses repress others, and some forbs (broadleaf prairie plants) inhibit various grasses. The experts term this allelopathy, which first drew attention when it was noted that desert plants somehow restrained seedlings and competing vegetation from establishing themselves in the vicinity of the parent plant (where the battle for moisture would be critical to survival).

The lawn is not only a world of plant life. Millions of "bugs" (bacteria) and small animals occupy each square inch of sod and soil. Larger creatures feed upon the smaller, in a food chain based upon the microorganisms. Insects such as aphids, ants, beetles, fritflies, and wasps find their niches. Isopods are at home in the soil, grubs feed on roots, mites suck plant juices from foliage, and spiders prey upon certain insects. Birds come down to feast; cats chase the birds; dogs run the cats away; children corral the dogs; and a few old curmudgeons chase the kids off the grass. A square foot of average lawn must support hundreds of kinds of organisms. Just which kinds they are will vary from place to place, depending upon moisture, fertility, shade, organic matter, mowing, use, types of stress, and so on. Earthworms aerate the soil, recycling organic matter; other "worms" may help, too, but sometimes they cause trouble (as do some eelworms [nematodes] which attack grass roots). All the while the fungi are fighting one another for sustenance and *lebensraum.* Some are parasitic, some subsist only on dead materials, and they seem to hold one another in balance. The lawn is indeed an arena for give-and-take, one full of life.

ADAPTATION

Obviously, from what has been said, the lawn, like agricultural crops, is a circumspect and contrived ecosystem, a limited weave of ecological relationships. It is controlled by man and superimposed upon a natural ecological framework which in turn has been altered to some extent by man. The hoped-for end result from the lawn ecosystem is a grass community having, as nearly as possible, all plants looking and behaving alike (a monoculture). These are kept attractively low (by mowing) and are expected to form a durable ground cover for outdoor living space analogous to the carpeting indoors. This outdoor carpet is to be functional at all times of year, never unpleasant, toxic, or hazardous. It's a pretty large order, one that ordinarily takes some doing! The requirements mostly go against nature's grain. Nature, for one thing, prefers diversity rather than uniformity. Natural grasslands, one will note, sport many kinds of grasses and forbs, and they have seasonal cycles in which now one, now another species predominates. Only where man sows crops, be it for lawns, farm fields, or forest regeneration, is monoculture imposed upon nature, requiring a constant battle to maintain it.

Of course, nature tolerates only the fittest, at least for the long term; what grows most efficiently in the local environment is what survives, even though it is not necessarily what man prefers. When we demand bluegrass or bentgrass elegance in our lawn, we may not be choosing the kind of plant which could cope best with the environment (often brush or trees would do better than grass). By insisting that the lawn keep us out of the mud year-round, we further limit our choice of species; aggressive summer annuals such as crabgrass are obviously unsuitable. Even most perennials are highly seasonal. Yet, whatever is planted must function in spite of being constantly decapitated (mowed), used (as for a playground), and frequently unintelligently managed (fertilizing or irrigating improperly may benefit weeds more than the grass). For imposing such strictures upon the ecosystem, energy (effort and cost) must be spent. The further one diverges from natural conditions, the greater is the effort likely to be necessary to achieve a good lawn.

Sometimes one, sometimes another ecological input will have major influence. In arid lands such as the Great Plains and the Southwest (Fig. 1-3), irrigation must come first if there is to be any presentable lawn at all. Once you can water, maintaining a lawn-like ecosystem comes easily. In another region the chief problem will be entirely different; it may be poor, sandy soil on the coastal plain that limits lawn making, a predilection for disease and water-loving weeds in humid, misty habitats leeward of lakes or ocean, or indecisive climate in the border states (where the weather accommodates neither northern nor southern grasses well). Sometimes one can do much to overcome adverse ecological factors, by improving a poor soil, watering a dry habitat, spraying for pests, or choosing special kinds of grass suited to less-than-ideal conditions. With enough "babying," turf can be maintained in almost any situation. Publicity has been given a lawn grown on concrete, with moisture and fertility supplied constantly, as to a hydro-

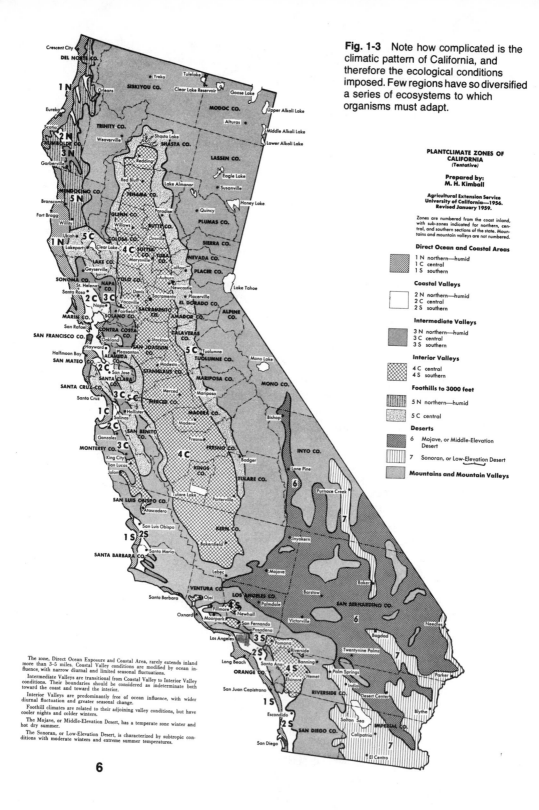

Fig. 1-3 Note how complicated is the climatic pattern of California, and therefore the ecological conditions imposed. Few regions have so diversified a series of ecosystems to which organisms must adapt.

ponic crop growing in the greenhouse. One can even alter the "climate" to some extent, by creating shade, protecting against desiccating winter winds, contouring the land (so that the slopes slant less into the summer sun and retain water rather than letting it run off quickly). Some such practices are simple and relatively inexpensive; others are complex and prohibitively costly. One must weigh the importance of having a top-quality lawn against these costs.

By way of example let's explore how making a lawn in Ohio jibes with or is at cross-purposes with nature's intent. The natural vegetation in Ohio, as in most of the eastern United States, was originally forest. This forest has been cut and cleared, but we build our lawns upon soils developed under deciduous forest. Such soils generally contain clay and silt, are not rich, but are retentive and have good capacity for improvement. Left alone the land would return to trees, but this reversion is prevented by cutting and mowing. Fertility of the soil is improved through fertilization, and the grass growth thus encouraged further improves the soil by infiltration of fine rootlets. Rainfall adequate to sustain forest is more than enough for grass; in this climatic belt lawns can generally survive without irrigation, although watering during dry spells keeps the grass more presentable. But adequate rainfall has its own disadvantages: Moisture can encourage disease, and it may leach fertility from the soil, even eroding the soil itself before a lawn becomes established. And habitat is equally as good for the weeds as for the grass. Weeds are abundant, and the battle against them unending. But on the whole pests are reasonably well controlled with pesticides, and by encouraging a thriving turf through timely maintenance (mowing considerately high, fertilizing especially in autumn, tackling the weeds before they overwhelm the grass). Growth may be so good that accumulated residues (thatch) becomes a problem, and must be removed or be controlled biologically.

All told, the lawn ecosystem is not so conservative of energy as letting the yard become a forest would be. But the climate is nonetheless reasonably conducive to success with turf and needs only moderate molding to yield an acceptable lawn. Chief input will be mowing, a prime consideration. Moderate fertilization (its intensity to depend upon the kind of grass and the luxuriance demanded) and the occasional elimination of weeds are the only other concerns of much moment. Most lawn owners will not find lawn keeping too onerous, even as costs rise and shortages develop; the attractiveness of a living grass carpet outdoors justifies what is a moderate expense for most people at current standards of living.

POLLUTION

Lawns are sometimes assumed to contribute to pollution of the environment, and occasionally they may. But on the whole they benefit their surroundings far more than they hurt it. Suburban lawns and urban turfs help make cities habitable. They insulate the ground, keeping it cooler in summer, warmer in winter. They protect against erosion and the clogging of waterways, and lessen cleanup of drainage channels. To some extent they free the air of pollutants by picking up things like sulphur dioxide and carbon monoxide and incorporating them into harmless molecules. They recycle noxious materials, constantly refresh the air, and make offending substances innocuous. They help to make tolerable "heat islands" such as our cities, reducing infrared surface temperatures by as much as 50°F., and air temperatures as much as 7°F. Where vegetation grows, child mortality, suicide, and energy consumption are less than in places where there are no plantings. A California study showed tall grass to measure 67°F on a warm day, short grass 83°F, bare soil 85°F, and plastic grass 125°F (about what a sidewalk would be). Turf supports "fun and games," including recreational complexes that are part of megalopolis. Plantings hold down dust, conserve rainfall (prevent flooding), and beautify harsh surroundings. This is quite a series of pluses, against which only a few negatives must be weighed.

An accusation often leveled against lawns has to do with fertilization. "Contaminating" nutrients are presumed to get into the runoff and seep into ground waters, with consequent eutrophication (choking with vegetation) downstream. Occasionally this might be true, but only in the very rare instances where lawns are overfertilized (increasingly unlikely with the rising cost of fertilizer) or where fertilizer is spilled. Tests of water seeping through sod show that very little in the way of applied nutrients escapes the grass itself, and secondarily the topsoil in which the grass is rooted, to become part of the ground water. Even surface runoff results in very little stream contamination, since fertilizer applied to the lawn is almost immediately absorbed by the grass or fixed by the soil and its microflora. More often than not fertilizer reduces rather than increases pollution, because it encourages the grass to more vigorous growth, enhancing all the benefits cited earlier. Research shows that of the nutrient charge in runoff, ninety-eight percent results from erosion (i.e., is linked to soil particle movement, which grass prevents), and only about two percent results from soluble nutrients dissolved in the water (less than is ordinarily found in rainfall). So, fear not pollution as a result of lawn keeping; it will in no way compare with that from industrial wastes and sewage.

In this era of power mowers, lawn keeping does add to noise pollution. But lawn equipment is no more offensive than are motorcycles and street traffic. Mower manufacturers are becoming more conscious of noisy motors, and better-muffled powerplants can probably be anticipated in the future.

Pesticides are feared by many, largely because they are poorly understood. "Horror stories" imply that the environment is being poisoned because laboratory tests administering thousands of times the concentration of chemical ever likely to be encountered by people or pets cause carcinogenesis or other effects in test animals. One scientific test revealed yogurt to be more harmful than a chemical being restricted, when force-fed at a similar concentration! Everything encountered can be hazardous at inordinately high rates, even though it is useful as normally utilized. Correct usage according to label directions should be the answer, not prohibition of helpful chemicals. Of course inherently hazardous materials should not be released generally, but with today's requirements for label clearance (needed for sale in the United States) the guarantee against this is almost certain.

DDT, once widely used for insect control, and similar chlorinated hydrocarbons have received much criticism because of their persistence and concentration in the food chain sufficient to interfere with the breeding of birds and to cause other ecosystem upsets. But newer evidence suggests that the assays which "find" these materials in the environment often give erroneous identification. Here again good judgment should prevail, and "hard" pesticides should certainly not be used unnecessarily. But there should be no cause for concern in using convenient weed killers, insecticides, and fungicides when really needed. Almost all that are offered today are biodegradable and will not become a persistent risk. Probably the tobacco you smoke and the coffee you drink are far more toxic than encounters with pesticides that are properly used.

Ecology

EXPERIENCE makes all of us ecologists to the extent that we soon learn that habitat shapes the plant and animal life occupying it. It is worth our time here to examine ecological definitions and lingo.

ECOLOGISTS view organisms as composing *communities*, and their environs and interrelationships as an *ecosystem*. Green plants, of course, capture the energy of sunlight through photosynthesis, the driving force of the ecosystem; all except a few primitive forms of life feed at the photosynthetic trough. Eventually a community reaches a relatively stable state in tune with "average" conditions. This is the *climax* phase, the assemblage of the organisms best adapted to the prevailing conditions. A community is usually less complex where conditions are more stringent, as in the Arctic compared to the tropics or in exposed thin-soil habitat compared to rich prairie. Land that is disturbed by man generally represents a stringent habitat and a less-complex ecosystem.

SOME living thing will occupy almost every bit of space in a climax community, taking advantage of any opportunity for sustenance; almost all *ecological niches* become filled. The penalty for disturbing an ecosystem is an increased expenditure of energy to maintain the alteration. Of course, energy in all its forms is becoming increasingly dear. In the lawn the use of specially bred low-growing cultivars, tolerant of disease, reduces the need for special attention (energy expenditure) and makes lawn keeping a lot easier.

THE ECOSYSTEMS man imposes upon former forest lands mostly utilize introduced species. Likewise, the most serious pests invading the lawn are typically foreigners. Some of the worst lawn weeds—crabgrass, dandelion, plantain, knotweed, chickweed, and purslane, for example—are all camp followers of the white man from the Old World. They are truly the world's most "successful" plants, self-starting and getting along famously wherever the land is disturbed. We don't like this rugged aggressiveness in weeds, but we admire it in our leading lawngrasses.

ECOSYSTEMS evolve in a slow, orderly fashion with one community gradually supplanting another in response to environmental change. This is *succession.* A lawn left alone would first grow weedy, then (in humid regions) change to scrubby brush, and eventually become woodland. To retain a lawn, a homeowner must keep it "juvenile," in an early successional stage. This, of course, is contrary to nature's bent, which trends towards complexity and a steady-state balance having little net productivity.

DARWIN long ago showed that nature selects the best-adapted organisms to dominate any ecosystem, *natural selection;* poorly adapted organisms face extinction. So it is in the lawn. Each bit of attention, or inattention, accorded the lawn has its influence. Excessively low mowing is to the lawn what overgrazing is to the range; grass consistently deprived of food-making green leaf gradually weakens, thins, and is supplanted by prostrate weedy growth such as spurge and knotweed. Under these conditions the weeds are better *adapted* than is the grass.

IT'S NICE to have solid stands of "the very best." But an ecosystem based on such *monoculture* goes contrary to nature's grain; complexity better equips the ecosystem to withstand disturbance and to persist (to have *survival value*). A monoculture can be all but wiped out by an affliction to which the identical plants are vulnerable. Because of their limited genetic leeway, monocultures are especially sensitive to change and variation; they are thus unstable and vulnerable to invasion by better-adapted species. It is costly to maintain a monoculture, and the risks are high.

A SHIFT away from rigid reliance upon pesticides towards letting nature handle some of the load seems to be gaining acceptance. Ninety-nine percent of all pests are estimated to be checked by natural predators or by environmental change (drought, seasonal sequence, and the like), anyway. But that remaining one percent can be pretty devastating, especially for a monoculture. *Integrated control* can help by pitting natural enemies against the pests whenever possible; chemical treatments are saved for important occasions or where pests get clearly out of hand. Sometimes pesticides worsen conditions: the predators are affected more than the pest, and freed from predators the remaining pest population *explodes.* Of course, biological controls offend purists who insist on eradication rather than containment. Obviously, the predator will die out if all its prey disappears.

PLANTED to delectable modern cultivars, nurtured with fertilizer, kept "immature" by frequent mowing, a lawn becomes a very *productive* plant community. Gross photosynthetic accomplishment is not, however, compensated for in most lawns by equivalent "predator" consumption. True, earthworms consume a lot of spent vegetation, and clippings decay, recycling their nutrients. But most lawns lean towards accumulation, with net productivity similar to crop plantings like a pasture. This can be remunerative if you want "hay" for mulch or compost. More often it spells extra effort to keep the ecosystem in balance. If accumulation much exceeds decomposition (or if you interfere with decomposition as by applying fungicides that restrain decay organisms) thatch tends to build up. Thatch is a bane of the modern, intensively maintained lawn. It consists of undecomposed tissues at the base of the sod which can get so thick as to impede fertilizer, even water, from reaching the rootzone. It interferes with aeration and encourages shallow rooting. In some cases thatch may harbor pest innoculae.

ADAPTED organisms tolerate moderate variations in the environment and still survive. As a rule there is little visual response to stress until a certain breaking point is reached. Homeowners frequently get into trouble by assuming that "where a little is good, a lot is better." Often, a lawn simply does not have the *carrying capacity* (the soil depth, the fertility, the minimal moisture) necessary to maintain a grass population of the density the homeowner would like. It's like overpopulation on a low resource base, resulting in a reduced standard of living for all.

POLLUTION comes from overloading the ecosystem with an imbalance beyond its capacity to absorb it. The most troublesome pollutants are entirely new substances with which the ecosystem has had no "experience," no opportunity to evolve either resistant or consuming organisms. Synthesized chemicals such as DDT are a prominent example; small quantities have a profound effect since few organisms have yet "learned" to cope with the strange molecules. Lawn insecticides and fungicides can easily upset the micro-ecological balance unless cautiously used.

BUT QUANTITATIVE pollution is a more general problem, the overloading of the ecosystem with too much of something or other. Modern technology provides many opportunities for pollution, but relatively few tricks for curing an upset once it has been triggered.

WE SOMETIMES forget that the lawn *microclimate* is not what the weather gauge records at the usual breast height. Seemingly inconsequential happenings impose stress upon the grass; as with the Sahara Desert, expanding even wider as the forest is cut and the land overgrazed at its borders, the lawn may relentlessly give way to its burdens. An interface no more than a few inches in depth dominates the lawn's ecosystem, so "think small" in your grass-tending operations and consider the many obscure forces operative there.

The Team:
Leading
2 Lawngrasses

That "lawns" are planted to "grasses" is generally taken for granted. There are some exceptions to the practice, such as the use of Dichondra (a genus of the morning glory family) in Southern California; and in some parts of the world low, trailing plants of any sort are left to compose the lawn, as was frequently the situation in America until well along into the twentieth century. But for the last half century, at least, grass has become so closely identified with "lawn" as to be almost synonymous. Indeed, the grass family is remarkably efficient as a ground cover, the mainstay for prairies, meadows, and pastures long before civilization had progressed enough for humankind to worry over lawns.

Grasses have worked out so well where land is grazed or mowed because the plant's growing point (meristem) hugs the ground and is not lost to grazing or clipping. New tissue develops from the base of the leaf and from the crown imbedded at soil level; then as tip growth is grazed or clipped, new leaf forms continuously at a reasonably steady pace. Contrast this with most plants, the growing points of which

Fig. 2-1 Lawngrasses are beautifully adapted to mowing. This is a mixed stand of Highland bentgrass and bluegrass.

are located at the tips of the stems; when the plant is sheared it takes many days for new buds to form in leaf axils farther down the stem. If defoliation is quite severe, the plant may even die. For grazed grasslands, grass plants that are especially low-growing have evolved through natural selection, and for lawns man has selected decumbent types for his turfs—not upright-growing species such as corn or bamboo (which are also grasses). The anatomical progression by which various turfgrasses assume their typical form and habit differs greatly, but the concept of "basal growth," even if oversimplified here, is certainly one of the chief attributes qualifying the leading lawngrasses for utilization in turf that must be constantly mowed.

GRASS ADAPTATION

Lawngrass species will be reviewed in more detail shortly, with particular adaptations noted. Some, for example, are well suited to low fertility, others to high. Some can stand a droughty habitat, others like moisture. Some withstand shade well, others do poorly out of the sun, and so on. These individual traits are mostly characteristics of species, or even of varieties (more correctly *cultivars,* a term derived from the words *culti*vated *vari*ety). But there are also broad adaptations, based upon the basic physiology of differing groups of grasses. Of most concern is whether a grass does well in a reasonably warm (subtropical) climate or in a cooler (temperate) one.

Grasses adapted to warm climates mostly have an efficient "four-carbon" scheme of food building; cooler-climate grasses have mostly adopted the "three-carbon" pathway. These respective groups are usually referred to as "warm-season" and "cool-season" grasses, al-

13

though it is realized, of course, that much overlap occurs. Cool-season grasses do withstand quite hot summers, and warm-season grasses relatively cold winters. Henceforth, we can simply refer to these two contrasting groups as "northern" and "southern" grasses, which, in North America, are best adapted to the regions indicated on the map (Fig. 2-2). Northern species are most productive when days are bright

Fig. 2-2 Black indicates the southern species of grass; gray indicates the northern species. Lighter shading west of mid-continent indicates that irrigation is necessary.

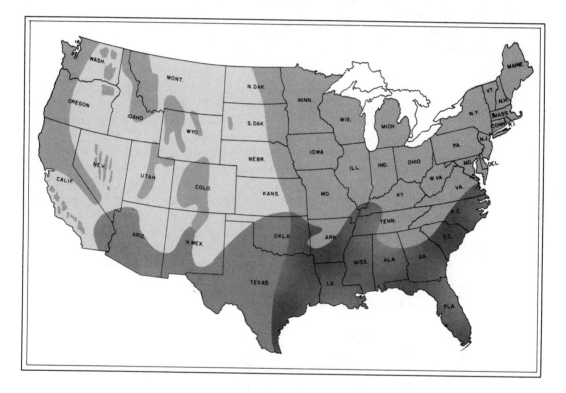

and moderately warm (60°F to 80°F), nights cool; at temperatures above about 85°F catabolism (negative metabolism sacrificing stored energy) tends to exceed anabolism (positive metabolism accumulating stored energy) causing a photosynthetic (food production) deficit. But the grasses do well at temperatures even so low as freezing. Southern grasses thrive even when temperatures approach 100°F, but they become inefficient in cooler weather, often beginning to yellow well above freezing and turning dormant (brown) with frost.

CAST OF CHARACTERS

While innumerable grasses serve special purposes, only four northern and five southern species have proved broadly important for lawns; one coarse field species is very useful where climate is neither truly southern nor northern, as in the border states. They are:

NORTHERN SPECIES

Kentucky bluegrass (*Poa pratensis*)
perennial ryegrass (*Lolium perenne*)
fine fescues (*Festuca rubra*, in three botanical varieties)
bentgrasses (several species of *Agrostis*)

SOUTHERN SPECIES

bermudagrass (*Cynodon dactylon*, and its hybrids)
manillagrass or zoysia (*Zoysia matrella*, and its varieties)
st. augustinegrass (*Stenotaphrum secundatum*)
centipedegrass (*Eremochloa ophiuroides*)
bahiagrass (*Paspalum notatum*)

"IN BETWEEN" (BORDER STATES)

tall fescue (*Festuca arundinacea*)

Fig. 2-3 Kentucky bluegrass, *Poa pratensis*.

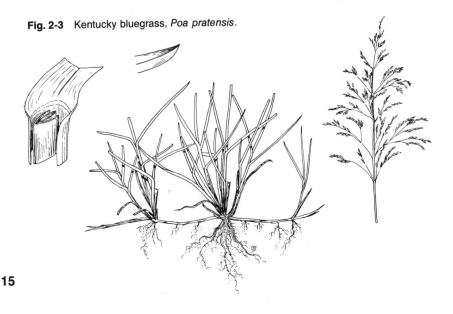

Fig. 2-4 Perennial ryegrass, *Lolium perenne*.

Fig. 2-5 Red fescue, *Festuca rubra*.

Fig. 2-6 Bentgrass, *Agrostis spp*.

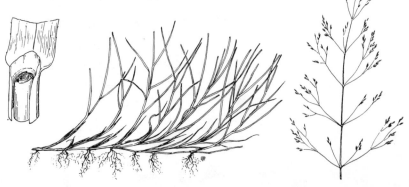

Fig. 2-7 Bermudagrass, *Cynodon dactylon*.

The Team

Fig. 2-8 Zoysia, *Z. matrella*.

Fig. 2-9 St. augustinegrass, *Stenotaphrum secundatum*.

Fig. 2-10   Centipedegrass, *Eremochloa ophiuroides*.

The Team

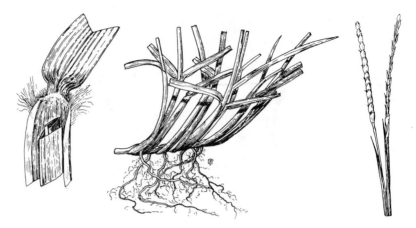

Fig. 2-11   Bahiagrass, *Paspalum notatum*.

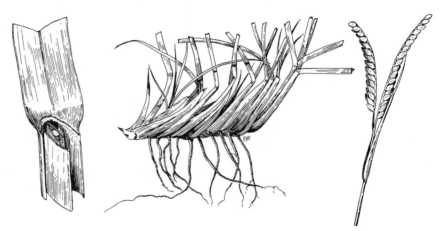

Fig. 2-12   Tall fescue, *Festuca arundinacea*.

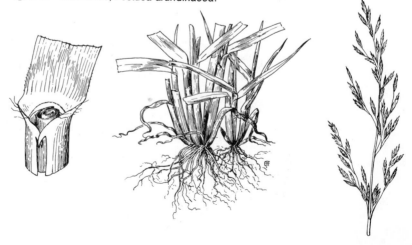

These are the turf mainstays, which will be discussed more fully later in the chapter. Some of the specialty grasses are important, too:

NORTHERN SPECIALTY LAWNGRASSES

redtop (*Agrostis alba*)—usually an impermanent "nursegrass" until permanent turf establishes, but surviving well in soggy situations from border states northward.

rough bluegrass (*Poa trivialis*)—well-adapted to shade and moist habitat in northerly climates.

annual or Italian ryegrass (*Lolium multiflorum*)—a temporary, coarse bunchgrass sometimes used for quick cover in mixtures and in winter-seeding dormant southern turf.

wheatgrass (*Agropyron spp.*)—not good turf, but survives in northerly drylands.

sheep and hard fescues (*Festuca ovina*, and its varieties)—used similarly to the fine fescues, but generally not so compatible or readily available.

alkaligrass (*Puccinellia distans*)—especially for saline habitat, primarily in arid climates.

SOUTHERN SPECIALTY LAWNGRASSES

buffalograss (*Buchloë dactyloides*)—primarily for midcontinent (Kansas) dryland habitat that cannot be irrigated.

carpetgrass (*Axonopus spp.*)—for soggy habitat in the deep South.

Fig. 2-13 Redtop, *Agrostis alba*.

Fig. 2-14 Rough bluegrass, *Poa trivialis.*

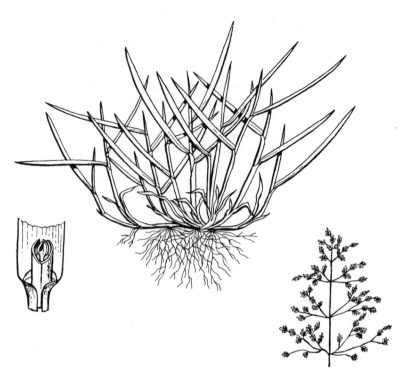

Fig. 2-15 Buffalograss, *Buchloë dactyloides.*

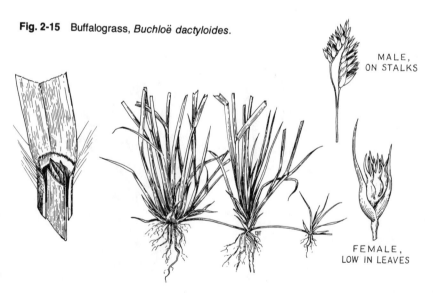

MALE,
ON STALKS

FEMALE,
LOW IN LEAVES

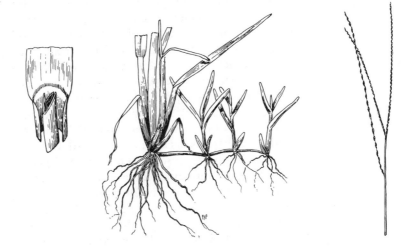

In addition there are many minor species, such as are sometimes utilized in Europe but only rarely in America. Among them are woods bluegrass (*Poa nemoralis*), for shade; crested dogstail (*Cynosurus cristatus*), for mixtures; and dwarf timothy (*Phleum nodosum*), especially for sportsfields. Propagated more as a horticultural item than as a seeded grass is beachgrass (*Ammophila spp.*), used for stabilizing dunes near the seashore. Various legumes (clover, vetch, lespedeza), and dichondra also are occasionally used for "turf," although they are not grasses.

LAWNGRASS PERSONALITY

Most of the lawngrasses are Eurasian introductions, only a few of the less important ones (sheep's fescue, some wheatgrasses, buffalograss) being domestic species. Many, such as Kentucky bluegrass, are so long escaped and naturalized in the New World as to be "native" for all practical purposes. Most of these grasses were introduced rather casually. They were familiar in the homelands of the colonists coming to America and were no doubt carried along almost inadvertently in shipboard hay and cattle bedding, or as packing materials protecting household and trade items. As the colonists felled the forest and disturbed the soil, these aggressive species, long an accompaniment of civilization, gained a toehold in the New World. They were better adapted to the newly disturbed ecology than were native grasses, which, in any event, were not abundant in forested country. When colonization reached the Great Plains where native grasses are well adapted, conquering the land was not so easy for the European introductions; nonetheless, even there native species seldom responded to plowed ground as well as did Old World introductions.

The reason so many Old World migrants end up in our lawns is not only that these species are aggressive, adaptable, and capable of persisting with little or no attention, but also because evolution in the Old World bequeathed them the habit of remaining green during cold weather. Practically all native grasses in America turn brown after frost; not so Kentucky bluegrass (which, incidentally, gained its name in the early 1800s because it thrived so well on the rich soils of north-central Kentucky), fescue, bentgrass, and perennial ryegrass. Even in the rigorous continental climate of mid-America, where the best of the northern grasses "bite the dust" when scorching winter winds sweep across the plains, these European species remain green long after frost, and perhaps all winter if there is a protective layer of snow. Not uncommonly Kentucky bluegrass lawns are only a bit off-color until Christmas in the Missouri and Ohio valleys, and in mild winters they may remain more or less green year-around. One of the characteristics highly thought of for new bluegrasses in the Rutgers University breeding program is good winter color; many of the cultivars bred there (Adelphi, Bonnieblue, Galaxy, Majestic, and so on) are outstanding for their dark color late into autumn and early in spring, if, indeed, not all through winter.

Another characteristic esteemed in a good lawngrass is the ability to spread from a small beginning, colonizing adjacent ground. With few exceptions the grasses enumerated earlier all have this ability to spread (the exceptions being bunchgrasses such as the ryegrasses and certain of the fescues). Spreading may be by underground stems called rhizomes or by trailing runners aboveground termed stolons. Rhizoming is perhaps a bit more advantageous than stolonizing, because there is less chance of the spreading stems "getting in the way" and building up a layer of thatch atop the soil. One of the great attractions of Kentucky bluegrass is its ability to weave a strong sod that resists tearing, because of its abundant rhizomes. The spreading and creeping varieties of fine fescue spread fairly well by rhizomes, and of the southern grasses the zoysias and some cultivars of bermudagrass produce rhizomes as well as stolons. Characteristically, all the southern grasses spread quite aggressively by stolons, a boon when establishing a stand, a bane when trying to keep them out of adjacent flower beds. In the North the bentgrasses are stoloniferous, with the creeping and velvet bentgrasses (like Emerald and Kingstown) spreading more prolificly than the rather erect-growing colonial sorts (such as Highland and Exeter). As was mentioned, the danger of thatch formation is generally greater with a stoloniferous grass than with a rhizomatous one or a bunchgrass.

Other factors do have an influence: for instance, in that the siliceous foliage of zoysia and the tough leaf sheaths of fescue are quite resistant to decay, they build up a thatch accumulation more than do species having tissue that is quicker to decompose.

PLASTIC GRASS

A phenomenon of our times has been "artificial turf" made from plastic-like materials. Fake grass such as Astroturf and Tartanturf is employed primarily for athletic fields, and many of the major sports stadia have such carpeting. For brutally used grounds, little else will stand the abuse. But cost of installing artificial turf is far greater than that of establishing live grass, and its upkeep, although different, is no less onerous than that for turf. Artificial turf deteriorates, even if gradually, while living grasses, by nature of their continuous growth, are constantly self-renewing. There is little argument with the view that natural grass is esthetically more pleasing than the man-made type. It fills an advantageous biological role of recycling filth and refreshing the surroundings.

One could argue endlessly as to which type of turf is preferable for athletic performance (certainly the play of the ball and the footing differ between live and artificial turfs) and whether the injuries sustained are more serious with one than the other. A big factor with athletes is the build-up of heat on a plastic surface. During one day game a member of the St. Louis Cardinals (who play on Astroturf) made that point by standing in a bucket of ice water between innings. A Purdue University study showed natural turf to average about twelve degrees cooler than artificial turf and to reduce thermal pollution approximately ten degrees over lawns in the city. At Michigan State University, Dr. Mecklenburg measured a temperature of 163°F on the Tartanturf of the football stadium near midday on August 18, while at the same time living grass around the stadium registered only 88°F, some 75° cooler!

SUCCESSION IN THE LAWN

In the previous chapter mention was made of ecological succession, in which plant communities replace one another in a progressive series until a reasonably persistent "climax" eventuates. This process will vary greatly from place to place even within a single climatic belt, depending upon local differences and such accidental happenings as may occur. The succession hypothesized for an ecosystem in Ohio in Chapter One could proceed in various directions so far as native tree populations are concerned. An abandoned field progresses through various stages of herbaceous weed dominance, to brush and aggressive trees such as hawthorn, elm, and crabapple. Thereafter relatively small local differences that satisfy the "likings" of particular species will determine the successional pathway. Generally the early trees are superseded by others that are slower to start, but which compete better for nutrients and sunlight. Eventually, the only seedlings that can persist in the understory, shaded as it is by a canopy of large trees, are those which are especially tolerant of shade (maple and beech, for example). In a moist, mesophytic Ohio habitat the climax forest tends to be dominated by beech-maple. But on dryer, hotter habitat tolerance of shade weighs less heavily than ability to endure such exposure, and oak-hickory dominates instead. Not that we are concerned here with forest ecology, but trees afford a more familiar and obvious example than do small organisms, demonstrating the interplay of the environmental factors which determines what type of vegetation will occupy a particular site. The same sort of thing goes on with grasses in the lawn, although of course the custodian keeps the turf community "juvenile" and highly "fired up," preventing development of a mature or climax condition.

A few examples of lawngrass response may be of interest. Bermudagrass is very intolerant of shade; it will succeed in the shade no better than does crabgrass. Yet it is exceedingly aggressive and fast-growing in the sun if provided reasonable moisture and fertility. Because of its aggressiveness it is not a very companionable grass mixed with other species, tending to squeeze them out, and it is certainly no good for shady parts of the lawn. But it is vigorous and quick to heal, making an excellent, recuperative cover (although at the cost of generous maintenance). Centipedegrass is almost the opposite of bermudagrass. It "resents" high fertility (being regarded as a low-maintenance species) and shows temperament about nutrient balances. It is slow to colonize and does not grow rampantly. It does well in the shade. Centipede's recalcitrance is compensated for by less demanding care!

The counterpart of centipedegrass in the North are the fine fescues. Most cultivars endure shade well, and poor-soil, dry habitats. They tend to dominate in such locations, even though initially planted on an equal footing with other species. Even in the open fescues don't give ground easily. But when they are in competition with bluegrass, the bluegrass usually wins out in time if the lawn is adequately fertilized; fertilizer confers greater advantage on bluegrass than on fescue.

Perennial ryegrass gains great initial advantage in mixtures because the seed sprouts so quickly and the seedlings are so vigorous. Yet ryegrass is not so broadly tolerant of some environmental stresses as is bluegrass. It often disappears during winter while bluegrasses and fescues survive quite well. Similarly, bentgrasses are at a disadvantage in dry climates, but given a toehold in moist habitat they, like bermuda in the South, overwhelm most other species. As bentgrass spreads by stolons and tends to form dense patches, it is not ordinarily a good companion in grass mixtures. Also, its need for lower and more frequent mowing makes for incompatibility in a bluegrass community.

Of course the lawnsman can modify the lawn habitat to some extent, usually enough to accommodate the grass of his preference. We've seen how mowing practices and timely use of fertilizer can favor one lawngrass over another. The lawnsman can certainly keep most weeds out of the lawn with the modern-day arsenal of herbicides. For example, picloram and siduron have been used to free turf of northern species from aggressive bermudagrass, which is one of the most pernicious weeds where not wanted. Bromacil takes orchardgrass out of bluegrass. Heavy fertilization has been utilized to eliminate perennial ryegrass from bluegrass in Pennsylvania (the ryegrasses are less hardy through winter when heavily fertilized) and to remove tall fescue from bluegrass in Ohio. Low mowing and watering often enables bentgrass to persist and dominate, even in habitat not particularly suitable for *Agrostis*. Sometimes a cultivar bred for vigor and low growth will withstand heavy use and moderately low mowing, while common grass fades under this regimen. The lawn (or any ecosystem), as I've said before, is a complicated weave of interrelating factors, each of which influences the others and which cumulatively determine the success to be had with any planting.

THE STAR PERFORMERS

The stalwarts for most lawns in America (pp. 15–21) merit specific review. The species themselves are newly risen from the ranks: Remember that even three decades ago lawn keeping was rather casual and without select cultivars or special maintenance products. Many of the cultivars selected or bred out of these genotypes have since arisen to lawngrass stardom. How lawn cultivars come into being is discussed more fully in a later section of this chapter.

The turfgrass "biographical sketches" which follow emphasize the basic qualities of the species rather than the myriad of special attributes which individual cultivars manifest. In general new cultivars of any species represent improvement over the old-fashioned parent grass, or the effort and expense would not have been made to bring them to market. Many are not particularly distinctive, however, nor necessarily outstanding in all environments and under all conditions. Most have yet to stand the test of time (resistance to disease, for example, is not "proven" until the cultivar is widely enough planted over a long period of time so that its performance can be assessed under many conditions and while exposed to newly evolving races of disease).

The qualifications of cultivars can seldom be thoroughly documented, for it is impossible to test them fully in all environments under competent judgment. Even were this possible, nature has a way of making no two seasons exactly alike, so that there is always the chance of a peculiar combination of weather, grass physiology, and means for infection suddenly making a disease virulent. But it is safe to say that, by and large, the new cultivars are more tolerant of disease than were their forebears, better looking, generally lower-growing, and more dense (making a prettier turf). While some may prove a disappointment under particular circumstances, on the whole they represent a major advance in the art of lawn keeping. Most commonly they are planted in blends or mixture to better "spread the risk"; if one cultivar proves disappointing, another in the blend with somewhat different heredity likely will surmount the adversity.

A few of the prominent cultivars will be mentioned by way of example for those grasses for which meaningful selections have been made. Keep in mind, however, that the breeding of new cultivars is constantly ongoing, and that new selections are continuously sought to replace fading older ones. Today's featured cultivars are likely to be superseded by others in time. But for the foreseeable future the major species reviewed here will provide the most satisfactory lawns possible.

NORTHERN GRASSES

KENTUCKY BLUEGRASS

Bluegrass is the most-used lawn species for the North, quite attractive, self-reliant, and easily cared for. Because of unsurpassed rhizoming, bluegrass forms an especially strong sod; it is stout underfoot year-round, resistant to wear, and amazingly recuperative (partly because its tenacious underground parts are protected in the soil) (Fig. 2-17). Bluegrass performs most capably on rich, neutral, or slightly acid soils. It does well in either sun or light shade (towards the southern limits of its range, light shade is advantageous). It grows best in cooler weather and is superlative through autumn when it tillers (thickens with new shoots) profusely, yet stays low in response to declining day length. The cool-weather stimulation carries over into spring; but the leaves grow longer then, which calls for more frequent mowing.

By early summer wiry seedhead stems form, their frayed appearance after mowing giving the lawn a tinge of "gray hair." Having expended food reserves in a seeding effort (growth of the stems bearing inflorescences is determinate, and they will die), bluegrass often

Fig. 2-17 Clones of Kentucky bluegrass freshly pulled from good soil. Note the abundant rhizomes (the snakelike white stems extending horizontally from soil), a few of which have turned up to become new plants (clump on left).

languishes a bit, with some of the secondary tillers withering away. If summer turns hot, the grass is even more at a disadvantage; it cannot produce food abundantly enough in hot weather to compensate for that used up for intensified respiration and other catabolic functions. Summer, then, is the weakest link in the bluegrass seasonal cycle, a time when the grass thins, and weeds often gain a toehold. Forcing the grass through fertilization and watering may weaken it further if the weather remains hot; often bluegrass prospers better if allowed to go dormant in summer, at least with common types in the southern part of its range. However, as the newer cultivars have been selected for ability to survive summer adversity, those truly tolerant of disease shouldn't suffer hot weather "fertilization ills" as the common grass does. Likewise, since the newer cultivars are low-growing, not so much green leaf—the grass' means of sustenance—is lost to mowing. In general bluegrass is favored by fairly tall mowing, which is especially important under adversity (hot weather, in the shade, where weeds occur, and so on).

The seasonal cycle of bluegrass, in contrast to that of weeds such as crabgrass, is graphed in Figure 2-18, which affords insight on how to manage a northern lawngrass. Obviously, the species will profit from fertilization in early autumn, the time of year when growth is most intense and when months of cool weather lie ahead. Fertilizing in early summer, on the other hand, when the grass is "going downhill," favors weedy competition. The graph strongly suggests that autumn is the best time of year for renovating, overseeding, fertilization, weed control, and other lawn repairs where bluegrass is concerned. Next best is spring, with summer least satisfactory (except in northerly locations and at high elevations where summer is short and cool).

27

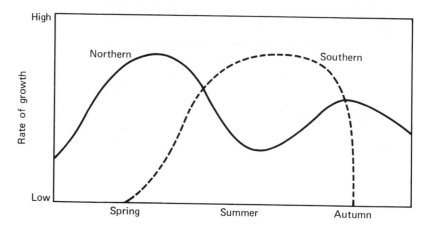

Fig. 2-18 Lawn growth cycles. The solid line represents a typical northern lawn of Kentucky bluegrass; the broken line, southern lawns such as Bermuda or Zoysia. The southern line can also represent summer weeds in a northern lawn; the northern line, winter weeds in a southern lawn.

Figure 2-19 depicts a bluegrass plant, naming its more familiar features. A distinctive feature of bluegrass is the boat-shaped tip to the leaf. You can often distinguish bluegrass from other species in the lawn by pulling a leaf gently between thumb and forefinger; the spoon-like leaf tip can easily be felt, a giveaway for Kentucky bluegrass (and most other *Poa* species as well). While bluegrass suffers its share of diseases, generally these are not fatal, and with change of weather afflicted grass "snaps back" vigorously. It is normal for the older leaves to senesce, turning yellow. Younger leaves arise towards the tip (center) of the culm, sufficient to maintain a complement of about three to five healthy, green, functioning leaf blades per culm. The oldest leaves, as they senesce, may appear to be diseased; but if the blemishes truly represent disease, it is of no consequence, for these are tissues "on the way out" in any event. Under good growing conditions a new leaf may form every few days, and the consequent contribution of the lowermost leaf on the culm to sod detritus may number during the growing season in the dozens. Fortunately, these add little to the thatch (organic residues at the base of the sod), for spent leaves decay quickly.

Bluegrass' growth habit is a nice compromise between density enough for good looks but looseness enough not to stifle companion grasses. The erect culms display themselves well for attractive appearance, yet are open enough to let clippings sift into the sod. The texture (a visual effect due to leaf width and position) is fine enough to give an impression of luxuriance, yet not so tight as to appear harsh and dominating. Leaf tissues are firm but not overly fibrous; thus bluegrass mows neatly (except during seeding season). All in all, bluegrass is

28

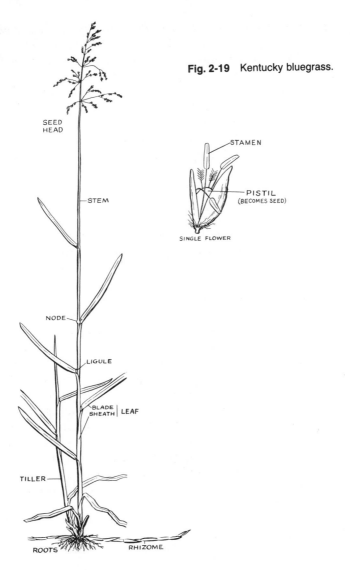

Fig. 2-19 Kentucky bluegrass.

SEED HEAD

STAMEN

PISTIL
(BECOMES SEED)

SINGLE FLOWER

STEM

NODE

LIGULE

BLADE | SHEATH | LEAF

TILLER

ROOTS   RHIZOME

probably the most flexible and accommodating species available for northern lawns. Its main disadvantages are summer weakness if hot weather is prolonged and slowness for a seeding to become established (at least compared to fescues and ryegrasses).

Kentucky bluegrass is complex genetically. It is a polyploid with a highly variable chromosome number (usually from 35 to 105), discrepancies occurring even within one cultivar. Seed production depends only to a limited extent upon sexual fusion (the typical fertilization of an egg cell), most seeds being formed apomictically (i.e., remaining unfertilized and unreduced, thus carrying the mother plant's heredity). This is advantageous for perpetuating a distinctive genotype without need for a lot of rogueing and inbreeding in isolation. But enough sexual crossing occurs to permit "hybridizing" of superior lines, a technique employed quite successfully at Rutgers University, the major center for bluegrass breeding. Promising offspring with apomictic tendencies are sought for practical perpetuation of the new genetic combinations.

Presumably Kentucky bluegrass originated in the mountains of southeastern Europe, from which polyploid forms spread throughout Europe by historical times. Evidence indicates that Kentucky bluegrass did not occur in what is now the United States at the time of colonization, but was introduced all but unintentionally from shipboard, and perhaps intentionally by the French missionaries ascending the St. Lawrence for trading with the Indians in Illinois country. In any event, by the early 1800s bluegrass had established itself as one of the chief crops in the newly colonized Midwest, where it became known as "Kentucky" bluegrass because of its admirable performance and importance in the northcentral part of that state. As colonization moved farther westward, so did Kentucky bluegrass—into Missouri and northward into Canada. Only since midcentury has it been taken to the Pacific Northwest, where today most of the lawnseed crop is grown.

In the United States bluegrass seed was for many years harvested from "wild" stands throughout the Midwest, from pastures from which grazing was withheld until a seed crop had been taken in late spring. Then Merion was discovered as a clone on a golf course near Philadelphia, beginning a new era for the searching out (and eventual breeding) of superior cultivars. A few cultivars prominent in recent years, both new and old, appear in the Lawn Institute's Variety Review Board "acceptances list" for 1976. The examples listed here are only a minor portion of the many named cultivars being offered commercially or under test.

ADELPHI—An attractively dark, low Rutgers University hybrid from Bellevue X Belturf parentage, quite dense and leafy but compatible in mixtures.

ARBORETUM—A mass selection from Missouri, especially recuperative for unpampered lawns; appearance is typical of old-fashioned bluegrass so long a favorite.

ARISTA—An attractive, fine-textured cultivar bred in Holland, especially used in blends; combines well with perennial ryegrass.

BARON—A bold, vigorous, high-rating European cultivar, quick to establish and economical for acreage; widely acclaimed for performance and disease resistance.

BONNIEBLUE—Another notable Rutgers hybrid out of Bellevue (X Pennstar), unusually low and dark, quite resistant to stress and disease.

FYLKING—A decumbent, misty-green Swedish beauty of refined elegance that withstands low mowing and tolerates disease well; widely adapted and acclaimed for mixtures as well as solo performances.

GALAXY—Another of the Rutgers hybrids from Bellevue (X Pennstar), notable for an exceptionally dark hue, low profile, lengthy season, and excellent winter performance; generally disease resistant but shows some susceptibility to stripe smut.

GLADE—A Rutgers selection of all-around quality, for shade as well as sun; decumbent, spreads vigorously, and is notably resistant to mildew (a serious disease in shade).

MAJESTIC—Another richly-colored Rutgers hybrid from Belturf X Bellevue, with lengthy season; very low-growing habit, producing a strong sod from abundant rhizomes.

MERION—Still a leading bluegrass of outstanding beauty; fairly broad-bladed, stiffish foliage is leafspot resistant but suffers from newer diseases (e.g., stripe smut); a heavy feeder that should be fertilized regularly.

NUGGET—A dwarfish selection from Alaska, unusually dense and stiffish (like a tight-pile carpet), "tops" for summer good looks (but a little slow in early spring and susceptible to dollarspot); does well in shade, and withstands low maintenance.

PENNSTAR—Highly refined from an European bloodline by Pennsylvania State University, exhibiting unusual grace and beauty; good disease resistance, and low thatching potential.

PRATO—A sprightly cultivar from Europe, tolerant of companion grasses and mostly used in blends.

PLUSH—A broad-bladed selection from Rutgers, which seems widely adapted; medium green, with reasonable resistance to disease.

SODCO—A dwarf, slow-growing, dark green, 4-line composite bred at Purdue University, useful in sun or shade, in blends or alone; genetic diversity aids disease resistance.

SYDSPORT—A highly rated broad-bladed Swedish cultivar, bold in texture and in color, quick to establish, making a "solid" sod.

TOUCHDOWN—Selected on a Long Island golf course; excellent overall quality (top-rating at Rutgers), tolerating leafspot and stripe smut.

FINE FESCUE

Like bluegrass, the fine fescues (Fig. 2-20) are believed to be of Old World origin, although their naturalization in the New World is rather obscure. For the most part they have occupied infertile, dry ground, not doing well towards the southern limits of the bluegrass belt (uncharacteristically, however, sometimes populating bogs and marshes,

Fig. 2-20 A Chewings fescue (as you might guess, the "Jamestown" cultivar), a very attractive fine-textured lawn species.

and extending scatteringly into the southern states). Traditionally, in America, the fine fescues had been divided into two groups, the "creeping red" (*F. rubra rubra*), and the Chewings (*F. rubra commutata*). Recent investigations, based mostly on chromosome count and time of flowering, distinguish still a third grouping (*F. rubra tricophylla*). Rutgers University breeders consider the Chewings types (subsp. *commutata*) to be particularly dense and to spread very little by rhizomes; Jamestown, Highlight, and Koket are typical cultivars. Creeping fescues (subsp. *tricophylla*) are somewhat less dense than Chewings and spread more readily by rhizomes; typical cultivars are Dawson and Golfrood. The spreading group (subsp. *rubra*) is even more open and rhizomatous and is represented by cultivars such as Ruby and Fortress. The average person will have difficulty distinguishing one fine fescue from another, however, although the Chewings types are the best looking for lawns. Where turf does not need a "spit-and-polish" appearance, such as for roadside seeding, spreading fescues are probably better suited. They and creeping forms are much utilized in seed mixtures in which bluegrass is meant to carry much of the load.

Fine fescues parallel bluegrass in general form and growth habits. Fescues are not so strongly rhizomatous as are the bluegrasses, and their foliage is a bit narrower and wirier, the edges tending to curl in, making the leaf almost tubelike in dry weather. Leaf sheaths persist as a brown or reddish accumulation at the base of the culm (tiller stem), a helpful clue for identifying fescue. The leaf tips are more pointed than with bluegrass, and not boat-like. When fescue is left unmowed it develops a delicate, wind-swept appearance. Seed sprouts and seedlings progress somewhat more rapidly than with bluegrass, but are not so aggressively competitive in mixtures as would be ryegrass (or, eventually, bentgrass). Better lawn seed mixtures usually include a modest percentage of fine fescue as backup for bluegrass, particularly useful in shade and for infertile, dry locations. On the whole bluegrasses and fescues are good companions, behaving much alike and responding generally to the same regimen of care (height of mowing, seasonal fertilization, and so on). On good soil in favorable locations bluegrass usually dominates and eventually suppresses the fescue, although the fescue can be remarkably persistent and once dominating a stand may give bluegrass little chance. Seed mixtures formulated for shade generally have fescue predominating, and the species is suggested for droughty or sandy soils where bluegrass is not at its best.

Fescues are subject to much the same assortment of diseases as is bluegrass. Selection aims for greater tolerance to disease, particularly ability to hold up in warm, humid weather, fine fescues' biggest failing. Fewer outstanding cultivars have been bred than with bluegrasses, although Dawson, Highlight, and Koket from Europe and Jamestown, Pennlawn, and Wintergreen domestically all do their bit for American lawns. Ruby from Europe and Fortress from New Jersey are spreading cultivars much used in mixtures.

THE BENTGRASSES

Cultivars of *Agrostis,* the bentgrasses (Fig. 2-21), are the finest-textured and most elegant of the northern turfgrasses, but they require

Fig. 2-21 A creeping bentgrass, one of the most elegant turf species, commonly planted for golf greens. This is a sod section of the cultivar "Emerald."

constant attention (especially to mowing) to look well. The colonial bentgrasses (usually considered to be *A. tenuis*) normally require less attention than do the creeping bentgrasses (*A. palustris*, or *A. stolonifera* in Europe) and the velvet bentgrasses (*A. canina*). Highland is a distinctive colonial ecotype considered by some European authorities to be a separate species, the same as occurs in south-central Europe and on the Chilean coast of South America. Highland is the "workhorse" of the bentgrasses, being available in steady supply, economically, as high-quality seed; most usage is in northern Europe rather than in America, however.

While the emerging leaves of bluegrass and fescue are folded, those of the bentgrasses are rolled (as with a newspaper sent through the mails). As bentgrasses spread by stolons rather than rhizomes, they tend to build up a mat of basal stem growth surmounted by a canopy of green leaves towards the tip. If the lawn is left too long between mowings, the leafy part of the stem may be cut off, leaving unsightly brown stubble for days or weeks until new growth regenerates from below; bentgrasses therefore should be mowed often, about twice weekly for lawns and at least every other day on very low-cut turf such as a golf green. Bentgrass leaves are shorter than those of bluegrass and fescue. They are narrowly arrowshaped, usually with a light green or bluish-green cast. Several veins are prominent (compared to one major central vein in a bluegrass leaf). Most bentgrasses grow as a dense colony rather than infiltrating openly and sparingly into other turf; thus bentgrass is seldom recommended for mixtures except where the turf is expected to be mostly bentgrass and to be cared for according to bentgrass requirements.

Drippy-moist weather for at least a portion of the year is ideal for bentgrass. In the United States this occurs chiefly on the west slopes of the Cascade-Sierra mountains from California to British Columbia, leaward of the Great Lakes, or where frequent mists develop due to elevation from the southern Appalachians into New England. Elsewhere, of course, bentgrass can be accommodated by irrigation. Colonial bentgrasses such as Highland don't require a great deal of care, but creeping bentgrasses are fairly demanding, often requiring occasional thinning to avoid build-up of thatch. Bentgrasses "prefer" acid soils, something particularly true for velvet bent. Compared to bluegrasses and fescues, bentgrasses should be mowed low, generally three-fourths to one inch for the colonial sorts, one-half inch or less for the creeping types. Most creeping bentgrass selections are propagated vegetatively since they do not come true from seed because of sexual reassortment; exceptions are Penncross and Emerald, the latter a pure-line out of Congressional (a vegetative cultivar) that is not so aggressive as Penncross and thus more easily cared for. The only available cultivar of velvet bentgrass is Kingstown, which can make an exquisite turf when well cared for.

Bentgrass seed is very small, running in most cases about eight million seeds to the pound. Seeding rates thus can be light (about one pound per thousand square feet). The grass should not be expected to compete strongly in its early stages of growth (most bentgrasses, however, are planted alone, or with only modest inclusions of bluegrass or fescue). Bentgrass is on the whole more susceptible to disease than bluegrass and fescue, partly perhaps because of the generous irrigation and fertilization normally accorded bentgrass. Creeping bentgrasses in particular require more attention than does bluegrass —more frequent mowing, thatch prevention (by thinning and topdressing), irrigation, and probably fungicide treatment for disease prevention. Bentgrass is quite sensitive to snowmold in winter, something that afflicts other northern species much less.

PERENNIAL RYEGRASS

Perennial ryegrass was not always well regarded for fine turf. But the new "turf-type" cultivars changed this, and today the better perennial ryegrasses are as good-looking and easily managed as bluegrass. As with bluegrass, perennial ryegrass leaves are folded rather than rolled in the bud stage, but they lack the boatshaped tip characteristic of bluegrass. They tend to be a slightly lighter shade of green than bluegrass and are shinier in reflected light. Of course rhizomes are lacking, ryegrass being a bunchgrass. Thus ryegrass should be seeded fairly heavily since it will not spread. Ryegrass is normally best held to less than twenty percent in mixture with bluegrass-fescue, enough to provide quick cover, yet not so much as to overwhelm the slower species completely. In mild maritime climates, where summer and winter extremes are not great, perennial ryegrass is not likely to suffer decimation; there it can be planted alone (although including a little bluegrass is good insurance). If the stand thins, or if parts of the turf are damaged, bolstering by spreading more seed will be necessary.

The great advantage of perennial ryegrass is its ability to sprout quickly, making a stand of vigorous seedlings in short order. The seed is large, only about a quarter million seeds to the pound, so sowing rate should be rather heavy (at least four pounds to the thousand square feet, and preferably six). While perennial ryegrass may not be so competitive against slower-starting species as is annual ryegrass, nonetheless it can, in mixture, crowd bluegrass and fescue and delay their establishment. Other disadvantages to ryegrass, compared to bluegrass, are a faster rate of growth (requiring slightly more frequent mowing), a narrower range of adaptation (winterkill is a risk in colder, continental climates), mowing is more difficult (the leaves of most cultivars are more fibrous than with bluegrass, fray instead of cutting neatly), and in certain seasons may not look as perky as does bluegrass (usually not being up to bluegrass' appearance in autumn and after early frost).

Perennial ryegrass cultivars look very much alike, the advantage of the better selections being chiefly greater hardiness, disease resistance, better density, and improved mowing qualities. Manhattan, a composite of fifteen selections taken mostly from Central Park in New York, by Rutgers University breeders, led the new perennial ryegrasses into their era of general acceptability. The very attractive Pennfine, from Pennsylvania State University, followed soon; later came such outstanding selections as Citation, Derby, Diplomat, NK-200, Yorktown, and so on.

SOUTHERN GRASSES

BERMUDAGRASS

Bermuda and its hybrids (primarily crosses of *C. dactylon* with *C. transvaalensis*) is the most widely planted southern turfgrass, not only important for lawns, roadsides, and pastures but also highly valued for golf greens and sportsfields. The leaves are folded in bud and arise in clusters along the trailing shoots, often densely enough to appear opposite one another. The ligule, where the blade joins the leaf sheath, is a fringe of hairs, and the sheath is sparsely hairy. Bermudagrass is notorious for throwing numerous seedheads, typically four or five fingerlike spikes, making a "crowsfoot." *C. dactylon* probably originated in Africa but acquired the "Bermuda" name by virtue of that island being a way station in migration to America. At least one cultivar, Sunturf, is thought to be a natural hybrid between *C. dactylon* and another African species and has been given the botanical name *C. X magennisii*.

Bermudagrass is very vigorous and aggressive and demands a good bit of attention if it is to perform up to its best capabilities (ample fertility and moisture, frequent mowing) (Fig. 2-22). The species suffers its share of diseases, but on the whole is not a prima donna about such things, recuperating quickly once the affliction eases. Bermuda turf is low and dense, a bit stiff and harsh compared to bluegrass, but an excellent ground cover. Diminutive selections such as Tifdwarf are so decumbent as to merit mowing at a quarter inch and enjoy usage similar to the finest-textured bentgrasses of the North. Bermudagrass is widely adapted, hardy cultivars surviving into the northern states (although bermuda is seldom desirable north of Kansas-Kentucky-Washington, D.C., because of the prolonged winter dormancy, even

Fig. 2-22 An improved bermudagrass in the South.

though hardy cultivars may not winterkill). Bermuda seems weaker in the very deep South, such as in southern Florida and along the Gulf Coast, although it is still widely used for such things as golf greens there. But north from the southern coastal plain almost to the Ohio Valley, and in irrigated parts of the Southwest, bermuda is a lawn mainstay. Unimproved "common" bermuda is easily grown from seed, making quite a presentable turf if reasonably cared for.

Bermudagrass does best on near-neutral, fertile soils, and it responds well to attention. It is intolerant of siduron (a northern crabgrass preventer) but tolerant of most other familiar weed controls. Being a southern grass, bermuda grows best under warm, humid conditions, and seems not to suffer from temperatures in the nineties. It cannot stand shade, however, and performs poorly when the temperature drops even to 50°F or thereabouts. It is generally mowed fairly low, much like colonial bentgrasses in the North—about an inch high for home lawns, down to a quarter inch for golf greens. The trailing stems mow best with a reel rather than a rotary mower.

37

The improved cultivars center about hybrids developed at Tifton, Georgia, by Glen Burton (primarily Tifdwarf, Tifgreen ,Tiflawn, and Tifway). Midway has been selected by Ray Keen at Kansas, especially for winter hardiness; Santa Ana was selected by Dr. Youngner in Southern California and is notable for its smog resistance. Numerous older selections are grown in Florida; a Texturf series in Texas; Sunturf, Tufcote, and U-3 (developed through USDA cooperation) in more northerly locations where they are recognized for their hardiness. All of these must be propagated vegetatively, for they will not come true from seed. Further details regarding bermuda cultivars can be found in suitable references such as *Turfgrass Science and Culture* by J. B. Beard (Prentice-Hall, 1973).

MANILLAGRASS OR ZOYSIA

Three intergrading zoysias are used for lawns, sometimes designated as separate species and sometimes as subspecies of *Z. matrella* The *japonica* group is highly variable and includes coarse forms: Seeded zoysia will be the japonica type because of sexual reassortment. More familiar for southern lawns are the finer-leaf *matrella* sorts, propagated vegetatively. An even finer-textured *tenuifolia* series is available, but usually is a bit more difficult to grow well than are matrella selections. The leaves are rolled in bud, but otherwise zoysia plants resemble bermudagrass. Also, like bermudagrass, zoysia spreads both by rhizome and by stolon. The seedhead is less conspicuous than with bermuda, being a short single spike. Zoysia is much slower growing than bermuda, getting by with less mowing than almost any other southern species. But it is very "tough" (siliceous), thus difficult to mow with anything but a heavy-duty machine. Reel mowers are preferred for neat clipping. Zoysia may grow so densely that it becomes almost impervious to applied materials such as fertilizer, even rainfall; consequently thatch can be quite a problem. When the grass is mechanically thinned, healing is much slower than with bermudagrass, perhaps giving weeds more of a chance for entree. Although zoysia is not a demanding species and provides a topflight turf when well tended, the few drawbacks it does have are rather hard to overcome. It is widely adapted, but finds its greatest use north of the southern coastal plain, such as from middle and northern Alabama to Washington, D.C.

Zoysia suffers from a number of grass diseases which are generally not too serious. In some areas it is badly smitten by billbug (hard to control because it burrows deeply into the thatchy sod). A japonica selection named Meyer is hardy even into the northern states where it is widely sold as plugs and sprigs; but it is not so good-looking as are the matrella selections for southern lawns. Emerald is a matrella cultivar selected at Tifton, Georgia. Midwest comes from Purdue University, where it was bred for open growth and winter hardiness (with the thought in mind that it might be interplanted with bluegrass). Zoysias, like bermudagrasses, are not often planted in the North because of the long winter dormancy that results in off-color turf from October until May. Also, in the North, Zoysia takes several years to fill to a solid stand, so slow-growing is it under the restricted growing season there. But once established, zoysia is attractive, tough, and durable—almost more than one bargains for, considering its tendency to thatch and difficulty in mowing.

ST. AUGUSTINEGRASS

St. augustinegrass is widely used only in the extreme South, primarily in Florida and along the Gulf Coast west to eastern Texas. It is fairly coarse, with a few serious problems (primarily chinch-bug and a tendency to turn "puffy" [thatched and "punky"] if not properly managed). But it is economical as sod, endures shade well, and is even fairly tolerant of salt spray. On the whole the grass is versatile and modest in its requirements, thrives under "average" fertilization and irrigation, and can be mowed with either reel or rotary equipment. While acceptable for lawns, st. augustine is not suggested for golf courses or athletic fields. St. augustine apparently originated in the American tropics and was introduced to the southern United States many years ago.

St. augustine leaves are folded in bud and have a distinctive "half-twist" petiole where they join the sheath. The blade is rather broad and blunt, the ligule a fringe of hairs. The grass spreads by stolons, the leaves being moderately separated or quite condensed depending upon the selection. Seedheads are simple spikes, few in number and seldom objectionable. Propagation is almost entirely vegetative, with "common" cultivars such as Roselawn most grown. A few select cultivars are available, including the older Bitter Blue, Floratine, and most recently Floratam (coarse, but resistant to chinchbug and to the SAD—"st. augustine decline"—virus which is serious west of the Mississippi).

CENTIPEDEGRASS

Centipede looks very much like a finer-textured st. augustinegrass, but lacks the half-twist where the leaf blade joins the sheath. The grass was introduced into the United States from China in 1916. The leaves are folded in bud, the ligule consists of short hairs, and the leaf blades are blunt and flattened. The grass spreads well by stolons. Seedstalks are spike-like and not much of a nuisance.

Centipede is highly thought of as a "poor man's" grass, requiring little attention. It is temperamental about soil conditions, however, and "resents" high fertility or alkalinity. It is slow to establish from seed, the lawn appearing to be solid crabgrass the first year, although the centipede normally takes over in the second year. It is perhaps more commonly propagated vegetatively. Centipede endures shade and heat well, but cold rather poorly. It seems to do best in the northern portions of the coastal plain, where it is mainly used for home lawns. Centipede frequently develops chlorosis and then requires a change of fertilization procedures, or special applications of iron, to turn green once again. Only one or two cultivars have been selected, of which Oaklawn (selected at Oklahoma State University) is best known.

BAHIAGRASS

Bahia is indigenous to South America and has come into lawn usage almost accidentally, having been introduced first as a pasture species. Bahia grows more openly than does st. augustine and has narrower, more elongate leaf blades. These are generally rolled in leafbud and have a short membranous ligule. The plant spreads horizontally by flattened rhizomes and stolons. Seedheads are very abundant and seasonally pestiferous, being difficult to mow.

Bahiagrass is highly adaptable and thrives on relatively low maintenance, not much more than is required for centipedegrass. It finds favor for home lawns, golf-course fairways, and similar uses where an elegant turf is not required. It withstands sun and heat well, but not cold. Shade tolerance is good. Bahia is generally mowed at intermediate heights (one and a half to two and a half inches), rotary mowers being acceptable.

Three relatively unselected cultivars are available from seed, with a fourth dwarf selection (Wilmington, perhaps the most desirable) generally unavailable because of poor seed production. Pensacola is widely used for pastures, and because of its ready availability is often planted to lawns as well as roadsides. Argentine is generally preferred for turf, however, having a softer "feel" (the leaves are more or less hairy), darker color, and more prostrate growth. Paraguay is somewhat coarser, the leaves quite hairy but lighter green; it is less tolerant to cold than Argentine.

41 **Fig. 2-23** Grass characteristics useful for identification. Adapted from University of Wisconsin Extension Service Circular 69.

The Team

culm

leaf blade

ligule

auricle

collar

internode

leaf sheath

node

PARTS OF A GRASS

stolon

rhizome

SOD-FORMING GRASS

rolled in young shoot

folded in young shoot

bunch grass

VEGETATIVE KEY FOR IDENTIFICATION
OF A FEW COMMONPLACE GRASSES IN LAWNS

(Choose The Most Appropriate Alternatives Progressively)

I COOL WEATHER ("NORTHERN") GRASSES, GREEN AFTER FROST
(EXCEPT CRABGRASS AND FOXTAIL WEEDS)

1a Leaf blades folded in the bud-shoot.

    2a Auricles (earlike lobes where leaf blade and sheath join) present. . . . Perennial Ryegrass (*Lolium perenne*)

    2b No auricles present.

        3a Leaf blades narrow and "bristly," often inrolled like a tube, the tip pointed; old leaf sheaths quite persistent at base of stem, usually brown. . . . Fine Fescues (*Festuca rubra,* and related forms)

        3b Leaf blades flat, not "bristly" or "tufted," the tips boat-shaped; old leaf sheaths withering quickly.

            4a Leaf blades elongate, deep green; seedheads not abundant below mowing height, seasonal in late spring; reasonably uncongested growth. . . . Kentucky Bluegrass (*Poa pratensis*)

            4b Leaf blades shorter, light green; buff seedheads usually present below mowing height; a tuft-like "weed." . . . Annual Bluegrass (*Poa annua*)

            4c Leaf blades elongate, delicate, light green, and notably glossy; seedheads seldom evident; grows in dense colonies. . . . Roughstalk Bluegrass (*Poa trivialis*)

1b Leaf blade rolled in bud-shoot.

    5a Auricles (earlike lobes where leaf blade and sheath join) present.

        6a Leaf blades glossy below; auricles not stiff; ligule smooth; bunchgrass lacking rhizomes.

            7a Leaf blades rough to the touch along the edges; ligule short (½ mm or less). . . . Tall and Meadow Fescues (*Festuca arundinacea, F. elatior*)

            7b Leaf blades smooth on margins; ligule prominent (1 mm or more). . . . Annual Ryegrass (*Lolium multiflorum*)

        6b Leaf blades not glossy below; auricles stiff; ligule lightly haired; rhizomes prominent. . . . Quackgrass, and some wheatgrasses (*Agropyon repens,* etc.)

    5b Auricles not present.

        8a Ligule a fringe of hairs; annual bunchgrass "weed." . . . Foxtail (*Setaria spp.*)

8b Ligule membranous, fingernail-like; spreading by stolons.

9a Leaf blade or sheath at least somewhat hairy; annual
"weed." . . . Crabgrass (*Digitaria spp.*)

9b Leaves smooth, not hairy; perennials. . . .
Bentgrass group (*Argrostis spp.*)

II WARM SEASON ("SOUTHERN") GRASSES DORMANT IN COLD WEATHER
(EXCEPT RYEGRASS AND TALL FESCUE)

10a Leaf blades folded in bud-shoot.

11a Ligule a hairy fringe, not membranous.

12a Leaves closely approximate, the sheaths greatly over-
lapping; usually rhizomes as well as stolons. . . .
Bermudagrass (*Cynodon spp.*)

12b Leaves more distant along stem, sheaths not greatly
overlapping; stolons but no rhizomes.

13a Leaves and sheaths not hairy, not notably stalked
(petioled) nor twisted. . . . Carpetgrass (*Axonopus
compressus*)

13b Leaf sheaths hairy along margins and midrib;
blades conspicuously stalked, with an obvious "half-
twist." . . . St. Augustinegrass (*Stenotaphrum
secundatum*)

11b Ligule a fingernail-like membrane.

14a Auricles (earlike lobes where leaf blade and sheath
join) present; blade shiny; "wintergrass" that sometimes hangs on. . . . Perennial Ryegrass (*Lolium
perrene*)

14b Auricles lacking.

15a Perennial, spreading by stolons; ligule short, with
prominent marginal hairs. . . . Centipedegrass
(*Eremochloa ophiuroides*)

15b Bunchgrasses without stolons; ligule prominent;
"weeds" in lawns. . . . Goosegrass (*Eleusine indica*)
and other species

10b Leaf blades rolled in bud-shoot.

16a Auricles (earlike lobes where leaf blade and sheath join)
present; leaf blades "shiny" beneath; bunchgrasses.

17a Leaf blades stiff and rough to the touch along edges;
ligule short (½ mm or less). . . . Tall Fescue (*Festuca
arundinacea*)

17b Leaf blades pliable and smooth on margins; ligule
prominent (1 mm or more). . . . Annual Ryegrass
(*Lolium multiflorum*)

16b Auricles lacking; leaf blades dull (not lustrous); stoloniferous and rhizomatous.

18a Sheaths flattened, often hairy; ligule membranous; coarse and relatively open. . . . Bahiagrass (*Paspalum notatum*)

18b Sheaths round, hairless except at throat; ligule a fringe of hairs; finer textured, dense, and durable. . . . Zoysiagrass (*Zoysia spp.*)

18c Sheaths round, smooth (but blade hairy and grayish-green); ligule a fringe of hairs; loose, open habit; male and female plants separate. . . . Buffalograss (*Buchloë dactyloides*)

TURFGRASS CULTIVARS

The range of turfgrass cultivars extends from adventive (natural) populations molded by the environment (viz., Arboretum Kentucky bluegrass) to highly sophisticated intraspecific hybridizations (and less frequently interspecific ones, which have not proved especially useful).

A cultivar may be maintained by any of a number of techniques, including clonal propagation (notable with golf-green bentgrasses and the finer bermudagrass hybrids), seed maintained essentially as a pure line by rogueing of off-types to a standard, and random crossing from proscribed parental lines (three clonally maintained lines in Penncross creeping bentgrass, sixteen "pure line" parent stocks in the multiline Manhattan perennial ryegrass, over a dozen mostly apomictic lines in Park Kentucky bluegrass). Maintaining reasonable genetic uniformity in crop after crop of polycross seed harvests requires frequent fresh planting into fields free of the species, lest one of the parental lines become dominant and overshadow others. In the case of Penncross, growers have agreed that for certification a seed field will be in production for three years only.

It is impossible to say which of these procedures is most satisfactory for yielding good turfgrass cultivars. For general lawn usage heterogeneity (as exemplified by the mixing of cultivars or the use of heterozygous material) has satisfied needs better than have homozygosity and a narrow genetic base. Durability is of more concern in the lawn than is exact morphological homogeneity. Moreover, some of the most important turfgrass species—notably Kentucky bluegrass—are so complicated genetically that established crop-breeding techniques accomplish little.

On the whole cultivars of southern turfgrasses are most "conventional." Where planted by seed a general population may be used that is not characterized by cultivar definition (e.g., common bermuda or centipede; with bahiagrass a few standard cultivars are used with little attempt to refine the bloodlines). Ready sexual crossing and recombination keeps bermudagrass selections from coming true-to-type from seed, and the finer cultivars (many of them developed by interspecific crossing) must be maintained by clonal separations. This is relatively simple with an aggressive, fast-growing species such as bermuda, the stolons of which can be scattered much as is seed for making new starts.

Very much the same system is used with zoysia. Local selections or ecotypes are maintained by clonal planting of sprigs or plugs. St. augustinegrass sets little seed, and the relatively few selections given cognizance as cultivars are, like the common grass, propagated vegetatively. Even with centipede, of which seed is available (although of very small size and quite expensive), vegetative propagation rather than seeding is usual.

With northern turfgrasses, the situation is more complicated, particularly with Kentucky bluegrass, a polyploid-aneuploid with an apparent base chromosome number of 7. Natural interspecific crosses and introgression are probably involved, and *Poa trivialis* may have played a part. So great is the potentiality for genetic variation in "wild" adventive stands of Kentucky bluegrass in North America that early plant breeders believed it rather pointless to attempt hybridization within the species. Dr. Funk has since, of course, shown the advantages of utilizing select genomes. But it is true that in the long course of evolution nature has played upon the tremendous variability within the species to create untold biotypes and ecotypes. Thus, the main source for bluegrass cultivars has been simple selection of "strains" showing outstanding features.

Bluegrasses are to a greater or lesser degree apomictic, seed generally being from an unreduced egg not fertilized by pollen. The degree of sexuality has been shown to vary, greatly from strain to strain, somewhat (at least in certain cases) with latitude, and with growing conditions (natural outdoor pollination showed less sexuality at Rutgers than did forced flowering in the greenhouse). Funk's work clearly indicates that the tendency towards apomixis can be inherited and that even highly sexual lines can sometimes have their better traits bred into highly apomictic lines to create a desirable hybrid sufficiently apomictic to merit commercial development. Cultivars brought to market are generally highly apomictic, often ninety-seven or ninety-eight percent so (and the remaining small percentage of off-types mostly represents weak recombinations that are overwhelmed in the population).

Sufficient bluegrass selections from nature have been made now, to create quite a bank of select germplasm. At Rutgers University, hundreds of thousands of selections have been evaluated; most of them have been discarded, with the remainder husbanded for breeding potentialities. Dr. Funk and his students have learned how to achieve crosses even of highly apomictic selections. It has been found with most strains that pollination must take place shortly after midnight (in the greenhouse) in order to have male gametes present sufficiently early during egg meiosis to achieve a worthwhile, though small, degree of fertilization. Hot-water emasculation has generally proved satisfactory for panicles of the female parent. Many of the hybridizations achieved seem to be of a triploid nature, probably involving an unreduced egg and a reduced male gamete.

The situation is a little less involved with fine fescues. Most cultivars are simply selections carried to pure-line standards. Bentgrasses constitute a rather complex group, with the ecotypic cultivar Highland probably descended from a south German bent introduction. Astoria is a similar chance selection from nature, while Exeter represents a more deliberately developed inbred from the University of Rhode Island (and hence is more uniform than Highland or Astoria). Creeping bentgrasses have, by and large, been picked up as successful clones on golf greens and perpetuated vegetatively by stolons. The better fine-leaf perennial ryegrasses seem to be mostly multiline combinations of ecotypes, though most older cultivars represent inbred selections.

Thus it is apparent that lawngrass cultivars represent many patterns of origination and practical propagation. Many are simply ecotypes of adventive grass, sorted out by natural selection. Some are honed to a fine edge by elimination of off-types through selection and inbred rogueing, their characteristics perpetuated as a pure line or protected through vegetative propagation (including apomixis). Still others are the results of deliberate breeding programs, for which sufficient germplasm has only in recent years become available. The trend is in this direction, with the diversification that has proven useful in lawn culture being obtained through mechanical blending of different varieties or through the polycross technique (whereby several outstanding selections are planted together and let cross as they will) rather than through use of highly variable, unselected strains.

3 Lawn Soils and Surroundings

Soil is so commonplace that it seldom attracts attention. We know that a thin layer of topsoil is all that separates humankind from starvation, yet around the home it is often regarded as mere "dirt." Soil is quite important, even away from the farm. Without adequate soil, yards, gardens, parks, and greenbelts are destined for less than satisfactory performance. After all, the soil is home for the hidden half of plants, the root systems. We don't want to get tangled up in the intricacies of soil physics and chemistry here, but what a soil "is all about" merits some attention. As we shall see, soils are by no means independent of their environment. They develop in certain ways in response to source materials, climatic conditions, exposure and position, and chance occurrences.

Soil is not a substance but a system—a sort of ecosystem, if you will. Major interacting factors are residual rock particles (clay, silt, sand), organic additions (humus, such as might be left when grass roots die), living organisms (myriads of small forms of life such as bacteria, to say nothing of bigger "beasts" ranging from worms to gophers), a soil atmosphere (air sucked into soil pores as water drains, and gasses that are emitted or absorbed by organisms), water (ranging from a molecular layer tightly fixed to soil particles to free water that percolates through the ground), and many other influences. It is important how a soil faces and where it lies; that on a hillside will be different from that forming on bottomland. And, of course, past history is very important: Was the area glaciated, did the soil develop under forest or under grass, how long (and how wastefully) has the ground been cropped, have toxic substances been added (such as wastes or pesticides)? And, as with our ecosystem of Chapter One, few soils are in any degree virgin. A Wisconsin study indicates that eighty percent of the home yards in that state are highly disturbed, from foundation digging or other alteration of the natural profile.

Fig. 3-1 Your soil may be light or heavy, good or poor; managed properly it will support a lawn. Soils are improved by growing grass on them.

SOIL CHARACTERISTICS

Soil can be described or classified in various ways. Geographically soils are identified by general characteristics of the soil profile (an imaginary vertical slice down to bedrock showing characteristic layers) (Fig. 3-2). We needn't concern ourselves with complicated series of definitions that soil specialists use to name and characterize various soils,

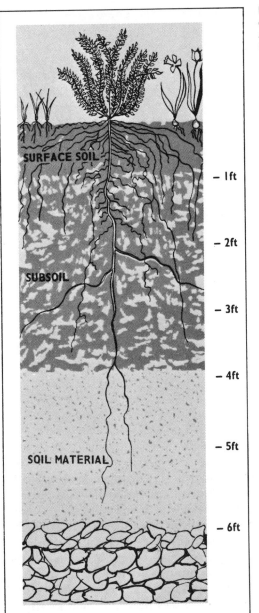

Fig. 3-2 Soils are made up of contrasting layers called horizons. Adapted from USDA Information Bulletin 320.

most of which are badly disturbed and unnatural in any event where lawns are planted. But the size of the soil's particles and the ways they interact have considerable practical significance. These characteristics will determine, among other things, how readily rain soaks in, how easily roots expand, how efficiently fertilizer is used, and so on (Fig. 3-3).

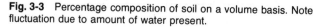

Fig. 3-3 Percentage composition of soil on a volume basis. Note fluctuation due to amount of water present.

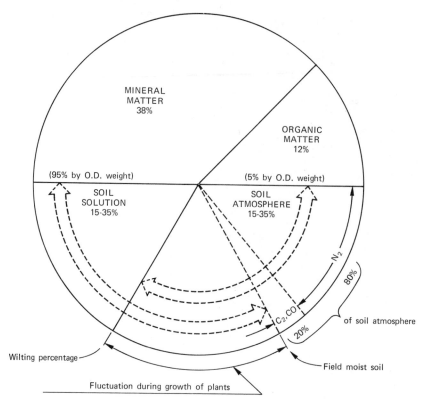

Obviously, the size of the mineral particles in a soil may range from rocks and pebbles down to the minutest clay fragments measured in millionths of an inch. Particle size determines the *texture* of the soil, in a range from coarse to fine. More coarsely textured soils, such as ones containing much sand, have comparatively large spaces between particles, or abundant large pore (macropore) space. Generally water runs through large pores "like a sieve," so free-flowing are they. At the opposite end of the scale lie fine-textured soils, mostly clay, in which micropores predominate. Clay particles are extremely small (less than 0.002 mm: See Table 3-1), and the spaces between them mostly so narrow as to be capillary rather than free-flowing. Although fine-textured soils have a tremendously increased pore network compared to coarse-textured soils, they can accept water only slowly (and drain equally slowly). But the tremendous internal surface these micropores represent makes such soil exceedingly responsive to physical and chemical interactions (such as fixation of fertilizer ions, which are held by electrical charges to the surface of clay particles). (See Fig. 3-5.)

Table 3-1 Soil texture classification by particle size.

Soil separate	Diameter, mm*	Number of particles per gram	Surface area in 1 g, sq cm
Very coarse sand	2.00–1.00	90	11
Coarse sand	1.00–0.50	720	23
Medium sand	0.50–0.25	5700	45
Fine sand	0.25–0.10	46,000	91
Very fine sand	0.10–0.05	722,000	227
Silt	0.05–0.002	5,776,000	454
Clay	<0.002	90,260,853,000	8,000,000

*United States Department of Agriculture System.

Few soils contain only a limited range of particles, of course, most consisting of combinations of clay-silt-sand (see Table 3-1 for a definition of these particle sizes). The soil texture triangle (Fig. 3-4) indicates

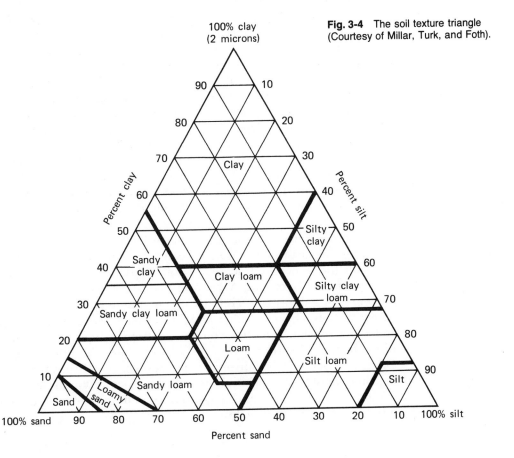

Fig. 3-4 The soil texture triangle (Courtesy of Millar, Turk, and Foth).

how certain textural combinations receive designations such as "clay," "loam," and so on. When soil is artificially compounded, as for golf greens, needing a lot of porosity and ability to withstand compaction, at least seventy-five percent sand is included. An attempt is made to achieve about a half-and-half apportionment between large (drainage) and capillary (water-holding) pore systems. Medium sands, with a particle size range from 0.1–0.6 mm, seem to serve best.

Equally as important is *structure*, the way the particles hold together. When chemical or electrostatic forces linking the soil particles are lacking, soil disperses (runs and *puddles*) when rained upon or cultivated. It is said to have "poor structure," tending to compact and become impervious (admitting little air or water and discouraging root penetration). Poor structure can often override the advantages of good texture. But when a soil has "good" structure it becomes tillable and highly productive, even if consisting almost entirely of clay particles (which could be rock-hard when dry and gummy when wet under poor structural circumstances).

Good structure results from soil particles adhering to one another, making loose aggregates or *crumbs*. We all recognize the advantages of a crumbly or well-aggregated soil, for ease of handling (cultivation) and crop response. It is not always clear just what makes a soil crumbly, but certainly organic materials assist in the accomplishment. Prized prairie soils may have only a few percent of organic (humus) content by weight, and other good agricultural lands only around two percent, but what a difference it makes compared to balky soil with little organic content such as southern laterites ("red clays") and adobes. Decomposing organic residues provide "gums" that cause soil particles to cohere; otherwise they would disperse and puddle. What this boils down to is that mixing organic matter into a soil ordinarily improves it, a maneuver practiced by gardeners since time immemorial. Organic residues are leaven for both coarse- and fine-textured soils; they make "light" (sandy type) soils "heavier" (more retentive, less porous) and "heavy" soils (ones abundant in clay and silt) "lighter" (more porous, less compact, and more manageable).

Still another characterization often heard is *topsoil* and *subsoil*. These are rather inexact terms that nevertheless have merit for positioning generally the respective fractions of soil. Topsoil, of course, refers to the uppermost layer (the A horizon primarily), which under most sequences of soil formation is fairly rich in humus and of rather good structure. Subsoil, on the other hand, represents deeper soil layers (B and C horizons), which often consist of extremely fine (clay) particles which have leached down with percolating water through the ages. Often a barrier is formed through which roots have difficulty penetrating. Since most biological activity in soil takes place near an air interface (within the top few inches of a topsoil), subsoils tend to be anoxious, infertile, and contain little humus.

Fig. 3-5 Structure of montmorillonite, one of the commonplace clay minerals. Note locus for fixation of cation nutrients. (After Hofmann, Endell, and Wilm, Marshall, and Hendricks.)

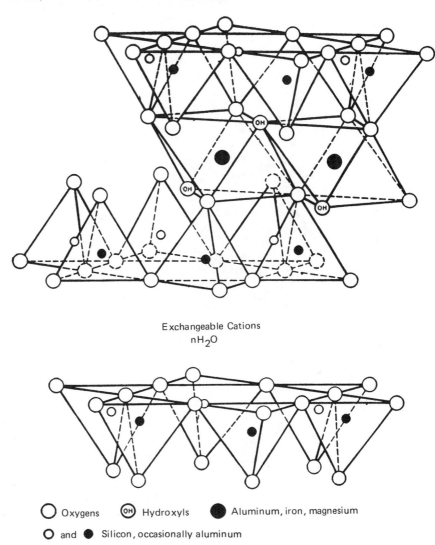

Exchangeable Cations
nH_2O

○ Oxygens   ⊙ₒₕ Hydroxyls   ● Aluminum, iron, magnesium

○ and ● Silicon, occasionally aluminum

SOIL BIOLOGY

By this time it is clear that we are dealing with complex microenvironment. Each square inch of soil is populated by millions of microorganisms, which react to everyday necessities much as do larger organisms (appropriating organic materials for food, utilizing water that seeps into the ground, and depending upon air which follows as the water percolates downward). Figure 3-6 affords an idealized diagram of this miniature world. Its functioning depends primarily upon air-water-particle relationships and their suitability for the "wee beasties" and plant root hairs subsisting in this microenvironment.

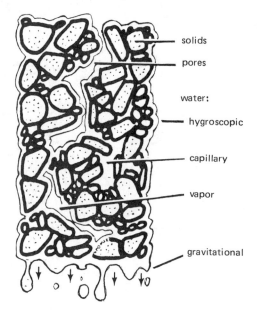

solids

pores

water:

hygroscopic

capillary

vapor

gravitational

Fig. 3-6 Stylized diagram of soil. Rock particles provide a framework housing the many soil components mentioned in the text. Adapted from L.A. Spomer, 15th Illinois Turfgrass Conference.

Obviously, the soil "weather" constantly changes. It is buffered somewhat, but still responds to what happens in our macroscopic world. If it rains, the soil pores fill with water, and only as this drains will air enter to sustain bacterial and root respiration. If above-ground weather is hot and dry, soil dries out, and biological activity mostly grinds to a halt, with the soil organisms "hibernating." Biological activity in the soil never ceases entirely, but it does diminish at high temperatures (as in the desert) or near freezing.

As microorganisms feed upon organic residues they release carbon dioxide, as do animals when they breathe. Carbon dioxide is absorbed by growing plants, which utilize the gas for making food. Many such obscure exchanges go on in the soil continuously, and the end result of some can be measured. Soil is a *sink* (i.e., a "rathole" into which the product disappears) for carbon monoxide, for example, a deadly poison when breathed. So soil is not something inert and indestructible, but a madly functioning biological system, disruption of which risks deteriorated structure and reduced productivity.

Lawn Soils
and
Surroundings

In a popular sense a fertile soil is one that is quite productive, although, as we have seen, productivity depends upon structure (which in turn determines air-water relationships) as well as upon abundance of nutrients. In a stricter sense fertility refers only to the availability of the mineral nutrients required by higher plants. Table 5-2 in Chapter Five indicates how many pounds of several nutrient elements are required for an "acre's worth" of grass growth. Nutrient condition is typically sustained and improved through addition of fertilizer, the subject of a later chapter. Keep in mind, however, that adequacy of nutrients is only one of the many needs of growing grass; without adequate sustenance in other respects a highly fertilized soil can still be quite unproductive (indeed, even toxic if the nutrients accumulate too heavily). The situation can perhaps be most easily visualized by the barrel of Figure 3-7, in which the least-ample stave will determine how well the barrel fills. There will always be some limitation to plant growth; the trick is to keep the various necessities pretty much in balance, so that a lack of one essential does not waste the potential of others.

Fig. 3-7 The limiting factor concept. Adapted from G.S. Smith, University of Florida, in Turf Bulletin of Massachusetts, Turf and Lawngrass Council.

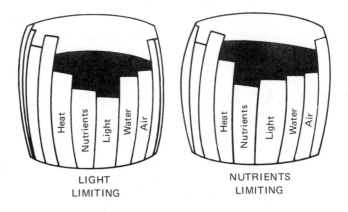

LIGHT
LIMITING

NUTRIENTS
LIMITING

SOIL ACIDITY–ALKALINITY

Whether a soil is alkaline or acid is generally indicated by a numerical pH reading. Technically pH is the inverse logarithm of the hydrogen ion concentration. But all we have to know is that a pH of 7 means the soil is neutral, anything higher alkaline, anything lower acid.

Each unit change represents a tenfold increase in acidity or alkalinity; thus a soil with a pH of 5 is ten times as acid as one with a pH of 6, or one with a pH of 8.5 ten times as alkaline as one with a pH of 7.5. Few soils ever become so alkaline as pH 9 (exceptions occur in alkaline deserts and the high plains of the West), and few soils become more acid than pH 5 (exceptions being some of the highly leached soils of the East, or where sulphurous leachate develops as in mine tailings). Most plants, including grasses, grow best under neutral or slightly acid conditions. Fine fescues, bentgrasses, and centipede "enjoy" acid soil more than do bluegrasses, ryegrasses, and bermudagrass, for example.

Acid soils are said to be "sour," neutral or alkaline ones "sweet." Sour soils can be sweetened by the addition of lime (usually ground-up limestone, but occasionally hydrated lime). Highly alkaline soils can be brought to a lower pH through addition of sulphur, or even the salt of a strong acid such as gypsum (calcium sulphate). Adjustment of pH will be discussed more fully in the chapter on fertilization, but it should be pointed out here that pH has an influence much farther reaching than its direct effect upon the growing plant. In fact pH helps regulate biological activity and chemical reactions in the soil. Certain nutrients become insoluble or "unavailable," others overly abundant (and hence toxic, as aluminum), if the pH becomes too high or too low. Centipede-grass in particular tends to become chlorotic if soil conditions turn alkaline, and lawns of the western plains can become chlorotic because alkalinity is high (which "ties up" the iron in the soil which is necessary for green chlorophyll formation). A soil test that readily indicates pH is a good starting point when planting a lawn. The comparative abundance of essential nutrients can also be determined by soil test.

FREQUENT SOIL PROBLEMS

Various things can "go wrong" with soil, leading to its deterioration. For example, constant cultivation causes oxidation of most of the organic material and may result in the breakdown of soil structure; many a garden soil, not given the relief of an interim green manure planting (vegetation plowed under to replenish organic matter) gradually becomes so intractable that it can scarcely be cultivated. It is sticky when wet, hard when dry. Mayan farmland in southern Mexico, abandoned over a thousand years ago, shows the soil still not to have recovered its original organic content and fertility! Fortunately, soil planted to grass usually improves. The grass roots and clippings gradually replenish the organic fraction. Prairie soils are among the richest, made so by eons of grass growth.

But even under grass soil structure can worsen, most of the time because of *compaction*. Compaction simply means that the soil is pressed or squeezed more solid, eliminating much of the macropore space. Compaction is mostly a problem on heavily used ground such as pathways, athletic fields, golf greens, and where equipment passes. Soil compacts more readily when wet and soft than when dry. Rainfall penetrates compacted soil poorly, gas interchange is inadequate, and root growth diminishes. In northerly climates annual freezing-thawing helps loosen and restructure compacted soil, at least to the depth that frost penetrates. For a home lawn this probably suffices to keep the soil adequately aerified. But for heavily used grounds, especially in the South where freezing does not occur, mechanical aerification may prove helpful. Certainly aerification is a standard practice for maintaining golf greens in all parts of the country.

Several types of aerification equipment have been developed, the simplest of which consists of spikes that are forced into the soil. These often loosen thatch more than benefiting the soil. As a matter of fact, such spikes must compress rather than loosen soil at the particular spot where they are forced into the ground, although there may be some lateral agitation that fractures hard ground and permits a better influx of air. Machines having slicing "knives" on a rotating cylinder probably are better than simply forcing spikes into the ground, for they move into the soil with a lateral cutting action that should not be so compressive. Both types of machine penetrate only shallowly, however, and fail to reach compaction areas two to three inches deep where the problem usually resides.

Deeper aerification can be achieved with coring machines. These have hollow tube-like penetraters that remove (and eject) a pencil-like core of soil. The better machines punch holes several inches deep. That the holes so made benefit grass rooting is attested by the fact that very soon they become filled with thriving grass roots. However, even the best of aerification techniques have a relatively short-lived influence. A study at Pennsylvania State University showed that after several years practically no influence could be detected from a wide range of aerification treatments. Still another soil-loosening device is the subsurface cultivator, a machine designed with vibrating probes that are pulled forcibly through the soil. Use on reasonably dry ground the vibration fractures the soil, the cracks serving as aerification channels. Such machines tear the grass where they slice through the turf, and their effectiveness is limited to heavy soils in dry condition.

Soil organisms, particularly earthworms, are great soil aerifiers and cultivators. Over a century ago Darwin noted that earthworms were quite beneficial in churning fields. One study indicates that about thirty tons of organic residues per acre are consumed and dragged into the soil by earthworms annually. Even on strip-mining soil banks in

Ohio as much as two tons of black locust debris per acre was buried or consumed by earthworms; their fertile casts (i.e., soil-and-feces passed through the gut) contributed appreciably to soil improvement. Numerous investigations have pointed up the usefulness of earthworms for keeping down lawn thatch. Where pesticides that drive out earthworms are used, such as some pre-emergence weed preventers, thatch accumulates (though not on adjacent ground populated by worms). Water infiltration lessens, the moisture-holding capacity of the soil is reduced, soil compaction increases, and grass growth suffers. Except for swards such as golf and bowling greens that must be perfectly true (where casts would become obstructions), earthworm activity should prove a boon to lawn keeping.

Occasionally failure of water insoak into a soil is due less to soil pore blockage than to water-repelling (hydrophobic) surfaces. Even sandy soils can become coated with water-repelling substances that interfere with rainfall acceptance, not an uncommon occurrence on some of the sandy soils of northern Michigan. Many soils are quite difficult to wet after a thorough drying out. And, as with a thatch roof shedding rain, a heavily thatched lawn may cause water to run off rather than letting it soak through to the soil. You have perhaps noticed how dry the soil can be, even after a heavy rain, where old grass clippings have been used as mulch. In such instances treatment with a wetting agent (Aqua-Gro is a non-ionic type much tested for turf) usually breaks down surface tension enough to facilitate water penetration.

REGIONAL FOCUS

It is apparent from the maps of Figure 2-2 and Figure 3-8 that North America experiences a general moisture gradient from abundance in the East to deficiency in the West, and a temperature gradient from warm weather and a prolonged growing season in the South to cooler weather with a short growing season in the North. These influences shape soil qualities in a general way.

Soils that have developed under ample rainfall tend to be leached of nutrients, and the finer soil particles gradually work down the soil column to the water table (where they often settle and become something of a barrier). The native vegetation usually consists of trees, which concentrate most ecosystem nutrients in their voluminous biomass, returning a portion sparingly as leaves and twigs drop and decay. From Minnesota-eastern Texas eastward most soils have developed under this influence. Of course their texture varies greatly depending upon the parent rock from which they formed (limestone and igneous

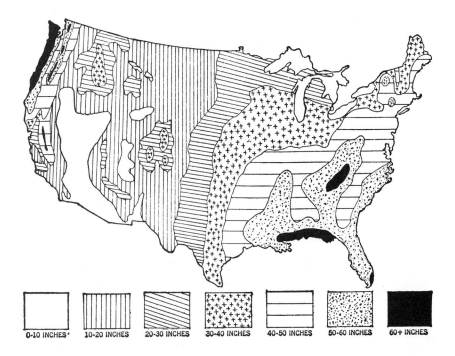

Fig. 3-8 General rainfall distribution in the United States. Average rainfall very much influences soil conditions. Irrigation is essential for convenient gardening where rainfall totals much less than 30 inches annually. Generally soils are alkaline at about 30 inches or less rainfall, although even with far greater rainfall soil need not necessarily be acid if in limestone areas.

0-10 INCHES   10-20 INCHES   20-30 INCHES   30-40 INCHES   40-50 INCHES   50-60 INCHES   60+ INCHES

bedrock often spawn clays and silts; sandstones and quartz-containing bedrock, or unconsolidated coastal plain deposits, usually yield porous soils rich in sand).

Where rainfall is not sufficient to leach appreciably through the soil but is approximately balanced by evaporation and transpiration, prairie develops. Prairies concentrate organic residues and nutrients in the topsoil. In the United States extensive prairie evolved west of the forested section to the Rocky Mountains. In even dryer habitat (arid plains and desert) rainfall sufficient to produce ground water flow is only occasional and will generally be evaporated through capillary rise from the soil. Salts accumulate at the surface (alkali flats). Except for high elevations the American Southwest and Great Basin are desert-like.

Temperature is equally determining. Soils formed in cool climates tend to accumulate organic residues (biological activity and the tempo of decomposition is not so great as under subtropical conditions). Glaciers, too, have overrun northerly locations, stripping some areas of

59

soil and depositing it elsewhere, often to the accompaniment of bogs and lakes which become traps for sediment and organics. In contrast soils of the southern United States, particularly those that have been cultivated, tend to have limited organic content and become eroded more easily.

In mountainous areas soil erodes very easily. It accumulates in the valleys and basins, but the slopes are thinly covered and rocky. Soils are usually less fertile when formed from hard-to-weather and scantily mineralized bedrock, such as the metamorphic formations of the Appalachians. By and large soil building will be harder in mountainous areas than in the flatlands. In the less favored locations through much of New England, hauling in of topsoil is required to create much of a lawn or garden.

As was noted earlier, heavier soils inland from the coastal plain are quite responsive to improvement; they hold moisture well, bank applied fertilizers nicely, and improve as grass is grown on them. But soils of the coastal plain—that flat fringe of country at low elevation from Long Island through southern Georgia to coastal Texas—are often sandy, pervious, holding moisture and nutrients poorly. They must be fertilized and irrigated frequently, with the exception of the rich alluvial soils deposited in deltas. The Mississippi Valley from the bootheel of Missouri southward is replete with transported alluvium bequeathed from northern uplands. Alluviums may be poorly drained, but they are generally rich, workable, and produce excellent lawns.

Rich soils are characteristic of the Midwest. Spottily in Ohio-Indiana-Illinois and abundantly westward from there, the rich prairie lands occur. The eastern prairies receive sufficient rainfall to produce abundant vegetation (the tall-grass prairie) and are among the most prized agricultural lands in the nation today, rich in nutrients and of excellent structure. The more westerly prairies (short-grass prairie) also developed good soil, although the less abundant rainfall sometimes results in salt accumulations, excessive alkalinity, and soil loss due to wind erosion.

From the Rocky Mountains westward to the Sierras-Cascades the country is too dry to support much other than desert vegetation. The exceptions are mountain ranges that intercept moisture, providing streamflow enough for irrigation. For the most part soils of arid lands are less than ideal, tending to be overly saline, rocky (the finer soil has blown away), and occasionally "poisoned" by alkali (usually where impermanent lakebeds form). Brick-like adobes (heavy soils of inferior structure) frequently develop. But west of the Sierras-Cascades again are found some of the most productive soils in the nation, particularly in the interior valleys of California-Oregon-Washington-British Columbia. In California topography is all cut up by mountain ranges, so it is difficult to generalize; but on the whole the soils have reasonably good structure and respond well to irrigation and fertilization.

Fig. 3-9 Yes, you can have a lawn here, too. But you'll need irrigation, maybe acidification. People have learned to manipulate the environment to satisfy grasses' needs.

Obviously, in a brief chapter such as this it is impossible to do more than highlight a few of the important characteristics of soils. Those wishing more elaborate discussion might consult a reference book such as *Soils: An Introduction to Soils and Plant Growth,* by R. L. Donahue, J. C. Shickluna, and L. S. Robertson, 3rd ed., 1971, Prentice-Hall, Inc.

Lawn Response to Soil and Location: A Capsule Summary

NORTH AND NORTHEAST

Northerly locations provide ideal cool-season turfgrass country. Bluegrass and fine fescues planted to heavier soils are largely self-reliant. Lawns on poorer soils require more frequent fertilization. Watering may spruce a lawn up but is seldom required for survival.

Bluegrass follows the same general growth cycle, whether in Providence, Dayton, or Denver. Providence has an equable marine climate causing little stress; but the soil is seldom rich, probably needing lime as well as fairly liberal fertilization. Dayton has a continental climate exhibiting greater extremes; growing grass is a bit harder. But the soil is generally deep and responsive, making good lawns quite possible. Denver must have irrigation, but the high elevation is very favorable to bluegrass. Soils may be overly rich in cations such as potassium and are often saline until irrigated (they will benefit more from sulfur or gypsum than from lime).

61

From Washington, D.C., and the foothills of the Appalachians westward through southern Illinois and Kansas City as far as the High Plains the country is difficult for both northern and southern lawngrasses. Bluegrass culture extends as far south as Georgia and Alabama in the mountains, and good bluegrass can be grown in St. Louis and Washington, D.C., with proper care. But bluegrass culture is more difficult there than in Michigan or Massachusetts. By the same token, southern grasses have difficulty so far north as Missouri and Virginia. Indeed, the belt of greatest difficulty for lawn keeping in the United States probably lies across the nation's midsection, where the variable weather rather than soil quality is determining.

In warmer weather irrigation helps to keep lawns green, but here, even more than farther north, watering encourages weeds, especially crabgrass. Some homeowners prefer to sacrifice quality for tenacity, planting deep-rooting tall fescue in this belt. The hardier bermudas and zoysias are also possible.

SOUTHEAST

Most lawns are planted vegetatively in the Southeast. Almost all benefit from fertilization, centipede (a poor-soil species) being an exception. Liming helps many of the southeastern soils, especially eastward. Much bahia and st. augustine are used in Florida, where soils are often poor and sandy. From northern Florida into the Piedmont temperamental centipede does well, too, on the light, acid, infertile soils predominating there. Carpetgrass is a "natural" for boggy land. Better soils of the uplands northward from the Coastal Plain, especially when improved by fertilization and liming, make excellent habitat for bermuda and zoysia.

SOUTHWEST

In the Southwest, lawn keeping involves the same practices mentioned for the East, but irrigation is more critical. Seldom is the need less than for an inch of water per week, but how fast this should be applied depends upon whether the soil is light and porous, or heavy and slow to absorb water. Recalcitrant adobe soils abound. More than anywhere else, aerification seems to aid southwestern soils. Many soils are alkaline and benefit from gypsum or sulfur. Blanching (chlorosis) of the grass due to tie-up of iron can be corrected with iron sulphate or iron chelate sprays.

In west Texas, New Mexico and Arizona lawn keeping is not overly complex. Bermudagrass is mainstay for the lowlands, bluegrass for the higher elevations. Problems troublesome in the East are mitigated by the drier climate and the reduced frequency of weeds. California is more complex. A series of climatic belts runs north-south, causing striking changes of habitat within a few miles. Even in the deserts it is possible to maintain bluegrass under irrigation because the nights cool nicely in the clear, dry atmosphere. But the San Joaquin Valley is clearly country for southern grasses. Elsewhere California is a grand mixture of habitat (Fig. 1-3), often with peculiar local solutions; for example, dichondra, a member of the morning glory family, is much used for lawns in the Los Angeles area.

Interior regions east of the Sierra and Cascade ranges are bluegrass country, handled in the same fashion as in northern Arizona and the Rocky Mountain region. Irrigation is essential, but performance is usually excellent.

The coastal belt from San Francisco northward, in which soils are almost waterlogged during winter, is dominated by bentgrass. In this maritime environment, lawn management follows the dictates for a mild, humid climate. Soluble nutrients are likely to be well leached from the generally heavy, acid soils, calling for generous fertilization and often liming. Humidity encourages disease, although the hazard can sometimes be minimized by keeping potassium levels up. As this is a benevolent climate, blemishes heal rapidly.

4 The Soilbed: Planting the Lawn

Earlier chapters reviewed climatic and vegetational patterns in North America, the development of the soils there, and the kinds of grasses most useful for making a mowed lawn. As was noted, this often involves replacement of a forest ecosystem with a grassland one, indeed with a highly artificial grass community that can persist only with special care. Even prairies have a radically altered ecosystem imposed upon them when fine turf grasses are grown instead of native species. The art of blending grass, soil, and climate into a reasonably durable lawngrass community, without extravagant effort or excessive upkeep, is our next order of business.

No lawn is exactly like any other. Rather, each is beset with its own peculiarities and requirements. While suggestions can be advanced, the person in charge of the lawn must weigh the many parameters affecting performance and adopt those which are useful for his particular circumstances. Planting a lawn merits a bit of forethought. Inadequacies glossed over in the beginning will be a recurring problem forever after. Most corrections are more economically made as the lawn is built rather than after it becomes established. They will be mostly of a physical nature, involving the moving of masses of soil, preparing a good soilbed, and choosing well the kind of grass and the means for establishing it efficiently.

With a new house on disturbed ground, procedures are relatively clear-cut. One starts from scratch, taking advantage of whatever technology is available each step of the way. But what if your grounds are mature, landscaped, with a lawn of sorts already existing? Should the whole thing be plowed up and a fresh start made with all the inconvenience and expense this entails, or can an improved turf be coaxed from the mishmash without such traumatic disturbance? Much will depend upon the nature of lawn problems. If fundamental deficiencies exist, involving pockets of poor soil, unsatisfactory drainage, slopes that are too steep, and so on, then a complete remaking of the lawn would seem the best solution. But if the old lawn is unsatisfactory only because it is weedy or lacks cultivars you prefer, correction should be possible without all this bother. In fact even a small residuum of spreading lawngrasses may be sufficient to recolonize the lawn once weeds are checked and the grass is encouraged through timely fertilization.

Let's assume first that we are dealing with the making of a brand-new lawn from scratch. For this the soil is best turned to make a receptive soilbed, providing opportunity for the mixing in of "goodies" such as a fertilizer, lime, and organics. We will not talk about the

Fig. 4-1 Small-area soilbeds can be cultivated by hand. The surface here is just right for receiving seed. The seed will tumble into the crevices and be ideally situated to sprout.

landscaping layout here—a separate art also worthy of advanced planning—other than to point out that a pattern which allows an easy flow of equipment will save untold hours in lawn upkeep later compared to blind passages, square corners, and odd-shaped designs the mowing of which necessitates a lot of time-consuming maneuvering or special trimming. Informal design with curved, sweeping borders lends itself well to easy upkeep, especially where large grounds are concerned that will be tended with riding equipment.

INITIAL GRADING

Shaping the lawn-to-be is almost invariably necessary, considering the piles of soil and irregular topography left from construction, excavation, digging for utility lines, and so on. This is a job for big equipment—bulldozers, front-end loaders, back-hoes, and the like. They can do a whale of a job in compacting your soil, too, especially if run on wet ground. But even if you are building your own home it is difficult to exercise much control over grading operations, at least without costs getting out of hand. Ideally, the operations would be carried out when the ground is dry, and provision made to scrape the topsoil to the side for replacement later. Special efforts may be worthwhile to protect trees and shrubs that are to be part of the finished landscape. Seldom will a tree flourish if its roots are greatly disturbed, or if buried by an overburden more than a few inches thick bulldozed in from elsewhere. Many operators of big equipment could "care less" if trees are bumped, the bark scraped, branches broken. A temporary protective fence before grading begins may help guard prized trees or shrubs.

The lawn should be made to slope slightly away from the house if this is at all possible. This helps to keep water away from the foundation and minimizes annoying seepage. The slope should be shaped to a "natural" contour, having swales to conduct excess rainfall efficiently to a lower grade. Slopes should be kept gentle enough so that mowing will not require special measures; they should be approachable from almost any angle, so that the mower won't always run on the same track (which would create soil compaction and a one-direction grain to the grass). Particularly watch out for depressed areas; locations where the soil is unsettled and likely to sink in time will become temporary impoundments, inconveniently boggy each time it rains.

DRAINAGE

In most cases lie of the land permits contouring such that surface drainage keeps the ground adequately free from excessive moisture. In some cases, however, subsurface drainage may be necessary. Cor-

Fig. 4-2 A contour map of the homesite helps determine a sensible landscaping layout. Avoid massive grading, if possible. Adapted from USDA Agricultural Information Bulletin 244.

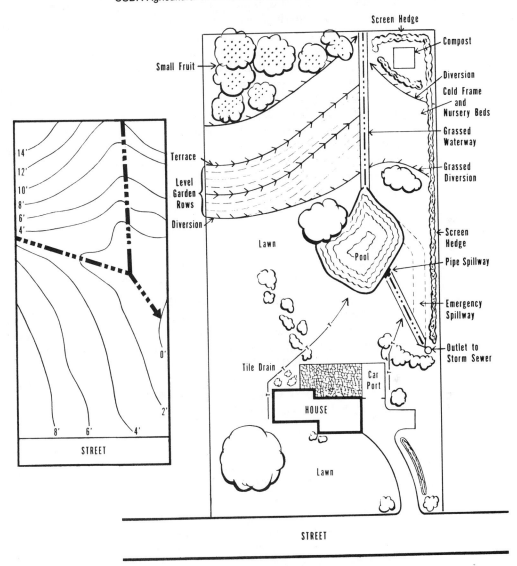

rection is usually accomplished by the laying of agricultural tiles a few feet below the surface to carry away standing water that would seep only slowly from a high water table. Tile laying is an engineering operation. Most homeowners will have no difficulty in laying tiles themselves, however, using a level to guarantee a continuous mild grade for the tiles. They should, of course, empty into a low-lying sewer or other outlet. Tile is typically laid in parallel lines about ten feet apart under waterlogged parts of the lawn, perhaps connecting to the outlet in some sort of herring-bone pattern. In most cases professional installation of drainage will prove more efficient than doing it yourself, since a homeowner seldom has access to the necessary trenching equipment.

In instances where subsurface water flow needs only a little facilitation, "French drains" or slit trenches often work out well. These are simply narrow slits perhaps a couple of inches wide dug into the soil with trenching machines such as are used for laying small-diameter pipe. The trench is filled with chunky rock loose enough to let water percolate easily along the channel almost as readily as if tile had been laid. The top of the trench may be overlaid with smaller pebbles (soil would tend to work into the crevices between the stones and block water movement). Narrow trenches are soon overtopped and obscured by growing grass.

STEEP SLOPES

Ditching and drainage are mostly flat-country problems. At the other extreme hilly land may also need special attention. As a rule it is impossible to maintain turf conveniently when the lawn slopes more steeply than about thirty-five percent. If the lawn cannot be graded so that the slope is less than this, probably retaining walls or terraces (with ground covers instead of grass on the vertical rise) will be worth considering. This is another matter for which expert advice and professional help is usually needed.

UNDERGROUND IRRIGATION

Many homeowners will want to install underground irrigation systems, particularly in the Southwest where watering is so essential. As with the laying of drainage tiles, this is best undertaken during soilbed preparation, rather than having to dig up the lawn later. Again, professionals in the business are best able to guarantee performance of the system. More will be said about automatic irrigation in the chapter on lawn watering, but it is well to note here that any installation must be calibrated for local water pressure and be tested for the pattern and coverage of the spray to ensure that there are no gaps or areas tending to become overwatered and soggy.

The Soilbed　　Grading is not occasion to bury piles of rejected plaster, bricks, or other debris. It pays to gather and remove these, for if they are only shallowly covered they may disrupt normal rooting of the grass and become perpetual "worry spots" in the finished lawn. Pockets of contamination resulting from such inadvertencies as the limey runoff from cement and plaster mixing, discarded oil or paint solvent, and so on, can so alter soil chemistry as to make grass growing very difficult. The contaminated soil should be removed, or at least loosened and scattered as widely as possible, so that there will be no one concentration having markedly different soil characteristics.

SOILBED CULTIVATION

Unless the soil is quite sandy, bulldozing will compact the ground enough to require cultivation of the incipient lawn. With small yards, and perhaps rich organic soils, cultivation can be accomplished rather easily with small equipment such as a rotary tiller. More often, however, practicalities dictate plowing or discing with tractor-drawn equipment. Some lawn-making firms even own machines that work the soil, level it, and seed it in a single pass. As a rule a disc harrow will loosen soil a convenient three or four inches deep, following final grading. Some touching up by hand may be necessary in corners and near obstruction where the big equipment can't go. A drag (such as a section of chain-link fencing) or a special leveling device (such as a York rake) will help achieve a smooth surface. Of course final cultivation is best undertaken at suitable soil moisture content so that the soil crumbles nicely rather than forming wet clods that will be like rocks when they dry.

Be aware, too, that soil structure can be destroyed by over-cultivation. Pulverizing the soil until it is fluffy and dustlike causes the aggregates to break down. Pulverized soil slakes ("runs") into a soup when watered, accepts further watering very grudgingly, and cakes as it dries. Rain tends to run off rather than soaking into the soil, causing surface rilling and wash of soil and seed. With heavy soils, at least, the soilbed should be cultivated only until aggregates of pebble size result, about as big as your fingertip. This texture will seem a bit rough and unesthetic, but it provides many cracks and crevices into which lawn-seed can nestle, ideally situated for sprouting. Of course such a pebbled surface accepts rainfall better than does a slaking one, and watering becomes much less tedious.

Fig. 4-3 After grading, loosen the soilbed and break up the clods.

SOIL STERILIZATION

Occasionally, where the cost is justified (such as for golf greens and athletic fields), soil is sterilized chemically. Most weed seeds, disease organisms, and soil insects are killed, as well as growing vegetation. The microorganisms so essential to soil "ecology" are no doubt decimated, but when conditions return to normal they repopulate the soil quickly even though there may be some temporary imbalances among organisms. Metham (Vapam) is a soil drench that can be used by the homeowner, soaked into a newly cultivated soilbed and "sealed-in" by watering. After a few days the toxicant dissipates enough so that lawn planting can proceed. More thorough sterilization is obtained by fumigating with methyl bromide. The vaporizing liquid is introduced under a tarpaulin that has been sealed by shallow burying at its edges. Since the vapor is very toxic and tarpaulin laying requires some skill, methyl bromide fumigation is for the most part left to the professionals. Here, too, planting can proceed in just a few days after the tarpaulin is removed and the gas dissipates. A large assortment of other chemicals can achieve partial sterilization, such as the killing of above-ground vegetation (but not necessarily weed seeds nor fungi in the soil). This can be of great aid in lawn renovation, as we shall see. More will be said about partial sterilization in the chapter on pest control. Few homeowners indeed will have reason to undertake complete soil sterilization, as technically involved, costly, and hazardous as it is.

SOILBED FERTILIZATION

While lawn fertilization will be discussed more fully in a later chapter, it should be pointed out at this point that soilbed preparation affords the best opportunity for introducing beneficial nutrients into the rootzone (Fig. 4-4). It also presents a good opportunity for making

Fig. 4-4   Soil amendments can be rotary-tilled into the rootzone as a final measure of soilbed preparation.

pH corrections without any risk of injury to the grass. Introducing phosphorus into the rootzone is especially appropriate. Phosphorus applied later on at the surface would work down the soil column only very slowly, since phosphatic compounds and radicals fix rather tightly to soil particles (at least with heavier soils). A minimum of around twenty pounds of phosphorus to the acre is necessary for grass seedlings to grow, so it makes sense to mix at least this amount into the soilbed while the ground is being cultivated anyway. Actually, about ten pounds to each thousand square feet of a lawn fertilizer rich in phosphorus should be used, to provide an adequate supply of the nutrient for some time to come (knowing, also, that a portion will become fixed and "unavailable" or only gradually available to the grass). As fertilizers for the established lawn are proportionately rich in nitrogen rather than phosphorus, for soilbed preparation be certain that the phosphorus content of the product you purchase comes to at least ten or fifteen percent. Unless a soil test indicates otherwise, other major nutrients are not so important at this stage; in any event they can be supplied after the turf is growing.

Liming (or acidification of alkaline soils) might well be undertaken at time of soil preparation, too. A soil test will suggest the amount of agent needed. Mildly acid soils should benefit from fifty to one hundred pounds of ground limestone per thousand square feet, spread before cultivation and worked into the soil during final discing. Some very acid soils will need more lime than this, but ordinarily it is better to raise pH step by step as the lawn program continues rather than to try for a several-point rise in pH all at once as the lime can't diffuse through the soil all that quickly. Table 4-1 suggests lime application rates for differing types of soil.

Table 4-1 Approximate amount of ground limestone needed to correct soil acidity. Figures indicate pounds per 1000 sq. ft. required to raise pH to 6.5, for three types of soil.

Soil pH	Light Soil (sandy)	Medium Soil (loam)	Heavy Soil (silt-clay)
6.0	25	35	50
5.5	60	70	90
5.0	80	115	160
4.5	115	150	200

Similar quantities of gypsum can be used for alkaline soils, less to lower the pH than to substitute calcium for sodium and improve soil structure. An over-supply of sodium is mainly responsible for the poor structure and barrenness of alkali soils. Elemental sulfur, which will gradually oxidize to sulfuric acid, has considerable acidifying influence. Ten to fifty pounds per thousand square feet should be used, the lesser rates for mild alkalinity and lighter soils, the stronger rates where alkalinity is great and the soils heavy. As a rule neutral soils tend to favor bacteria over fungi. Since certain bacteria fix or transform nitrogen beneficially, liming acid soils may improve soil fertility aside from whatever contribution the calcium ions from the lime may make.

Ordinarily fertilizer will be dispersed with a spreader just ahead of final cultivation. Avoid fertilizing before grading is completed lest fertilized ground be bulldozed into certain locations only. A spreader accomplishes fertilizer distribution much more accurately than can hand-casting. Large agricultural equipment is best used for large properties, but home yards can be fertilized quickly with nothing more than an inexpensive centrifugal "whirl-cast" spreader such as the Cyclone. A Cyclone-type spreader throws reasonably heavy fertilizer particles in a ten-foot band at each pass; at this rate is doesn't take long to parcel out the necessary nutrients.

SEED AND SEEDING

Seeding is the most economical way of starting a lawn, although the initial care until seedlings are well established can be very taxing.

Fig. 4-5 After final tilling, level the soilbed for seeding.

Most lawn seed mixtures call for about three pounds of seed to each thousand square feet, assuming uniform distribution (best achieved with a spreader). With something so lightweight as grass seed, the drop-from-hopper type of spreader may prove more accurate, although the centrifugal type will sow more rapidly. Whether utilizing a mechanical spreader or casting seed by hand, it is a good idea to distribute half the designated amount of seed in one direction, the other half at right angles. This assures a more even distribution and avoids misses. Very fine seed, such as that of bentgrass or centipede, which would ordinarily be sowed one pound or less to the thousand square feet, can be made to handle more easily by mixing with the seed some inert ingredient (such as sawdust, sand, or cornmeal) to extend its volume. That way, mixed one part to two, let's say, three pounds of mixture is available for spreading over a thousand square feet instead of a meager single pound using seed alone.

If the surface of the soilbed is loose and chunky, as was recommended in a previous section, the tiny seeds will settle neatly into the soil cracks and crevices, deeply enough imbedded for a perfect start. Ordinarily nothing more need be done, except the expected watering, and perhaps provision of a mulch (to be discussed in a moment). Rolling is seldom necessary and, in fact, can prove detrimental because it crushes the loose soil, impeding water insoak and seedling emergence. If the soilbed is very dusty or very sandy, however, rolling after seeding may help restore capillarity to the soil, drawing moisture up into the rootzone. With such soils the seed is generally tumbled into the top half-inch of the seedbed by raking or dragging ahead of rolling. Seed located at the very surface will have difficulty in sprouting because it dries out so easily. Also, it may wash or blow away. Most lawnseeds are quite small and, if buried deeper than about half an inch, lack the stored energy to force a youthful sprout all the way to the surface. This is especially so if the soil slakes, making a crust, or is compacted.

Some lawngrasses are much quicker to sprout than are others, as was noted in Chapter Two. Of the northern grasses ryegrass sprouts most quickly, with ideal warmth and humidity in as little as four or five days (Fig. 4-6). Fescues are only slightly slower, but the seedlings are not quite so robust, giving a less forceful visual impression. Bluegrasses and bentgrasses are still more reticent and may not show for a couple of weeks under good conditions, or even longer if the ground is cold or watering niggardly. In the South bermudagrass seed with the hulls removed sprouts rapidly, but that left unhulled is slower (at least for a high proportion of the seed). Zoysia and centipede are slow to appear, although zoysia sprouting can be hastened if the seed hulls are "scorched" in an acid bath. Bahia is medium-fast. Of course st. augustine and improved cultivars are vegetatively planted as clones, to be discussed in a moment.

Fig. 4-6 Perennial ryegrass is one of the fastest-starting lawngrasses. This seed was in the germinator less than two weeks!

CHOOSING LAWN SEED

Having gone to the trouble of preparing a good soilbed, it doesn't make sense to sow anything other than the exact kinds of grasses you want to have. Not only should the appropriate cultivars be included

Fig. 4-7 Sowing seed to well-prepared soilbed—cultivated, fertilized, and carefully leveled.

in a blend or mixture, but the seed should be reasonably free from weed seeds or other contaminants (such as seed from leftover crop plants, perhaps forage grasses, which may have once grown in the seed field). Thus there are two aspects to seed quality: its genetic make-up and its mechanical purity. Let's review these aspects one at a time.

As was indicated in Chapter Two, improved cultivars of most major lawngrasses are now being selected for lawn attributes, even though the ancestral parent was adjusted to pasture or meadow. We have noted that not all cultivars are "world beaters" or necessarily more durable than common grass would be if suitably managed. But on the whole the new cultivars are more tolerant of disease, more attractive, denser, and lower-growing. These are meritorious attributes, which stand the new cultivars in good stead even though they may face an uncertain future. Ordinarily it is well worth the premium that select cultivars command, in order to take advantage of the hereditary characteristics important for lawn use that are bred into such grasses.

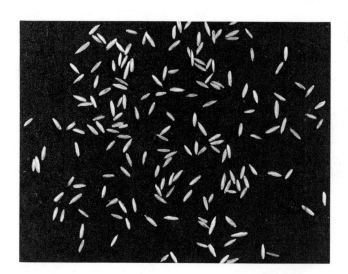

Fig. 4-8 What bluegrass lawnseed looks like when properly spread.

We also noted in earlier chapters the advantage of genetic heterogeneity, in order to avoid some of the disadvantages incumbent in maintaining a monoculture. The selection of improved cultivars of course sacrifices a measure of heterogeneity. So the seed mix formulator reintroduces diversity by combining several cultivars of the same species (a blend), or cultivars of different species (a mixture). On the whole blends and mixtures are more "foolproof" than are monocultures and are easier to maintain for a person who is not expert in fathoming a particular cultivar's requirements. Blends and mixtures are suggested for most lawn seedings, the apportionment of the cultivars corresponding to particular needs. We saw in earlier chapters, for example, that fescues adapt well to shade and poor dry soils, ryegrasses make quick cover, bentgrasses "prefer" humid climates and acid soils, bermudagrasses must have sunny habitat, and so on.

When seed is purchased under reliable brand, one assumes it will have been compounded in a way to satisfy stated purposes and local conditions. But you will still want to read the label listing, required by law, to be certain exactly what cultivars are included. Or you can purchase cultivars individually, and combine them in whatever fashion suits your needs and wishes. For most northern lawns bluegrass will be the mainstay, with a bit of fescue to take over under the trees, perhaps a bit of perennial ryegrass to provide quick cover initially. Bentgrasses and the southern lawngrasses ordinarily are planted alone so that their individualistic needs can be better met. We can anticipate that some day southern lawngrasses, too, will be more available as select genetic lines combinable into blends and mixtures, an opportunity so far little realized.

The physical quality of lawnseed depends upon how carefully the crop has been grown and how meticulously it has been handled through the cleaning, shipping, and blending operations. It all starts in the farmers' fields, with most seed nowadays expertly produced by specialists in the Pacific Northwest. Practicing fallowing and crop rotation, and using herbicides, growers plant seed crop cultivars to fields reasonably free of vegetation, especially free from other cultivars that are similar but of differing genetic persuasion. The fields are carefully watched during the several years they are productive, with constant rogueing (removal) of off-type plants and assiduous weed control. At harvest a few weeds and some crop seeds always seem to be collected by the combines; most are of little consequence because they're not plants which would persist in a lawn. Nevertheless, seed of high quality will be carefully cleaned by a series of blowing, sieving, and electrostatic operations to ensure that the final product is essentially pure seed of the particular cultivar, quite free from dirt, dust, chaff, stems, and, most importantly, foreign seed.

Obviously, the more careful the growing and cleaning, the more costly must be the product. You are not taking advantage of the industry's best technology by buying seed on the basis of cost. Rather examine the label carefully, to see that purity is high (i.e., that weed and crop seed content is infinitesimal). Remember, too, that the better cultivars usually yield seed poorly (who wants a cultivar that sprouts a lot of seedheads, stemmy and hard to mow in the lawn, determinate in growth?)! So, not unexpectedly, seed of such cultivars must sell at a higher price than high-yielding sorts with dubious lawn qualifications.

Someone is always willing to buy up and offer on the market poor lots of seed, opulent in weeds, crop, and lightweight (weak) seed. It doesn't make sense to plant such trash in order to save a few dollars, considering the expensive investment of seedbed preparation and how much more costly it will be to maintain a weak lawn full of weeds. We are encouraged that a Consumers Union investigation showed that seed offerings nationwide are much improved over what they were only a few years ago. Still, it behooves the purchaser to look the label over carefully and to be willing to pay a fair price for merchandise of quality.

GETTING THE SEEDLINGS STARTED

A touch of warmth and humid surroundings are all the magic needed to trigger seed sprouting. Not much can be done about temperature outdoors, except to choose an attractive season. For northern grasses the best time to sow lawns is in autumn, which not only fits the growth cycle of the grass quite well but also takes advantage of residual soil warmth, a hangover from summer. Ordinarily the soil is dry enough in autumn to cultivate well, making a good seedbed with a minimum of effort. Summer weeds will be at the end of their cycle (no more crabgrass to contest the lawngrass!), and of course the weather is ideal for northern grasses which relish bright days and crisp nights. Seed sprouting is apt to be a bit slower at the next-best seeding season, early spring, because the soil hasn't yet warmed. Seeds sprout very slowly when temperature is below 50°F; it might take months at this rate of growth before you would see much grass. But when daytime temperatures reach about 70°F, even with cool nights, the action really picks up. As was noted earlier, ryegrasses may make a pretty good showing in only a few days. Slower species require more time, but there are stirrings within any viable seed almost immediately, once it is moistened; tiny rootlets emerge in only days, even though green shoots may not be much evident for weeks.

Of course you can do something about the moisture. Frequent light sprinklings on the new planting are the key. Even after a generous initial soaking it may be necessary to wet down the planting daily, if the weather turns hot and dry. In cloudy, cool weather, of course, the seedbed will not dry out so quickly. Use a light spray, applied carefully, so that the water soaks into the ground rather than running off, eroding soil and washing seed.

The Soilbed   You can give your new lawn and yourself an assist by mulching the new seeding. A mulch is some inert material that protects the surface of the new seeding. Its greatest importance is as a moisture barrier, keeping the surface (where the seed resides) from drying out quickly. Secondarily, it breaks the force of raindrops and so helps keep the soil from washing.

Fig. 4-9   A straw mulch is held down in a breezy location with onion-sack woven netting.

Before the nation was so heavily urbanized, straw from threshing operations was readily available. Straw free from weed seed and residual grain makes an excellent mulch when spread loosely four or five straws deep. In much of the country straw is still the favorite mulch for roadside seeding, purchased by the carload and blown upon the berms with special machines, often "tacked down" by an asphalt emulsion to keep it from blowing in the wind. A straw mulch used in windy locations around the home can be tied down with string between small stakes, or something like onion-sack netting (itself something of a mulch) can be laid on top of the straw and be fixed into the soil with bent wire wickets. For most urbanites, unfortunately, straw is neither readily available nor inexpensive.

Fig. 4-10 Keep the newly seeded and mulched lawn moist, sprinkling if rain fails. Adequate moisture and warmth will determine how rapidly the new seeding establishes itself.

But you can improvise mulches from various materials around the home, or you can purchase special lawn mulching materials from the garden center. Some of the better purchased mulches are thick burlap, excelsior mats, even fiberglass layers. Stringy sphagnum (peat) moss works reasonably well when wet down to give it weight. Grass clippings applied thinly do some good, although if applied thickly enough to really retain soil moisture they may prove impervious to watering and smothering to sprouting seed. Where pine branches are available, these make an excellent mulch. So do chopped twigs (if you have a shredder), or garden residues (plant stalks of various kinds). In tobacco country, tobacco stems are often available in autumn. Actually, anything that is loose enough to let water and air through to the soilbed and not so dense as to impede emergence of the seedlings will make a very satisfactory mulch. Sheets of clear polyethylene plastic have been used for their greenhouse-like effect. The plastic lets light through but doesn't allow moisture to escape. Unfortunately, unless watched carefully, the temperature under plastic gets quite high on a sunny day. As seedling grass cannot survive very long when the temperature rises much above 100°F, the plastic cover must be lifted for ventilation quite frequently. This makes plastic-cover mulching too cumbersome for general use, although it can speed up grass establishment on small areas amenable to special attention.

Fig. 4-11 After a few weeks of good weather the new seeding becomes quite visible through the mulch (a few weeds, too). Straw can be left in place to decay.

VEGETATIVE PROPAGATION

While northern lawns are frequently started from seed, southern ones are often vegetatively planted with live stems or sections of sod. If the expense is sustainable a whole lawn can be covered with sod, in effect an established sward brought to maturity elsewhere and moved to the lawn. Bluegrass sod growing in the North has become very important and is a far cry these days from the old practice of lifting volunteer bluegrass from pastures for sale in the suburbs. The sod grower is now a specialist, planting improved cultivars and keeping them free of weeds or other pests. Whatever the mode of propagation, vegetative planting is nothing more than perpetuation of the parent clone by living fragments, the same as if "slips" were made from a geranium or chrysanthemum clumps were separated. The progeny from such divisions will have heredity identical with the parent; this, of course, is the reason that select cultivars of southern grasses (which don't come true from seed) must be vegetatively propagated.

Grass plants are remarkable in their ability to sprout from the joints or nodes, even after being chopped into fragments. It's usually not necessary that the stem sections be rooted, for roots develop from the joints. Bentgrasses in the North and bermudagrasses in the South are especially amenable to starting from stem fragments ("stolons"). These grasses often are simply shredded, cast on a prepared soilbed, covered with a little topdressing, and held moist. Other species are not so easily started from fragmented stems and must be more laboriously planted as individual sprigs or plugs.

The chief advantage from vegetative planting is the certain start of true-to-type cultivars. In the North, sodding, or less frequently plugging into bare spots, is best done in the early spring or autumn, the most favorable season for bluegrass and its companions. Grass strikes root more certainly with less attention at that time of year, and the sod requires less care in handling when the weather is cool. During summer sod can be transplanted, but the chances that it will dry out or be killed from overheating are much greater. In the South a vegetative planting is perhaps best undertaken in the spring, allowing for a long growing season to complete filling-in. Plugs or sprigs started very late in summer may not have time to root securely before onset of dormancy. The new starts then may heave or winterkill.

That lawns are propagated vegetatively does not mean the lawnsman can escape the same measures of soilbed preparation discussed for seeding. If a vegetative planting is to be successful, the soil should be cultivated, providing a fertile soilbed into which the plants root easily. Elimination of competing vegetation helps achieve rapid establishment. The new vegetative plantings must be nursed along just as are new seedings, and especially must not be let dry out.

Sometimes new grass is introduced into an existing lawn by planting a scattering of plugs. These are likely to survive, even though sprigs seldom stand much of a chance interplanted into congested vegetation. If conditions are well suited to the new grass, it can be expected to gain ground through the years and eventually to dominate the lawn. This may take a long time, but some lawns have been changed over to zoysia, for example, precisely by this technique. However, it is ordinarily much better to grant new starts every advantage, without competition from other grasses.

Live starts should be kept cool and moist until planted and should be watered soon after planting. A mulch may help to retain humidity. Once the grass is well rooted, moisture is not so critical, and watering can taper off. However, weed competition will be quite serious for some time. Mowing automatically eliminates tall field weeds, and cultivation or treatment with herbicides between the expanding clumps of new grass facilitates their expansion. Mowing should be high enough not to scalp the grass, permitting it to retain as much green leaf as is possible. Even bermudas and zoysias are best mowed no shorter than two inches until they have filled to a thick turf.

SODDING

Machines have been developed for cutting sod which slice the turf at any depth. Commercial sod is cut relatively thin, less than an inch thick. Although this trims off most of the grass roots, in transplanting the roots would probably die anyway and would have to be regenerated from the joints. Thin sod has proven to develop new roots more quickly than thick sod. There are several economic advantages to thin sod, including less weight to handle and haul, easier hefting, and less loss of topsoil. But thin sod must be laid quickly and watered assiduously.

Sod is cut in several standard widths and lengths and is transported rolled or as squares stacked on pallets. Sod rolls or sections survive

Fig. 4-12 A rhizome-producing turfgrass is best for making a strong sod that can be hefted. Here an inverted section of "Majestic" Kentucky bluegrass has had the soil washed from the roots to reveal the rhizomes (at tip of knifeblade).

well for several days if the weather is cool and the sod is not let dry out. Much commercial sod is now shipped in refrigerated vans. Sod should be unrolled or unstacked as quickly as possible, to avoid yellowing of the foliage and possible demise from heating. Sod is laid on a prepared soilbed with successive strips meeting end-to-end near the midpoint of an adjacent section, providing reinforcement much like tiers of over-lapping bricks. A light top dressing of weed-free soil, especially along junctures, fills chinks and assures a level surface. Rolling and watering should follow immediately. Continue to water for the next several weeks, by which time the sod should be well rooted. Thereafter fertilization and other care follow the same pattern as for any established lawn.

PLUGGING

The planting of plugs is rather intermediate between sodding and sprigging. Plugs are nothing more than small sections of sod, usually circular as they are dug up with a plugging tool. Spaced through the

Fig. 4-13 Simple plugging tool in action. Plugs work up the hollow handle as cut, and they can be inserted into holes of the same size cut into a bare or thin lawn. They are then firmed into place with a stamp of the foot.

lawn, they provide centers of growth which are supposed to fill into a complete turf eventually. This may take a few months with fast grasses such as bermuda, or as much as several years with zoysia in cooler climates. Plugging is more economical than is sodding so far as raw material is concerned. A square yard of sod can yield some three hundred two-inch plugs; planted at one-foot spacing, these cover about forty square yards.

The same preparation of the soil should precede plugging as is done for seeding and sodding. Planting is simplified if a plugging tool of the same size as that used to cut the plugs is also used to make the planting holes. The plug is fitted into the hole, its surface level with the soil, and is firmed in place by stepping upon it or by later tamping or rolling. The rapidity with which plugs spread into a solid stand depends upon how closely they are spaced, as well as upon the kind of grass. Plugs planted only six inches apart should join more quickly than those a foot apart. Larger plugs might be expected to have greater reserves than smaller ones which, if cut very small, may have most runners or rhizomes decapitated.

Fig. 4-14 Sod plugs: Above, a fine fescue; below, Kentucky bluegrass.

The Soilbed

Sprigs are sections of stem derived by tearing apart sod, during which the soil is shaken or washed away. Long runners are generally cut into smaller pieces of from two to four joints. Obviously, sprigs require extra pains to keep alive since they are devoid of sustaining roots. As received from a nursery they are generally packed in moss or polyethylene bags to escape drying out. They should be kept cool and moist until planted. A common practice is to dump the sprigs into a bucket of water for carrying to the planting site. Individual sprigs are pulled out only when it is time to imbed them into the soil.

A planted sprig should have one end above ground, the other below. Most sprigs are about three or four inches long and can be stuck into the loose soil on the slant. The buried end is about two inches deep, the exposed joint slightly above soil level. Sprigs can be individually planted in checkerboard fashion as are plugs, or shallow furrows can be made the length of the lawn, into which the stem sections are properly spaced and lightly covered with soil. These rows will spread laterally to join in time. The soil should be firmed about the newly planted sprigs by tamping with hand or foot or by rolling. Machines have been developed for sprigging extensive swards such as golf fairways.

Fig. 4-15 Sprigs may be planted in furrows, the lowermost joint buried but buds of upper joint exposed.

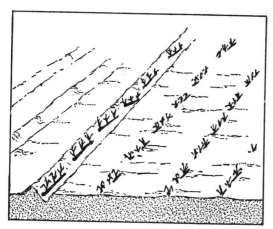

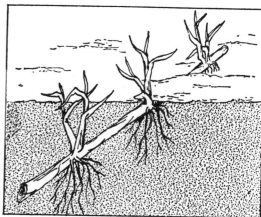

A square yard of sod may yield over a thousand zoysia or bermuda sprigs, and several hundred of st. augustine or centipede. It is obvious that almost a whole lawn could be planted from sprigs derived from a few yards of sod and spaced six inches to a foot apart. In spite of the rough treatment sprigs suffer, they nonetheless seem to start and spread more quickly than do plugs, perhaps because plugs are self-sustaining within their own biscuit of soil, while the sprigs must immediately strike new roots and start growing in their new environment. Kept free of weeds, watered, and fertilized, a sprigged lawn should knit to as adequate a turf as one which was sodded or plugged.

STOLONIZING

Very similar to sprigging is the planting of "stolons," as chopped runners of bentgrass in the North or bermudagrass in the South are called. Sod is generally shredded, and the resulting stolons are sold by the bushel. Often nothing more than clippings from bermuda turf let grow tall are the source of stolons. Shredded sod of non-apomictic bluegrasses is sometimes offered for starting this grass vegetatively.

As with other vegetative plantings, the soil should be prepared beforehand for stolonizing. The stolons are scattered lightly over the surface and should receive a light topdressing of soil, sufficient to partly bury the stems. One technique used on golf courses is to throw a wire mat on top of scattered stolons, which forms a secure surface on which to walk while soil is sifted through the meshes. The mat also firms the stolons into the base soil. The planting must be constantly watered until rooting and new growth are evident. Five bushels of stolons will generally plant one thousand square feet, although two bushels may get you by; or as much as ten bushels might be wanted for a quick, thick stand.

LAWN RENOVATION

Renovation seems to require "less sweat" each advancing year because of improvements in equipment and techniques. Mechanical thinners and powered soil scarifiers greatly lighten the physical burden, and chemical aids help assure a start for the new seeding.

Chemical knockdown before scarification is recommended for old lawns containing much unwanted vegetation. Little is to be lost by such "scorched earth" treatment, since not much useful grass exists. In most cases a contact rather than a systemic herbicide is used. Then rhizoming grasses such as bluegrass and fescue usually revive from underground parts. Most bunchgrasses and annual weeds are killed from treatment to ground line.

Fig. 4-16 Chemical knockdown prior to mechanical scarification. Grass in foreground has been sprayed to give the new overseeding a greater chance.

Strong fertilizer solutions sometimes have been used successfully as contact agents for killing unwanted vegetation. Concentrated nitrogen solutions or soluble fertilizers sprayed on the lawn should be appropriate around a home, as fertilizer rather than pesticide kill is appealing in these times of ecological concern. Moreover, it is often difficult to procure some of the more effective knockdown chemicals, even for agriculture.

Paraquat, the arsonates (cacodylic acid), and glyphosate are among the more promising herbicides for "scorched earth" treatment. With them, any chemical reaching the soil is inactivated almost immediately. Amitrol and dalapon have a systemic effect and may persist sufficiently in the soil for several weeks to inhibit a new seeding. Sodium arsenite, ammate, and cyanamid have long been used for vegetation knockdown but are required in much greater quantity than the newer compounds. However, many of the new, more efficient materials have not yet been licensed for home use, having received label clearance only for certain agricultural applications.

Autumn is probably the best time of year for renovating northern lawns, spring or summer for southern ones. The farther north the lawn, the earlier in autumn renovation should start. Late August is none too early in the northernmost plains states. The cooler weather of early September might be awaited in most of the northeastern United States south to the Ohio River Valley—even late September in the border states and the upper South.

Have the necessary supplies on hand well before the target date for renovation. Allow the necessary time for dissipation of chemicals if "scorched earth" knockdown is used. You will need the chosen herbicide (and the means for its application), top quality seed, and some sort of a "power rake" (powered thinning or scarifying machines). In addition, fertilizer, a means for irrigation, and possibly mulch materials will be wanted.

Begin renovation by scalping the lawn, i.e., mowing to cut the old vegetation as low as possible. If a lot of debris results, sweep it up for the compost heap. Apply the knockdown chemical, if one is being employed, within a day or two if possible; the hotter the weather the more likely it is to be effective. Follow up with mechanical scarification, after a waiting period suited to the chemical you have used. If a systemic herbicide having long-lasting effects in the soil was used, the whole operation should be initiated a month earlier than would be necessary for herbicides immediately inactivated by the soil.

The turf thinner or soil scarifier should be sufficiently powered that it cuts into the topsoil (Fig. 4-17). Depending upon how resistant the

Fig. 4-17 A motorized turf thinner removes thatch. Note the loose duff "raked" out between cart and dethatching machine.

old vegetation may be, make as many passes as necessary to create numerous soil striations. With thatch-filled lawns it may be advisable to sweep or rake the debris before the final pass to be certain that mineral soil is within reach of the seed.

Unfortunately, most mechanical scarifiers fluff the surface considerably, which may result in a dusty matrix into which seed does not settle so well as it would into cultivated seedbed. Pulling a drag over the new seeding should help to imbed the seed, or you can even run the scarifier over the lawn one more time. Any old vegetation kicked to the surface and old stem stubble still rooted in the soil can remain as a protective mulch. Where little such protection is left, an applied mulch is suggested.

Thereafter, moisture and time govern success. Try not to let the lawn dry out. Some of the old vegetation can be expected to revive. But if aggressive new grass varieties have been introduced, they will probably get off to a fast start and crowd the old plants substantially. Renovation seldom brings instantaneous change as would be expected from seeding a cultivated soilbed, but it does provide a reasonably inexpensive means for upgrading "tired" lawns.

What To Do, in Brief

THE NEW LAWN

PRELIMINARIES—You may want to lay an underground irrigation system, or tile poorly drained spots. It may prove helpful to knock down weedy vegetation chemically.

PREPARE THE SOILBED—Loosen the top three or four inches, preferably raking off old vegetation. Mix in fertilizer during cultivation. Add lime, too, if a soil test shows a pH much below 6. Rake soil level, and try to maintain a loose surface into which seed can sift. Let soil settle through one soaking; level, and loosen the surface again if necessary.

SOW GOOD SEED—Mixtures are most foolproof for home lawns. Good seed has little weed or crop content. Bentgrasses are seeded one or two pounds per thousand square feet, bluegrass and its mixtures about three pounds. Sow half in one direction, the other half at right angles. A lawn spreader distributes seed more evenly than can casting by hand.

MULCH—Mulch if possible with any loose material that protects the seedbed from drying. Clean straw three or four straws deep is an old favorite. Woven nettings, fiberglass, excelsior, or stringy sphagnum can be bought for the purpose.

ESTABLISH THE STAND—Soak a new seeding, then keep the surface moist by regular light sprinklings. It is not necessary to remove an organic mulch; it will soon be overtopped by grass and will decay.

AFTERCARE—Mow new grass before it begins to flop, at least one and a half to three inches for taller species such as bluegrass, three-fourths to one and a half inches for bentgrass-bermudagrass types. Watering can be less frequent, more prolonged. Don't worry about weeds in young turf. Mowing and crowding by grass will eliminate most. Survivors can be treated with weed killers later. You may want to fertilize young grass again after a few mowings.

IMPROVING OLD TURF

If the lawn contains a lot of thatch you may want to remove it mechanically. You can rent powered lawn thinners for this. Sweep up the duff dragged to the surface.

The quality of the lawn can be upgraded by introducing better grasses. Overseed at half rate, best in tandem with thinning and scarification so that new seed contacts soil and is not insulated from it by thatch or duff.

Fertilize northern lawns at least once in autumn (consider a second late autumn or winter feeding). Fertilize only lightly through spring and summer, enough to maintain good color. Space fertilization of southern lawns through the growing season.

Eliminate broadleaf weeds such as dandelion and plantain with 2,4-D (often "souped up" with silvex, dicamba, or MCPP for broader effectiveness). Crabgrass preventer must be used before crabgrass seed sprouts (when soil temperature reaches about 60°F in spring). Apply herbicide only to grass old enough that it is being mowed.

Water and Fertilizer
5 Keep the Lawn Growing

WATER AND WATERING

Water is so commonplace that we take it for granted, yet it is so integral to life that desiccation is tantamount to death. Living tissue is more than ninety percent water. Water is the universal medium and solvent; it influences every aspect of growth. So it may seem strange that plants are profligate in their use of "life's elixir." Probably because water has been so constant where life has evolved, there has been little cause for conservation.

A large member of the grass family, corn, can perhaps be visualized more easily than can an individual lawngrass plant. Its tissues embody approximately half a gallon of water. Through the growing season it utilizes another fifty gallons or so to complete its growth. An acre of lawn doesn't expend much less water than an acre of corn, about two thousand tons during the growing season, and a lot more where the season is long and irrigation generous, as is often the case in California. This represents a lot of an increasingly scarce and expensive commodity! Why so much water?

92

Plants are so demanding of water because their leaves are designed not so much for efficient water use as for efficient photosynthesis (the making of food through the good offices of chlorophyll in the presence of sunlight). To best accommodate photosynthesis leaves ordinarily grow flat, expansive, and exposed to sunlight (and to drying winds as well). Moreover, to keep the sapstream flowing, leaves must transpire ("evaporate") water. Sap is thereby "sucked up" from the roots through the cellular system of the stem, transporting nutrients even to leaves at the top of trees hundreds of feet tall.

Transpiration takes place through tiny pores on the surface of the leaf, the stomata, about one hundred thousand to the square inch and constituting perhaps 1–2% of the leaf area. The stomata are bounded by guard cells which, when turgid (distended with water), bow into an arc that keeps the pore open; when they turn flaccid and flabby the stoma more or less closes. Thus water loss is partially self-regulating; the stomata open in times of plenty, close as wilting threatens. Of course many other factors regulate guard cell performance, including hormonal control over potassium salts that in turn affect turgidity. But the point is that, in the course of evolution, plants have become a bit reckless with water because "attention" has been focused mainly on photosynthesis.

Of course transpiration, although exhaustive of water, is not without its benefits. It serves as the driving force for sap rise. Transpiration also exerts quite a cooling influence on the leaf. Leaves without transpiration would be "cooked to death" on a sunny day; protoplasm does not function properly nor even survive when temperature rises much above 100°F. Just as sprinkling cools off the garden because heat is absorbed to evaporate water, so transpiration draws heat from the leaf as sap is transformed into vapor.

Chemical treatments that reduce transpiration have been discovered. They generally operate by stimulating closure of the stomata. One such for turf is a phenyl mercuric acetate formulation used primarily to prevent wilting of golf greens. Of course nature provides a measure of protection against drying out for plant leaves, epidermal cells being covered with a waxy cuticle impervious to moisture. Cuticle is generally very thick on desert plants. Plants have evolved helpful forms and habits for dry habitat, too, such as photosynthesizing through green stems rather than thin leaves (as with a cactus in the desert), having stomata deeply sunk in fleshy tissues away from exposure, and accumulating watery storage organs to tide the plant over times of difficulty. In a way grasses are a compromise between the profligate users of water exemplified by lush tropical vegetation and the stingy plants of the desert. Grasses are well suited to prairie which is seasonally dry, and they often display physical adaptations designed to conserve water (like the curling-up of leaves in dry weather, hairy coatings to minimize evapotranspiration, and so on).

Of course grass picks up most of its water from the soil, through its root system. Tiny root hairs near the tip of the roots are the active sites of absorption. Chapter Three mentioned how important soil structure is for governance of water relationships through its matrix-and-pore system. Large pores provide fast drainage of excess (gravitational) water, but the smaller capillary pores are responsible for most of the retained water which constitutes the soil's reserve so important to plant growth. Fine-textured soils of good structure might hold as much as three inches of water in the top foot of soil; coarse-textured sandy soils may retain only half an inch (Table 5-1). Obviously moisture stress will show up more quickly on a sandy soil than on a heavier one! Following saturation by a good rain, a heavy soil can usually sustain a lawn for two or three weeks before grass begins to wilt; light soils may need watering every three or four days.

Table 5-1 Water-holding capacity of Florida soils and evapotranspiration losses from turf seasonally. After Horn, Florida Turfgrass Bulletin.

	Soil Moisture Holding Capacity		
Soil	*Field Capacity %*	*Wilting Point %*	*Water Storage, Upper 6 Inches*
Clay	30	15	1.4 inches
Loam	20	10	0.9 inches
Sand	8	3	0.4 inches

	Evapotranspiration Losses	
Period	*Loss per Day, Inches*	*Total Loss for Interval, Inches*
December–March	0.07	8.4
April	0.14	4.2
May	0.22	6.6
June	0.30	9.0
July–August	0.32	19.0
September	0.28	8.4
October	0.17	5.1
November	0.12	8.6
	Total for year	63.5

LAWN IRRIGATION

There is no question but that lawns require irrigation in drier climates if they are to survive; the minimum needs of the grass plant (at least half an inch per week on average) must be met (Table 5-1).

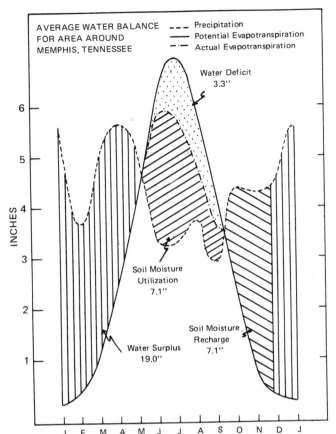

AVERAGE WATER BALANCE
FOR AREA AROUND
MEMPHIS, TENNESSEE

- - - Precipitation
——— Potential Evapotranspiration
—·— Actual Evapotranspiration

Water Deficit
3.3"

Soil Moisture
Utilization
7.1"

Soil Moisture
Recharge
7.1"

Water Surplus
19.0"

INCHES

J F M A M J J A S O N D J

Fig. 5-1 A water deficit occurs seasonally even in regions of ample rainfall.

Although lawns of the familiar lawngrasses may get by with as little as twenty inches of annual rainfall in climates that are not too hot and with a rainfall pattern reasonably frequent in summer, some irrigation is generally necessary where annual rainfall falls below thirty inches (Fig. 3-8).

In more humid parts of the country seasonal deficit occurs (Fig. 5-1), though watering is undertaken more to keep the lawn "presentable" than to insure survival. Here watering is a mixed blessing. When dry spells occur, of course watering is going to keep the lawn fresh and green compared to unwatered turf. An unirrigated lawn may even dry out enough to turn brown and dormant. This is nature's way, and grasses are well adapted to survive temporary water deficits. Indeed, in many ways drought is therapeutic for a lawn. Disease is held down, since fungi thrive on moisture. Water-loving weeds are discouraged, and seeds of hot-weather species fail to sprout. Weed seedlings that would survive under ample humidity often wither away. Some soils crack and fissure, a form of natural aerification. Nitrification usually intensifies, providing a "fertility boost" for the lawn when rains return. And, dry soils compact less than do wet ones if traffic is heavy. So don't assume that watering is necessarily "the answer" to achieving an improved lawn, as many homeowners are wont to believe. How often have you heard the plaint, "We have a hard time watering," as if this explains why the lawn is ill-looking, no matter what the real cause of trouble might be? Probably more lawns suffer from unwise or excessive watering than from drying out! Especially troublesome with an over-watered lawn is the cropping up of water-loving weeds—such species as annual bluegrass (*Poa annua*), rough bluegrass (*Poa trivialis*), unwanted bentgrasses (*Agrostis*), nutsedge (*Cyperus*), clover (*Trifolium*), pennywort (*Hydrocotyle*), and many other species adapted to moist ground.

Lawns use about an inch of water per week in warm weather, most of which is transpired, although some is lost directly through evaporation. Evapotranspiration is the term covering this form of disappearance. Even in humid regions rainfall is generally inadequate to match evapotranspiration losses on a consistent basis through summer. Through winter when plants are not active, rainfall accumulates and soil becomes thoroughly saturated by spring. A saturated soil with good water-holding capacity contains enough moisture within the rootzone to make up for rainfall deficits for as long as several weeks; a soggy spring soil can "carry" a lawn for some time even without rain or watering. But as spring becomes summer the grasses draw down soil moisture reserves, how fast depending upon rainfall. Lawns usually exist "hand-to-mouth" by August, so far as water is concerned, depending upon what rainfall occurs. The lawn may green up for a few days after a meager quarter inch rain, only to turn semidormant again awaiting the next revival. Repeated production of such flushes of foliage uses up food reserves and weakens or can kill the grass. The soil is often bone dry as deep as roots go, the grass having exhausted the water reserves there. Under such circumstances irrigation pays dividends by way of a better-looking lawn, even though watering may contribute little to the long-range health of the grass. Thorough drying out can have side effects, too, through influence on the soil ecosystem. It may favor the nitrifying organisms, which release a burst of fertility at just the wrong time, causing grass under stress to experience additional pressures (encouragement of disease, for example).

Grasses signal when they are about to dry out. The turf loses its resiliency; footprints remain outlined long after you've crossed the lawn, and mower tracks may persist for days. The grass assumes a bluish cast, rather than being bright green. Growth is much reduced, noticeable by the paucity of mower clippings. It is time to begin watering. As a general rule letting the lawn get this dry before irrigation is therapeutic, for reasons cited earlier (a dry surface restrains weeds and diseases). Most authorities recommend thorough but infrequent watering rather than light and frequent sprinklings, even though the same amount of water may be applied either way. Infrequent watering is more appropriate for heavy soils than light. A heavy soil can soak up as much as three inches of water before turning soggy, if irrigation is sufficiently slow and persistent. Watering should always be adjusted to the soil's absorption rate in order to avoid runoff. There would be no point in watering a sandy soil this much, since at best it might be able to hold half an inch of water. This it can soak up quickly in just a few minutes, so porous is a sandy soil's texture; pouring on more water than can be held contributes nothing to the grass and results in percolation loss that takes fertility with it. Thus each lawn must be judged according to its ability to absorb water and the reserves it can hold, before an irrigation schedule is decided upon. This is your guide for choosing a sprinkler, whether for large volume quickly or for light application slowly.

WATERING APPARATUS

Most people are aware that little is accomplished watering a lawn hose-in-hand. An exception would be a new seeding that should be syringed lightly quite frequently in order to keep the surface moist. Water from a hose nozzle is just not sufficient, nor in most cases uniformly and gently enough applied, for a workmanlike job of irrigation. But various sprinklers are attachable to a garden hose that have the "patience" necessary for more thorough watering. Good sprinklers will apply water uniformly within the coverage pattern, something that can be checked by placing tin cans in various locations and noting whether all accumulate about the same amount of water in a given time.

Many types of sprinkler are available, ranging from simple water roses with no moving parts to rotating heads and oscillating fans. Some elaborate devices creep across the lawn, winding themselves up on a fixed cable. Sprinklers with impeller-activated nozzles usually have stops that can be set for a fixed arc of the circle they would otherwise cover. This permits watering the lawn from a dry footing at its edges, especially helpful with new seedings that become mushy and should not be tracked up. Whatever sprinkler is chosen, check its pattern of coverage and whether its rate of discharge suits your particular circumstances, i.e., does its coverage fit the shape of the lawn, and does it disperse water uniformly at a rate that can be absorbed by the soil without runoff?

Underground sprinkling systems are more complex, but they come with both fan-spray discharges or pop-up heads that cover circles or part circles. Inexpensive plastic-pipe systems needing no plumbing expertise for installation are offered by firms such as the Moist O' Matic division of Toro. Even these, however, are generally more satisfactorily installed by a professional house. A relatively inexpensive unit of this type will have time-clock-activated valves near the inlet, which turn on each sprinkler head independently in sequence, for whatever duration the dial is set for, as frequently as is wanted. Watering can commence any time of day or night and can be programmed to skip as many days as desired between irrigations. Even more elaborate systems are available, of course, for such installations as golf courses and commercial properties; these are often automated to the extent hat they require highly trained technical personnel just to keep them functioning properly. Soil moisture blocks inserted into the soil can be "hooked in" to such systems, to automatically turn on the water whenever the soil dries to a particular moisture content. Most of the really elaborate irrigation schemes are utilized in California and the Southwest, where watering is so vital.

WATERING "SUBSTITUTES"

Mention has already been made of antitranspirants such as phenyl mercuric acetate, which, when sprayed on grass, stimulates closing of the stomata with consequent reduced transpiration. Grass treated in this fashion will wilt less quickly, but the treatment can hardly be considered conducive to normal grass physiology.

Sometimes grass is simply let go dormant and is then colored with a green dye. Dyeing turf is a regular practice with football fields which are to appear on TV. Most of the time such dyes are used for zoysia and bermuda when they brown in winter in the South. But they can also make drought-singed northern turfs look better and may be used even on such extensive swards as golf fairways when a tournament is being telecast.

FERTILIZERS AND FERTILIZATION

Fertilization of the lawn is handmaiden to watering so far as encouragement of grass growth is concerned. In the chapter on soils we saw that fertility, the supplying of nutrients, is equally as important a function of soils as is provision of a rooting medium the adequacy of which depends upon texture, structure, and other factors. We saw that now one need, now another may limit grass growth (the barrel of

Fig. 5-2 A. The difference fertilizer makes. This area received none. Contrast it with (B), an area being fertilized regularly. B. Here turf of the same age received regular feeding.

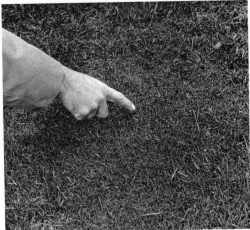

Fig. 3-7). So that nutrient unavailability not be limiting, lawns are usually fertilized. The modern tendency is to use light-weight but high-powered products (nearly half nutrient) that are convenient to handle and spread. Whatever the fertilizer formulation, suggested application rate is ordinarily such as to supply about one pound of nitrogen to the thousand square feet of a lawn at a time.

Seldom are soil nutrients so deficient that grass will not grow at all. But nutrient insufficiency commonly limits vigor more than do inadequacies of air, water, soil structure, light, or temperature. With grass nitrogen (N) is the key element, essential for the luxuriant leafy growth wanted in lawns. Yet it is the one nutrient most often insufficiently abundant for the vigor and color demanded. The lawn is therefore almost always bolstered with fertilizer featuring nitrogen. Nitrogen must be in balance with other nutrients, however, or upsets will occur. Nevertheless, when one is buying fertilizer, the emphasis (and most of the cost) is on nitrogen.

NUTRIENTS

At least sixteen nutrient elements are necessary for plant growth, and probably many more in such infinitesimal quantities that they are always available as a "contaminant" of the environment. The sixteen proven to be essential are: (1) carbon, hydrogen, and oxygen, basic for an organic molecule, the carbon absorbed by plant leaves from the air as carbon dioxide, hydrogen derived from splitting the water molecules absorbed by roots from the soil; (2) nitrogen, phosphorus, and potassium, the major fertilizer nutrients needed rather abundantly; (3) calcium, magnesium, and sulphur, the secondary fertilizer nutrients required in only modest quantity; and (4) iron, zinc, copper, molybdenum, boron, and chlorine, micronutrients or trace elements required in only small quantities (indeed, some are highly toxic when at all abundant). Many nutrient elements are important to the internal workings of plant physiology but don't accumulate to any extent in the finished plant tissues. The approximate frequency with which some of the nutrients occur in grass foliage is given in Table 5-2.

Table 5-2   Top: Mineral content (for selected elements) of Kentucky bluegrass foliage, in pounds per acre, based on two tons of dry clippings per acre. Bottom: Fertility elements in Merion bluegrass and fescue clippings from composite test turf at Pennsylvania State University sampled in July (From Waddington, Turner and Duich, Progress Report 350).

Kentucky Bluegrass (lb/acre)	
Nitrogen	60.00
Potassium	60.00
Phosphorus	20.00
Calcium	16.00
Magnesium	7.00
Sulfur	5.00
Manganese	0.30
Zinc	0.08
Copper	0.02

	Merion Bluegrass (%)	Pennlawn Fescue (%)
Nitrogen	3.79 %	3.48 %
Phosphorus	0.49 %	0.60 %
Potassium	2.19 %	2.32 %
Calcium	0.55 %	0.34 %
Magnesium	0.24 %	0.17 %
Manganese	78 ppm	146 ppm
Iron	100 ppm	55 ppm
Copper	18 ppm	19 ppm
Boron	13 ppm	11 ppm
Aluminum	88 ppm	34 ppm
Zinc	53 ppm	46 ppm
Sodium	21 ppm	31 ppm

ppm = parts per million

Maintaining a proper nutrient balance is as important as having nutrients present at all. The uptake of one nutrient ion is invariably related to other ions. Positive ions (cations) such as calcium (Ca^{++}), potassium (K^+), and ammonium (NH_4^+) become electronically attached to the surface of clay particles and soil colloids and are therefore not so subject to loss through leaching as would be negative nutrient ions (anions) such as nitrate (NO_3^-). Weak acids secreted by roots can release fixed cations, substituting the hydrogen ion (H^+) for the useful cation. While this is an oversimplification of a complex situation, it is practical to realize that heavy soils (with adequate clay and fine silt fractions) or soils rich in organic colloids are much better at "banking" nutrients than are light soils. Ordinarily they need not be fertilized so frequently.

That nutrient elements can be toxic when out of balance has already been mentioned, and often the efficiency of one nutrient depends upon the presence of another (for example, phosphorus uptake is greater from Ontario soils if ammoniacal nitrate is present). Cases are numerous where "too much" or "too little" of a micronutrient completely upsets the pattern of growth. Fortunately, with lawns, imbalances of nutrients are not so likely to occur as with crop plants which are sent to market, their nutrients thus being removed from recyclement rather than being returned to the soil. This is particularly true of micronutrients, which are almost always sufficient in lawn soils having a favorable pH. Thus lawn fertilizer formulation is more concerned with the major nutrients than with minor ones.

FERTILIZERS

Some drastic changes in "life style," including lawn keeping, came with the final quarter of the twentieth century. The transition from an era of fertilizer opulence at low cost to one of tight supplies at high cost was particularly jolting to lawn maintenance. The cause, of course, was the "energy crisis." Petroleum hydrocarbons had been an inexpensive raw material for synthesis of ammonia, in turn basic for fertilizer nitrogen. Fertilizer had been so inexpensive before the 1970s as to have been used almost wastefully; there was little financial reason for not employing it liberally. Attitudes have since changed. Concern now is more with how little fertilizer can be used to yet achieve satisfactory lawn performance.

Most lawn authorities feel that approximately four pounds of elemental nitrogen (N) to a thousand square feet (M) annually is required to keep grass reasonably competitive against weeds. This is not a lot of fertilizer, but still much more than the majority of homeowners have ever used on average (statistics from Pennsylvania and Virginia indicate only about one quarter pound of N/M to be utilized, all turf considered; many lawns must not be fertilized at all to bring the average this low). Of course, some grasses demand more fertilizer than do others, and so do some soils.

On the whole, conservative fertilizer usage is "not all bad." Using fertilizer abundantly enough to force maximum growth and deepest color often puts heavy stress on the grass. The grass may come down with disease more readily, and its physiology may become "discombobulated" in hot weather! Turf authorities usually deplore heavy nitrogen fertilization of bluegrass in spring, feeling that this triggers a surge of growth that draws down food (energy) reserves within the plant. Difficulties ensue as weather warms, making cool-season grass physiology less efficient (not so with warm-season grasses, however).

One might guess from these few inklings that fertilizer is a great device for manipulating the lawn ecosystem. It is a means for stimulating the grass, when applied at the right time of year, to make it more competitive against the weeds. It can encourage one grass to dominate another (generous fertilization favors bluegrass over fescue, bermudagrass over centipede, for example). Even proportionment of the major nutrients helps direct the lawn community's course, such as when ample phosphorus helps bluegrass to prosper in the shade.

A Michigan study involving a large series of samplings showed bluegrasses to average 4.2 percent nitrogen in their foliage, fine fescues 3.2 percent, and bentgrasses 4.6 percent. Phosphorus differences were not so great, all grasses averaging close to 0.5 percent of this nutrient. They were fairly similar in potassium content, too, varying a little above and a little below 2 percent. If soil fertility is not adequate to provide enough of these elements for approximately this percentage in the grass foliage, turf quality can be expected to decline. The potential value of adding nutrients through fertilizer, particularly in autumn for northern lawns, is apparent. Keep in mind, however, that nature supplies a modicum of nutrients continuously, through breakdown (mineralization) of soil particles and by pick-up of about six and a half pounds of nitrogen per acre annually in rainfall.

Soil tests reveal nitrogen adequacy poorly; a better indication is growth and color of the grass itself. But a soil test can be very helpful for assessing available quantities of other major and secondary nutrients, for which the minimum amounts needed for satisfactory turf performance have been pretty well determined. Smith, University of Florida, suggests that for the reasonably "heavy-feeding" grasses grown there (bermuda, zoysia, and st. augustine) a minimum soil nutrient content (expressed in pounds per acre) should be calcium 1200, magnesium 150, phosphorus 50, potassium 150; less "greedy" grasses (bahia, carpet, centipede) are satisfied with calcium 600, magnesium 100, phosphorus 40, potassium 100.

As for nitrogen, creeping bentgrasses and improved bermuda-grasses are regarded as quite "heavy feeders," needing in the neighborhood of six to eight pounds N/M annually as a minimum for top performance. Improved bluegrasses, perennial ryegrasses, st. augustine, common bermudagrass, and dichondra require only slightly less, at least half this much. Zoysias, colonial bentgrasses, common bluegrass, fine fescues, bahia, carpet, and centipede grasses fall still lower on the scale in about this order, often prospering with as little as two pounds N/M annually.

FIGURING OUT FERTILIZERS

It will be necessary to digress a bit in order to characterize fertilizers, keeping in mind the following definitions:

Complete fertilizer: one containing all of the major nutrients.

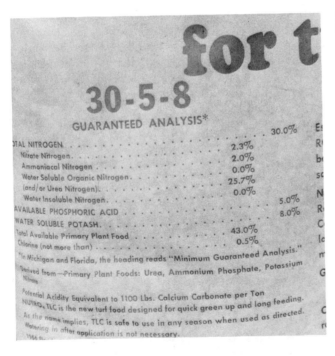

Fig. 5-3 Analysis on the bag of a complete fertilizer.

Ratio: the proportion in which the major nutrients occur.
Analysis: the actual percentage of nutrient (usually calculated as elemental nitrogen and as the oxides of phosphorus and potassium).

The nutrients in fertilizer are always listed in this order: nitrogen (N)–phosphorus (P)–potassium (K). Thus a ratio of 3-1-2 would indicate 3 parts of nitrogen to 1 part of phosphorus to 2 parts of potassium. A N-P-K ratio on this order (or perhaps where phosphorus is fairly abundant in the soil, something like a 5-1-3 ratio) would be good for turfgrass. Invariably a fertilizer formulated for grass (as contrasted to one for fruiting or flowering plants in the garden) is high in nitrogen compared to the other components.

For the most part nutrients are absorbed by unicellular root hairs near the tip of the roots. The roots grow to the nutrient more than the nutrient diffuses to the root. Approximate diffusion distance in soil is only 2 mm for P, 6 mm for K, and 1 cm for N.

Nitrogen

Nitrogen is the nutrient that stimulates growth strongly. It is especially desirable for grass or other leafy crops. (You wouldn't want so much for a tomato, however, because the tomato fruit is more important than the foliage; nor is nitrogen overly important in a seedbed, where phosphorus is especially required by seedlings.) Nitrogen is subject to rapid turnover; it is readily absorbed by the grass and often quickly sacrificed (as part of the protein) in clippings. Where clippings are left on the lawn much of the nitrogen is recycled; clippings provide nutrients equivalent to one or two fertilizations annually. As a rule the lawn could "care less" in just what form it receives its nitrogen, just so that the nitrogen is available to the plant in proper quantity when needed.

Fig. 5-4 Spreading fertilizer.

Nitrogen is something of a "plaything" in the ecosystem. Although gaseous nitrogen constituting nearly eighty percent of air is inert and not usable as a plant nutrient, small amounts are transformed (as by lightning) into soluble ions absorbed by rainfall that have fertility value. In the soil, nitrogen is oxidized or reduced with facility by soil organisms. The nitrifying species change ammonia and other reduced forms of nitrogen to nitrate, highly soluble and mobile in the soil solution, the form of nitrogen most used by higher plants. But the soil is full of denitrifying bacteria, too, which reverse the procedure and may cause nitrogen loss by volatilization. They are most active when oxygen is deficient (as with soil that is waterlogged for a protracted period). Nitrogen-fixing bacteria and algae also occur, which are capable of changing gaseous nitrogen into forms usable by plants. They often live in special nodules on plant roots, especially of legumes (the clover or bean family).

A study in Illinois utilizing radioactive nitrogen as a tracer showed that nitrogen applied to a lawn is quickly incorporated into organic molecules where it may remain for years, cycled and recycled again. Seven pounds of N/M was applied each year for fifteen years in North Dakota, with no loss due to leaching by ground water (although surely there must have been some volatilization to the air). In Kansas, on agricultural soil, nitrogen stabilized in the soil at a 0.1 percent concentration no matter how generously or sparingly fertilizer was applied.

Fertilizer nitrogen is basically of two types, organic and inorganic. Organic compounds are those fairly complicated molecules characteristic of life based upon a concatenation of carbon atoms. They are typically derived from tissues that were once living (vegetable or animal wastes). However, natural organic molecules are now simulated synthetically, providing a new class of organic fertilizers, the "synthetic organics." The ureaforms (UF) and isobutylene diurea (IBDU) are familiar examples. Urea, a very simple molecule, is technically "organic," but it is so soluble and similar in its behavior to inorganic types like ammonium salts and nitrates that it is grouped with the inorganic or "chemical" nitrogen sources.

Certain advantages and disadvantages reside with each of these fertilizer groupings. Inorganic nitrogen is typically lower in cost, quickly available to the plant, and fairly uncomplicated in its effects. On the other hand it ordinarily is leached readily, increases soil salinity, can "burn" foliage, cannot be applied at high rates (thus intensifying labor costs because of its need for frequent application), and tends to lower the pH. Organic nitrogen has the advantage of gradual release of nitrogen (avoiding flushes of stimulated growth and leaching losses); it is not likely to burn the turf, can be applied more generously (thus reducing labor costs), and often carries additional nutrients (especially micronutrients) as part of the organic substance. Disadvantages include a tendency to be more expensive, to be less "available" in cool weather (i.e., it requires a longer time for breakdown by soil organisms), and often to have a low percentage of nitrogen (excessive bulk needed to supply a requisite quantity of nitrogen).

Gradual-release or slow-release nitrogen sources have gained considerable favor for turf. Both UF and IBDU, like natural organics, provide a gradual feed-out of their nitrogen. So do prills of soluble nitrogen coated with wax or sulfur to restrain dissolution (viz., sulphur-coated urea, or SCU). Such materials are generally expensive, but unlike natural organics they carry a high concentration of nitrogen. Moreover, they are clean, light in weight, and easy to handle. The "gradual-release" feature results from a slow breakdown of fairly complex molecules (e.g., ureaform), slow dissolution (e.g., IBDU), or gradual "leakage" of the coating (e.g., SCU). The end result, in each case, is parcelling out of the nutrient over a prolonged period, rather than the "feast-and-famine" cycle involved with soluble nitrogen. A single fertilization often suffices for months, and with ureaform there is a bit of carry-over for a year or two. The slow-to-break-down fraction then accumulates in the soil as a reserve, which can continue to nourish grass for a number of months should fertilization cease. A graph showing this process appears as Figure 5-5. Generally both UF and IBDU are more efficient on acid than on alkaline soils. UF is slower to release nitrogen in cold than in warm weather, while IBDU may play out sooner and be more dependent on optimum moisture.

Fig. 5-5 Rate at which nitrogen becomes available from different fertilizer sources. Note nearly complete availability of soluble nutrient (ammonium sulfate) within two weeks, but slow release from ureaforms "A" and "B" over several months.

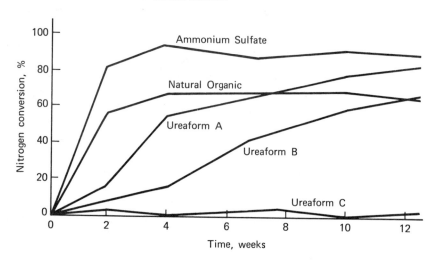

Phosphorus is a "tricky" nutrient, becoming available or unavailable according to a wide range of happenings in the soil. As it is fixed quickly and tightly to soil particles, usually in complex chemical combinations, it moves very tardily through the soil in ground water. We noted in Chapter Three that phosphorus is best mixed into the rootzone, since it may be years working down from the lawn surface. Phosphorus diffuses very little from a fixation site compared to potassium and especially nitrogen (see page 104).

Soil pH markedly influences phosphorus availability, as is noted in Figure 5-9. Fortunately, plant roots seem able to transfer phosphorus into the plant when root hairs contact fixation sites, even though the phosphorus may be technically unavailable (insoluble by soil test). One probably shouldn't be too concerned about the solubility of fertilizer phosphorus, since in most cases it will become immobilized when it contacts the soil in any event, yet be somewhat "available" to grass nevertheless.

Soils containing less than twenty pounds of phosphorus to the acre are not well suited to grass growth. Few soils have a content this low, however, most being in the "medium" range with a sixty pound or so average. Much depends, of course, upon the phosphorus content of rock minerals from which the soil evolved.

Application of phosphorus seldom results in observable change in the grass plant. Rather it contributes to better "tone" and the healthy growth resulting from nutrient balance. Adequate phosphorus is particularly important for encouraging good rooting. Seldom, however, is a lawn so deficient in phosphorus as to restrict growth, especially if the turf has ever been fertilized. At the other extreme, very high rates of phosphorus—over a thousand pounds to the acre—seem not to upset grass physiology. One seldom gets into trouble applying fertilizers rich in phosphorus or superphosphate alone.

Phosphorus, derived as it is from acidification of phosphate rock, has not been so expensive a nutrient as nitrogen. But phosphate rock deposits are limited, and fertilizer phosphorus can be expected to become less available and more dear as time goes on. Yet it is not needed by lawngrasses in large quantity, and ratios for turf fertilizers generally call for only one-third to one-sixth as much phosphorus as nitrogen and potassium, which is close to the proportions of these nutrients in grass tissue (Table 5-2). Fertilizer phosphorus comes in many complex chemical forms, but the main concern is simply the total phosphorus percentage (usually expressed as the oxide) listed on the label.

Potassium, the third of the major nutrients, is reasonably available in most soils. It is very abundant in plains soils where limited rainfall has forestalled its leaching. In most lawns it is not so scarce as to limit grass growth, though seldom so abundant as not to need occasional additions. Potassium also helps with the general "tone" of the turf and seems to make grasses more winter-hardy, less susceptible to disease, and a bit stiffer (less floppy) even when overfertilized with nitrogen.

An "adequate" amount of potassium would be about two hundred to two hundred fifty pounds per acre; most western soils run above this, and many eastern soils are somewhat below it. Unlike phosphorus, potassium is only weakly fixed to soil particles and may be displaced by other ions and moved by soil water fairly readily. Therefore, trying to build up huge reserves in the soil is rather pointless. Where rain or irrigation is sufficient to cause leaching, periodical replacement of potassium by fertilization is a good idea. Western soils will probably not need potassium additions, and even most eastern soils receive some replenishment continuously through mineralization of rock particles.

Because potassium deposits are more abundant than phosphorus, supplies should continue to be available at reasonable cost. Most fertilizer potassium is provided as the chloride, the most economical salt. The slightly more expensive sulfate would probably be preferable, given a choice, since sulfur is often a valuable nutrient conferring advantages in soil and grass alike.

Other Nutrients

The secondary nutrients, calcium, magnesium, and sulfur, are generally adequate in most soils. Calcium and magnesium derive naturally from rock mineralization and, of course, are added when dolomitic limestone is used for liming. Moreover, they often come "unannounced" in fertilizers, as part of the carrier or as unclaimed residues from the preparation of superphosphate. If a near-neutral pH is maintained, calcium (and magnesium) will probably prove adequate in the majority of lawns.

When coal was widely burned for fuel, sulfur occurred significantly in rainfall. Even today sulfur dioxide and other "fumes" get into the atmosphere from industrial operations and contribute to the newly recognized "acid rain." Probably most lawns receive ample sulfur from these sources and natural happenings. Response to sulfur additions has been noticed, however, especially in Florida and the rainy parts of the Pacific Northwest. The grass often experiences less disease then, and certain weeds are better contested.

None of the micronutrients, except iron in certain regions, are much of a problem. Probably adequate amounts already occur in the soil, or are recycled by clippings and added as traces in fertilizer. Iron, however, is frequently unavailable in alkaline soils (and may even be a problem with centipedegrass on acid soil, a grass notoriously temperamental about fertility balance). Soluble iron sulfate, sprayed onto grass made chlorotic by iron deficiency, will green it up in a matter of hours. Just two or three ounces per M are required. Other salts of iron can be used, and also chelates (in which the iron is bound into a complex molecule that presumably prevents its becoming "tied up" by the soil). Oftentimes, however, response to iron application is not long lasting. Better than supplying additional iron might be the reduction of pH, which often frees iron already present in the soil. We noted that both sulfur and gypsum have been used for soil acidification; they often correct iron chlorosis more efficiently than does piling on a lot of iron salts or chelates.

APPLICATION OF FERTILIZER

Lawn fertilizers should have certain common-sense characteristics. Dust-free granular products are better than dusty ones. Particles as fine as dust blow in the wind and coat grass foliage, causing burn. Particles about the size of buckshot, i.e., prills, make for easier, more efficient application. As with lawnseed, granular fertilizers are quickly and efficiently spread with a centrifugal spreader where the exact demarcation of borders is not of prime concern (Fig. 5-6). Feathering

Fig. 5-6 Servicing the lawn with a centrifugal "whirl-cast" spreader, in which a rotating plate beneath the hopper "throws" particulates metered onto it (through an agitating slot) quite widely.

one pass into another, as occurs with spreaders casting fertilizer, avoids "striping" due to skips. However, gravity-drop spreaders respect borders better (Fig. 5-7). If a fertilizer is dusty, and particularly if it contains soluble nutrients, watering the lawn immediately after application to wash salts off of the grass foliage and into the soil is suggested.

Fig. 5-7 Spreading with a gravity-drop spreader. Particulates are fed out through adjustable slots at base, agitated by a spindle between the wheels.

The timing of fertilization has frequently been cause for comment. It is just as important to apply a fertilizer at the right season as to apply it at all. Figure 2-2 contrasted bluegrass growth with southern grasses and hot weather weeds; it was quite evident that autumn fertilization benefits the bluegrass, summer fertilization the weeds. Not all situations are this clear-cut, however, since each lawn has its own personality and differs from all others in its needs. The soil, the weather, the kind of grass—all make a difference. But one generalization is possible: Fertilizer should be supplied to the grass on a schedule such that the grass can make the best use of the nutrients. In the case of northern

Fig. 5-8 Summer damage from using a soluble fertilizer in hot weather.

lawns typically this means generous feeding through autumn, sparing fertilization (just enough to keep up color and modest growth) through spring and summer. With southern lawns an early spring fertilization would provide a "shot in the arm" for quick green-up, with summer feedings corresponding to the kind of grass and adequacy of soil nutrients. Generous feeding in summer intensifies mowing. Autumn fertilization helps lengthen the growing season, but too heavy feeding late in autumn can turn southern grasses more susceptible to winterkill, in those regions where winter weather is severe.

LIME AND LIMING

As was noted when discussing soil, the level of acidity-alkalinity (expressed as pH) is important for regulating the availability to the plant of many nutrients. Certain essential micronutrients, such as iron, often become unavailable to growing grass when the pH rises to levels of moderate or strong alkalinity. Similarly, a pH that is quite acid can both make needed nutrients less available and "free up" less soluble elements to the point of toxicity. In general strong acidity reduces the availability of all major and secondary nutrients; alkalinity is less repressive of major and secondary nutrients, but can seriously curtail the availability of micronutrients (Fig. 5-9).

Fig. 5-9 How lime affects plant food availability.

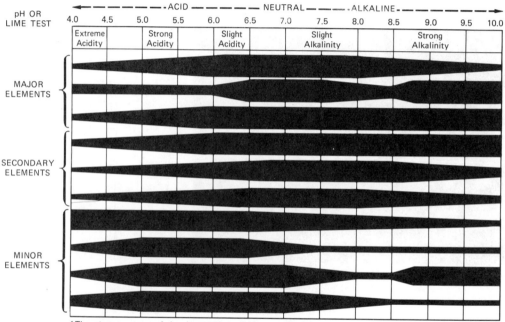

*The greatest amount of the elements is available at a pH of 6.5 to 7.0.
The soil should be limed and the pH corrected to suit the crops grown.

The different colored bars represent elements as indicated. When the soil is acid or sour the bars are thinner; meaning less food is available to the growing plants. The same is true when the soil is too sweet or alkaline.

Most fertilizers have an acidifying influence on the soil (Fig. 5-10), tending, with persistent use, to drop the pH as much as a unit or two. For quicker correction of alkalinity, of course, sulfur or other acidifying materials may be used. More often, however, the correction needed is for acidity. The oxides and hydroxides of calcium and magnesium have a strong neutralizing influence on acid soils. Most commonly limestone (calcium carbonate) or its derivatives are used. A favorite liming material is dolomitic limestone, a carbonate containing both

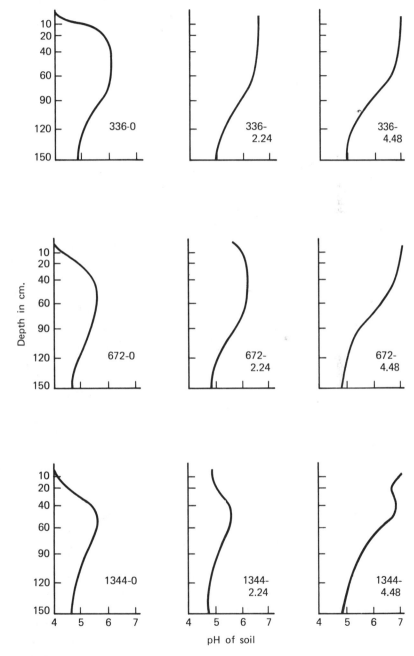

Fig. 5-10 The effects of four years' application of N from NH_4NO_3 (at annual rates of 336,672, or 1,344 kg/ha) and lime (at annual rates of 0, 2.24, or 4.48 metric tons/ha) on pH of the soil profile. After Palazzo and Duell.

calcium and magnesium. Calcium oxide, quicklime or hydrated lime, obtained by heating limestone, is nearly twice as "strong" as limestone. It is more difficult to spread than limestone because it is powdery rather than granular. Marl, an accumulation of sea shells in ancient lake or sea bottoms, is a good liming material, chemically about the same as limestone. Chalk is a soft form of limestone found in certain geological beds that can also be used. Liming at rates suggested in Chapter Three is often advisable in the acid soil regions shown on the map of Figure 5-11.

Fig. 5-11 Regions generally needing or not needing lime.

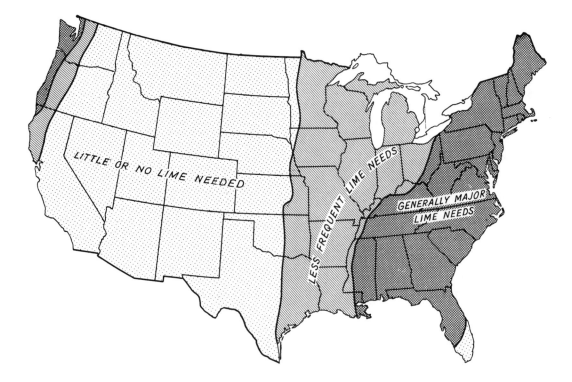

Ground limestone is spread in much the same fashion as is fertilizer. However, lime is best not applied with fertilizer, for it sometimes interacts chemically, causing volatilization and ammonia loss. Since ground limestone is quite heavy, it is well to spread it on firm ground. In northerly climates a favorable practice is to spread it on frozen soil, which not only avoids soil rutting but any danger from burn as well. The more pulverized the limestone is, the quicker-acting it will be (since more total surface is then presented for interaction with the soil). Many people favor a coarsely ground limestone, which brings about gradual neutralization over a period of years.

Watering and Fertilizing Checklist

Irrigate infrequently but thoroughly (light soils each few days, no more than one inch; heavy soils every one or two weeks, about two inches).

Water when grass begins to show stress (loses resiliency, develops bluish cast).

Adjust sprinkling to lawn and soil (all water applied should soak in; if it runs off, reduce the rate).

Time of day makes little difference (water the lawn when convenient, and when water pressure is favorable; more loss by evaporation occurs in the heat of the day, but less succor is given to disease).

Check out sprinklers for pattern, rate, and uniformity of application (place cans or jars within area of coverage to determine quantities).

Fertilize according to soil, kind of lawn, and esthetic demands (a soil test points up needs but nitrogen will invariably be wanted at least 2-4 lb./M annually).

Apply no more than 1-2 lb. elemental N/M at a time (base rates for complete fertilizers on the nitrogen).

Fertilize northern lawns generously in autumn, sparingly in spring and summer (long-lasting "gradual release" fertilizers have advantages, especially in warm weather).

Fertilize southern lawns during spring, summer, and early autumn (frequency depends on the kind of grass; summer feeding intensifies mowing).

Use granular rather than dusty fertilizers for convenience and to avoid burn (lawn service contractors often use liquids or slurries).

Choose fertilizer formulations rich in nitrogen for turf (analyses such as 30-10-10, 33-6-9, or 24-5-8 would be appropriate).

Lime markedly acid soils, acidify alkaline ones (a simple pH test tells you how much lime or sulfur will be needed).

Mowing and Equipment for Neatness and Efficiency

6

Sometimes it seems that modern America has too many gadgets. A homeowner can become snowed under by the clutter of infrequently used devices that seem to accumulate in every garage, many of them in faulty repair or out of date. Some of them cause more inconvenience to clean, store, and service than they save in operations. As a matter of fact, commonplace gardening tools can often accomplish small tasks in the time it takes to activate complicated equipment. There may even be increased satisfaction for a homeowner to have direct contact with a gardening chore, rather than be separated from it by an impersonal mechanical barrier or mysterious procedures.

However, the tremendous advances made in lawn and garden equipment cannot be denied. Modern labor-saving devices are blessings the homeowner should fully appreciate. They are especially apparent in the spreaders and sprayers now available to get the "spruce-up" tasks more easily done and in mowers that make mowing "fun." Because mowers are so fundamental to lawn keeping and so much a part of the hours spent on the lawn, they will be discussed at some length.

MOWING AND MOWERS

By and large mowing is an innovation of this century. Earlier, livestock did the job. Even today on some of the famed golf courses of Scotland, sheep roam the fairways to keep the roughs down. Later came sickles and scythes, skillfully wielded by gardening craftsmen. In 1830, the English engineer Budding fashioned the first lawn mower, patterned after shearing machinery in the textile factory where he worked. His principle, a reel rotating against a bedknife, is still used, though rotary mowers that resemble in principle the even older sickles and scythes now predominate. It wasn't until early in the twentieth century that a Detroit industrialist put a gasoline engine from a washing machine onto his lawn clipper to usher in the age of the power mower. Now almost every suburban home sports power equipment.

MOWER CHOICE

A number of factors must be weighed when one is choosing a lawn mower, some of them not directly related to the lawn (e.g., what can the budget stand, or how husky is the wife?). Seriously, though, keep in mind the "field of battle" at its most obstreperous season. You will want a mower that can handle the toughest grass growing at its fastest clip—even if it be exceptionally dense, excessively long, and perhaps mowed when damp (thus requiring more power). Chosen in anticipation of the worst circumstances, a mower should certainly be able to take care of other seasons quite easily.

Fuel Economy in Mowing

Reduced speeds and lower horsepower, where appropriate, can save on fuel.

Reels require less power than do rotaries or flail mowers, which put higher loads on the engine per unit of mowing swath.

A moderate lengthening of the interval between mowings should save on fuel, although still longer intervals might consume more fuel (the extra growth requiring a higher power output than would two easier mowings).

Higher clipping generally requires less work than does lower mowing that cuts tougher tissues. Low mowings on uneven ground may cause the blade to brush the thatch and soil. High clipping is less likely to dull the blade; blades sharper for longer cut more efficiently.

Regular maintenance, including lubrication, helps. Adjust reels for smooth, free-moving performance. Keep motors clean and tuned up.

Avoid carelessness that results in fuel spillage.

The size of the lawn must be reckoned with. An acre lot contains almost forty-four thousand square feet. Even assuming about half of this is occupied by house, drive and shrub beds, over twenty thousand square feet of lawn still remains to be mowed. If you attempt to mow this much grass with a lightweight, eighteen-inch rotary you will walk nearly three miles, allowing a bit for overlap and trimming. Walking three miles is more healthful than disabling, considering that you set your own pace; but doing it every few days can soon become tiresome, particularly when the weather turns oppressive. People with lawns of a half acre or more are usually prime candidates for a riding mower (Fig. 6-1). But for smaller lawns of four to five thousand square feet—the average size in New Jersey—capitalization of an expensive riding mower hardly seems necessary. Yet you do see many lawns no bigger than a postage stamp being tended with a riding mower; riding mowers are fun!

Fig. 6-1 Increasingly popular for larger lawns is the garden tractor with (multiple-blade) mowing attachment on hydraulic lift.

One bit of mower philosophy at this point. Whatever your lawn and inclinations, choose a mower that is strongly built and apt to be trouble-free, even if the machine may cost a bit more. It should have the capacity to complete the mowing in about half an hour or so, in a relaxing fashion. So much lawn-keeping time will be devoted to mowing that it should be made as pleasant an occupation as possible. A mower of high quality, for which there is good local service, of a size suited to the lawn, is a worthwhile investment, not a luxury.

Still another decision involves the mode of cutting, chief choices being reel or rotary. The kind of grass guides you to some extent. So does your temperament—whether you are a perfectionist, or content merely to keep topgrowth in bounds! For rough mowing akin to that given roadside berms, sicklebar, and hammerknife (flail) mowers can be used. The sicklebar is typically an extension to the side of a tractor with toothlike triangular cutting blades that agitate horizontally between guides; sicklebars are much used for cutting hay and other farm crops that are to be cured in the field. The hammerknife works from T-shaped blades that swivel loosely around a drumlike horizontal spindle; when the spindle rotates, centrifugal force extends the blades to form a peripheral "cutting surface." Mowing results from the impact of the rapidly rotating T-blades which, if dull, may tear and mash more than slice. Being pendulous, however, the T-blades "give" if they hit something and are thus less of an irresistable force upon collision than might be a rigid rotary blade striking a rock, for example. The sicklebar and hammerknife are not commonly used for mowing lawns, and we will not dwell upon them.

A walk-behind reel or rotary mower is generally selected for a home lawn of modest proportions. Reel mowers have a rotating cylinder of curved blades adjusted to barely touch a stationary bedknife, much as scissors cut (Fig. 6-2). When properly adjusted and sharp (not full of

Fig. 6-2 The way a reel mower cuts.

nicks or out of alignment), the reel mower performs the neatest job of cutting. Unfortunately, reels are a bit more difficult to maintain than rotaries, generally having to be sent to a lapping machine for sharpening. Often adjustment is more necessary than regrinding the cutting edges, however! Reels are frustrating to use where twigs, pebbles, or other foreign objects abound, since these will wedge between cutting blade and bedknife, halting the reel or nicking the cutting edge. Nor can a reel mower approach obstructions very closely for trimming, since the wheels invariably extend well outside the cutting blades.

Rotary mowers, in contrast, mow by impact, as does a sickle. The blade must revolve at high speed to cut cleanly. Minimum speeds of about ten thousand feet per minute are customary, and many mowers operate at double this. So much momentum can be hazardous; it is able to throw pebbles or metal fragments with the speed of a bullet, or sever fingers and toes without difficulty. A whirling blade becomes dull if it strikes objects in the lawn. Fortunately it can be sharpened with a file at home, although the blades should be balanced from time to time lest one arm come to outweigh the other, causing wobble. Rotaries are more versatile than reels. They sidle up to obstructions more closely and are better suited for tall-mowed turf. Unlike reels, which blow tall foliage down in front of the cutting blades, most rotaries develop a strong sucking action that lifts the grass into the cutting chamber.

Reel mowers are most suitable for well-kept, low-mowed lawns of bentgrass, bermudagrass, and zoysia; rotaries, for taller turfs not so meticulously watched over. Table 6-1 compares several aspects of reel and rotary mowers. Both types are available either in small sizes for the home (able to get into corners and do most of the trimming) or as large units for mowing acreage (reels generally grouped in tractor-drawn gangs; rotaries utilizing multiple blades, usually three). Large reel-mower gangs have no trouble mowing five acres an hour; they work best on open swards such as golf fairways. Large rotaries cannot be made to cut so wide a swath, although larger units can handle twenty acres a day without much difficulty.

Table 6-1 Reel and rotary mowers contrasted.

	Reel Machines	*Rotary Machines*
Cutting Quality	Excellent for low cut, with "scissors action" of reel blade against bedknife giving clean clip if mower is well-adjusted. Not so good on high cut, because reel "blows down" rather than "sucks up" grass.	Impact cutting can be adequate if blade is sharp and sufficiently powered, but there is apt to be more leaf tip fraying ("gray hair"). Well-designed machines "suck up" floppy grass into cutting chamber.

Power Requirements and Design	Less power required, and automatically adjusted to forward speed. Some models are under-powered for tough-to-mow grasses such as zoysia, and have insufficient reel blades (should have six or more for best mowing of bents and zoysia).	Need for power increases rapidly the wider the blade; for broad swaths mowers generally have two or three (staggered) cutting blades. Power needed for cutting unrelated to forward propulsion, so that hand pushed machines are generally preferred, allowing slower approach and no stall on tough grass.
Maintenance	Sharpening must be done on a lapping machine, so the mower must be sent out at appreciable service charge. May need frequent attention in poor lawns full of twigs, nails, toys, stones, dog bones, etc.	Blade is usually sharpenable at home with a file when it becomes dull, although care must be taken to maintain proper balance.
Safety	Reel mowers have the advantage, with slower moving blades that do not kick up debris.	On occasion blades break and whir out from the housing at high speed; or they may pick up and throw wire, stones, etc., with a lethal force. Can amputate toes or finger if carelessly handled.
Mowed Surface	Reels operate on two wheels, so that the cutting edge holds a uniform distance above ground level; the mower follows the swales and humps, scalping only if a rise occurs between the two wheels.	Rotaries generally have four wheels, maintain a rather level stance over irregular soil; at dips the grass is cut taller, over mounds it is scalped.
Manipulation	More cumbersome, heavier, less able to trim (as noted opposite).	Usually lighter, more easily maneuvered, more handily lifted and stored.

Other features worthy of scrutiny include a simple means for adjusting mowing height, ease of starting the motor, and the type of motor (gasoline or electric). We have repeatedly emphasized the importance of mowing height on grass behavior. In this day and age a good lawnmower should certainly have some sort of simple lever for quickly regulating clipping height, through a range from less than one inch to at least three inches. Reels lend themselves less well to simple changes of height than do rotaries, since the wheels are typically geared to the reel.

Recent years have witnessed vast improvement in the means for starting mowers. In many cases the pull-rope has been abandoned in favor of electric starting; but even if the mower must be started by tugging on a rope, good machines now "snap to" at the first pull. Nothing is more frustrating than a balky mower eating into time set aside for mowing!

Manufacturers have come a long way, too, in designing machines that can be simply serviced. Some of the older models required a contortionist to get at the stopcocks for changing oil, adding gasoline, and so on. The two-cycle gasoline motor is not widely used for lawn equipment, although it is in many ways a simpler power unit than is the four-cycle type. Two-cycle motors, much used for power saws, need to be revved up in order to supply the necessary power. Of course oil must be mixed in with gasoline for fueling. Most mowers use the typical four-cycle motor, which requires occasional oil changes but no special compounding of fuel. Such motors can be "gas hogs," however, at least at the higher horsepowers used for garden tractors and large riding units.

Electrically powered mowers may be a coming thing, but as yet they are not commonplace. A battery-powered garden tractor is available which can mow a sizable lawn before needing recharging. As battery power becomes better perfected, electrically powered equipment can be expected to gain favor. Certainly the silence, lack of stench, and low servicing requirements of electric units are features much to be desired. Electric mowers requiring a cord are seldom convenient, particularly where there are trees. The future of electric mowing would seem to depend upon the development of longer-lasting lightweight batteries that are more efficient and less bulky than heretofore.

Fig. 6-3 Underside of an "air cushion" rotary mower that "floats" on the lawn or does an airfoil on the water. This wheelless mower has found more acceptance in Northern Europe than in America; turf is typically mowed too tall in America for this device to be effective.

Fig. 6-4 The lightweight air cushion mower (see also Fig. 6-3).

MOWING HEIGHT AND THE GRASS

That the grass root system grows below ground proportionally to the height of the foliage above ground has long been recognized. Thus clipping height has a direct influence upon depth of rooting, which in turn influences the lawn's ability to plumb deeply into the soil in search of water and nutrients (Fig. 6-5). A deeply rooted lawn should require

Fig. 6-5 Dr. Robert's solution culture of lawngrass shows clearly that depth of rooting is closely related to height of mowing.

less attention than does a shallowly rooted one and be better able to shrug off trouble. In most cases it is wise to mow the grass as tall as is esthetically permissible. Obviously, appropriate mowing heights will differ for different grasses. Newer cultivars are mostly bred for low growth and generally thrive under lower mowing than would common grass. It is especially important to mow the lawn tall under stressful circumstances, such as in the shade, when weather or climate are less than ideal, or where disease is prevalent. Sometimes mowing height will make the difference between survival or loss.

One study in Missouri showed that low mowing of tall fescue depleted the grass's energy reserves, as could be demonstrated by regrowth failure in a dark chamber. The foliage and culms must therefore store reserve food, which is sacrificed with low mowing. That mowing height makes a measurable difference in the amount of roots, rhizomes, and foliage with several bluegrasses is shown in Table 6-2, based upon research done in Vermont.

Table 6-2 Comparative weights of roots, rhizomes, and foliage of five bluegrass selections mowed at the height indicated for three months. After Wood and Burke.

Variety	Yields in grams of dry weight								
	cut at ½ inch			cut at 1 inch			cut at 1½ inch		
	Roots	Rhiz.	Tops	Roots	Rhiz.	Tops	Roots	Rhiz.	Tops
Merion	2.2	0.3	24.3	2.2	0.5	27.9	3.3	0.7	33.7
Newport	2.3	0.2	22.7	2.8	0.2	22.8	3.4	0.6	28.6
Park	2.3	0.3	21.9	3.9	0.3	25.3	4.1	0.4	30.4
Delta	1.9	0.2	22.2	3.0	0.3	30.3	2.8	0.4	29.4
Common	2.8	0.3	24.5	3.6	0.6	28.0	4.1	0.6	32.4

As was noted in Chapter Three, bentgrasses and bermudagrasses are generally clipped shorter (one inch or less) than zoysia, improved bluegrasses, perennial ryegrasses, fine fescues, centipedegrass, and st. augustine (generally mowed at from one to two and a half inches); common bluegrass, unselected fescue, bahiagrass, and tall fescue are often mowed three inches high or higher, especially in difficult climatic zones.

Frequency of mowing ties in with clipping height. The few days between mowings, when green leaf is comparatively more abundant, can assist grass vigor. On the other hand, if the grass is let grow too tall, such that most of the foliage is sacrificed at the next mowing, clipping can prove traumatic; then most of the food-making green leaf is lost all at once, along with whatever energy reserves were husbanded in the tissues. As a general rule mowing should be frequent enough so that green leaf decapitation amounts to no more than fifty percent at any one mowing. Since most of the photosynthetic tissues are in the upper canopy of the lawn, mowing a lawn from a normal two-inch height down to one inch may sacrifice a lot more than half of the green leaf. But a lawn customarily kept at two inches, mowed when new growth reaches three inches, would probably not suffer unacceptable defoliation. If it is necessary to reduce mowing height, do so gradually, a fraction of an inch at a time, rather than scalping the lawn all at once and leaving only stubble.

Many homeowners insist on mowing the lawn quite low, in the mistaken belief that less mowing will then be required (i.e., it is reasoned that it will take longer for the grass to grow tall enough to need another mowing). Actually, the irregularity of turf growth is what calls for mowing. A freshly mowed lawn looks well whether low or tall. But the low-mowed one will probably become unkempt sooner than the tall-mowed one because differential new growth shows up so quickly by contrast in a low-clipped sward. As a rule labor is not saved by mowing low; rather, the grass is weakened and weeds are favored.

MOWING MISCELLANEA

Mowing patterns designed for the quickest, most efficient mowing in conformity with the shape of the individual lawn come with experience. If possible vary the direction of mowing so that the mower passes one time in one direction, the next in another. If mowing is practiced consistently in the same direction the mower may cause the grass to decline in that direction, showing "grain" that makes the lawn seem striped. In extreme cases lengthy shoots lying close to the soil may remain uncut. With most lawns it is possible to reverse directions at least occasionally, even if not to develop alternative right-angle mowing patterns.

Mowing experiences seasonal differences, of course. Obviously mowing must be more assiduous in seasons when grass growth peaks. But seasonal differences also show up in the "quality" of mowing. Young grass, or the fresh growth of spring, mows easily. The leaf tissues are soft, little lignified; the leaves are severed without much expenditure of energy. They may even be so soft and "mushy" as to wad up in a rotary mowing chamber rather than disperse neatly! Later in spring and summer stiffer, wirier stalks develop, meant to bear the seedheads. These are quite difficult to mow. You may think that your mower has suddenly turned dull for a three-week interval in June (bluegrass lawns), simply because the tough seedhead stalks fray rather than cut cleanly, showing "gray hair" even when freshly mowed. A

Fig. 6-6 An intermediate-size riding mower suited for "main-job" suburban lawn mowing.

well-adjusted mower with sharp blades helps, but things will get better as this growth phase passes in any event. Still, summer leaf contains less protein and more cellulosic cell wall than does the new growth of spring or autumn and is apt to be a bit "tougher" to cut.

Lawns mow most attractively if quite level; irregularities and scalpings may develop where a wheel dips into a depression or a mound rises under the cutting blade. Uneven lawn surfaces can be corrected by filling in the low spots with additional soil (but don't add more than a quarter inch at a time, to avoid smothering the grass). This is a better solution than mashing the ground with a roller, which will compact the soil. Mowers having large wheels and broad tires are less apt to reflect irregularities than their opposites. Flotation-type "balloon" tires are commonplace these days on big equipment, allowing its use even on damp ground that would show narrow tire ruts.

It really shouldn't be necessary to issue a caution about servicing the lawn mower on the grass. Yet, many people thoughtlessly "gas up" or tinker with the machine on the lawn instead of on the driveway. Almost inevitably some gasoline or oil will be spilled, disfiguring the grass. It pays to get in the habit of servicing all equipment off the lawn. It also pays to police the lawn regularly for sticks, dog bones, toys, and other obstructions that will at the least be an impediment to efficient mowing, or at worst injurious to the mower (or to its operator if something is hurled by a rotary blade).

Thriving grass wears better than that ill cared-for (or at least it recovers better from injury). But whatever attention a lawn receives, constant hard use in the same location will wear out the turf. No grass can stand up to such things as daily football play. So it is wise to move playgrounds from place to place and to barricade shortcut pathways (place shrubbery strategically or lay stepping stones).

Different grasses have differing degrees of wearability. One test at Michigan State University showed this progression: Manhattan ryegrass better than tall fescue, better than Merion bluegrass, better than fine fescue, better than rough bluegrass (*Poa trivialis*). Fine fescues and *Poa trivialis* were especially hurt by "crushing," such as when a "sled" was dragged over the turf. The percentage of cell-wall substance makes the difference. The leaf sheath has more cell-wall cellulose than does the leaf blade (i.e., more heavy-wall lignified sclerenchyma tissue). A comparison of several bluegrasses in Washington showed that groundhugging, densely growing cultivars such as Merion, Nugget, and Sodco wore better than the common types.

CLIPPINGS AND THATCH

Whether to collect clippings or leave them on the lawn has always been a matter of dispute. That the clippings have fertility value worth recycling is beyond question (Table 6-3).

Table 6-3 Nutrients recoverable in clippings from an acre of lawn during the growing season.

Nutrient	Pounds
Nitrogen (N)	120
Phosphorus (PO_5)	40
Potassium (K_2O)	100
Calcium (CaO)	40
Magnesium (MgO)	8
Sulfur (S)	8

But neither is there any question but that clippings can be unsightly if they are so long or abundant that they remain perched atop the sward. In that case they probably should be raked for the compost pile. Here again the type of mower can have some influence. Mowers that fragment the clippings before ejecting them and those that blow the clippings evenly rather than leaving them in windrows assist greatly in keeping the lawn neat. With fertilizer costs increasing, recycling the

Fig. 6-7 One means for collecting clippings (and leaves, using larger bag). Air stream from the rotary carries clippings into the air-permeable bag.

clippings would seem to have considerable appeal. One study made by the USDA at Beltsville showed that leaving the clippings was beneficial to the lawn, all things considered. That clippings are not very instrumental in building thatch has become quite clear. The cut tips of grass leaves consist of fairly delicate tissue which decomposes quickly when brought in contact with moist ground. Ligneous leaf bases, surface roots, and rhizomes are largely responsible for thatch.

Even if clippings contribute little to it, thatch can be a problem. When at all thick it becomes a barrier between lawn and soil. Slow-to-decompose grasses such as zoysia and fine fescue are notorious thatch-formers. Thatch can become so impervious that it insulates the rootzone from normal air interchange; fertilizer, even rainfall, can't penetrate uniformly. Emergence of new shoots may be blocked. Soil is insulated from the warmth of the spring sun, delaying green-up. Thatch may harbor insect pests and disease spores, which on occasion may attack living grass. Protected in thatch, pests are harder to reach with pesticides. Grass rooted mostly in thatch is neither drought resistant nor well anchored.

Yet thatch is not all bad. It is nature's means for recycling plant tissues. As it decays it does serve as something of an organic fertilizer. Some experts feel that thatch contributes importantly to biological balance, too, by helping prevent diseases from becoming epidemic. Certainly it can restrain the sprouting of weed seeds, and in moderate amount may aid wearability much as does a pad beneath a carpet.

Thatch was never paid very much attention until the modern demand for improved lawns arose. An undecomposed agglomeration of debris at the base of the sod is always an accompaniment of grass growth, whether lawn or prairie. This constantly decays at its base while receiving additions above. Like the compost pile, its thickness depends upon how quickly the old stuff decays and how ample are the new accumulations (Fig. 6-8). In recent years the new grasses, bred to

Fig. 6-8 Pencil points to area where thatch forms, typically an accumulation of ligneous leaf sheaths and roots rather than clippings. Here thatch is not at all excessive.

grow densely, have intensified the accumulation, while decomposition continues at nature's leisurely pace. Even so, approximately forty percent of prairie thatch disappears during winter, and similarly lawns shouldn't be much different. In Manitoba the increase of prairie biomass (mainly thatchlike residues) proved to average only ten percent annually, so there had to be a ninety-percent natural disappearance due to decay and recycling.

Fungicides may temporarily slow down the "bugs" responsible for decomposition. But the elimination of earthworms, as when arsenicals and certain pre-emergence herbicides are used, seems more often to be the cause of thatch build-up. USDA research at Beltsville showed no measurable thinning of thatch during a five-year span, no matter what treatment was tried in an attempt to reduce the accumulation. In later years aerification, or liming to a pH of about 7, helped a bit. Thatch can be eliminated by burning, as was commonplace with native prairie; burning about doubles the new growth. Burning of zoysia lawns during winter has been tried in the upper South, with fair success so far as removing the thatch is concerned, but with considerable unsightliness and dirtiness, and often an increase of winter weeds.

In a broad sense all vegetation develops thatch. It is as natural as the change of season. Green leaves serve their life span, then wither and shed. Thatch accumulates most rapidly where the growth pace is heady, the "crop" juvenile—exactly the case with a constantly mowed and fertilized lawn. There seem to be microbial repressants in thatch itself, probably polyphenols, which discourage decay; watering (leaching) helps to get rid of them and provides the moisture needed for decay.

Incidentally, senescent tissues destined to become thatch are generally not very rich in nutrients. Nutrient withdrawal into the storage regions of the plant seems to occur before a leaf ends its useful life. Tests on fallen leaves show that nitrogen, calcium, and potassium are the three most abundant nutrients in spent foliage, accounting for approximately eighty percent of its nutrient content. These, of course, are precisely the nutrients most often replenished by fertilization and liming. Next most abundant are manganese, magnesium, sulfur, phosphorus, and the trace elements, in that order.

Creating a microclimate conducive to decay is the best means for controlling thatch. Humidity, fertility, pH, aerification, and the like should all be made as favorable as possible. Topdressing (the scattering of a bit of weed-free topsoil over the turf) achieves this pretty well. But as topdressing is expensive and its application complicated, it is a practice more appropriate for the golf course than for the typical home lawn. Home lawns are more often freed of thatch by mechanical removal. Some dethatching machines comb out the thatch with flexible tines, others slice into the sod with toothed discs, and some simply poke holes into the ground (see Chapter Three). The debris ordinarily kicked to the surface should be swept up for use as a soil amendment, mulch, or for compost. Turf is rejuvenated by dethatching, and fresh growth encouraged. Stimulation comes not only from the "pruning," but because stirring things up mineralizes organic material and releases nutrients. A newly dethatched lawn assumes a fresh appearance in just a few days.

Fig. 6-9 A simple foot-powered coring device illustrates the principle behind the better aerification machines. Perforations are made through the thatch and several inches into the topsoil, the soil cores being removed.

Fig. 6-10 A powered thatch remover in action.

Thatch is best removed during seasons in which the turf is growing actively. That way the scars from treatment are quickly healed, and gaps are filled where weeds might get a start. Early autumn or spring works well with bluegrass lawns, while southern turfs can be thinned in spring or summer (late autumn if winter overseeding is to be practiced). Even small lawns yield unbelievably large piles of fluffy thatch. But in spite of the tremendous volume removed, don't be surprised if it reaccumulates within a relatively few months. Thatch removal is not a cure-all, but it does "release" the lawn so that it becomes more responsive to other measures.

"CHEMICAL MOWING" AND GROWTH RETARDANTS

A chemical means for restricting grass growth, as an alternative to mowing, has great theoretical appeal. Even so simple a measure as eliminating contrasting weeds (Chapter Seven) is "chemical mowing" of a sort; it often satisfies the viewer, as is frequently the case with roadside berms. A retardant, maleic hydrazide, that directly affects grass growth has been available for some years. However, its costliness and the need for precise application at just the right stage has limited its usefulness. Maleic hydrazide is occasionally used on roadsides, and for repressing bahiagrass seedhead formation in the South.

More recently intensive research has unearthed other growth-controlling chemicals which do indeed restrict grass growth if properly applied at just the right time. But for reasons that are not always clear, results can be erratic. Timing is important; the same application, made weeks apart, can produce decidedly different results. The exact rate needed to restrain but not injure the grass varies with season, stage of growth, and the weather. Moreover, one grass may be restrained but not another, or the weeds may escape entirely (especially annuals sprouting after treatment, which have an easier time when the grass is restrained). Also, it is very difficult to retard growth without weakening a plant. Thus retardation may increase susceptibility to disease, or make the grass more vulnerable to inclement weather. Sometimes early repression is followed by stimulation later, which then calls for more, not less, mowing!

Agronomists at Southern Illinois University find that retardants may be useful for roadside grass but seldom for fine turfs. They have this to say: "Pronounced color losses of the grass, serious stand reduction and resulting weed infestations occurred after the use of higher rates of several chemicals. A concurrent herbicide application may be necessary to control weeds in Kentucky bluegrass if treated with growth retardants—most retardants tested showed some degree of phytotoxicity. . . ."* It was also noted that different cultivars responded differently to a given application, making it difficult to develop product directions for general use. Similar findings have been reported from various parts of the country. It appears that the factors governing grass growth are too numerous for effective integration by any single growth-control spray.

OTHER EQUIPMENT

The lawn ordinarily does not require a lot of special equipment beyond that which has already been discussed (sprinklers and irrigation apparatus, aerifiers and turf thinners, spreaders for seed and granular materials). Lawn keeping can take advantage of familiar garden tools, and the usefulness of spades, shovels, rakes, hoes, and so on, for handling soil, patching, edging, and the like need no discussion. Hand shears, several models of which are now powered by a battery, may help in the tidying up of small properties. A wide assortment of attachments are offered for garden tractors, including fertilizer spreaders, sprayers, and tillers attachable to the power takeoff. For commercial operations special machines have been developed which finish the soilbed and properly place the seed in a once-over operation. Some equipment, such as aerifiers, is used so seldom that owning it rather than renting is probably unwise. Let's look briefly at a few types of equipment bearing upon lawn tending, even though of secondary importance compared to mowers and spreaders.

LAWN EDGING

Grass can be prevented from encroaching on walkways and drives either mechanically or with chemicals. Perhaps the simplest edging device is a spade or a special half-moon "hoe" designed for edging. One merely digs the border, turning over grass that has extended beyond its allotted boundary. Powered edgers similar to a small mower work well for straight or slightly curving borders, such as along driveways (Fig. 6-11). Most have a cutting disc much like a buzz saw that can be oriented either horizontally or vertically. The device is simply wheeled along the border where the cut is to be made, set for the depth required.

*D. M. Elkins, J. A. Tweedy, and D. L. Suttner, *Chemical Regulation of Grass Growth,* Agronomy Journal 66:492-7, 1974.

Fig. 6-11   A motor-powered trimmer-edger.

Chemical edging has in many cases supplanted mechanical edging (Fig. 6-13). A nonselective vegetation killer can be sprayed with pin-

Fig. 6-12   Chemical edging with a wax bar impregnated with herbicide.

point accuracy by a good sprayer to kill all succulent vegetation that it contacts. The future of chemical trimming may be uncertain, for EPA restrictions increasingly prevent sale of the more useful chemicals to the homeowner (although many have clearance for agriculture). Gasoline and kerosene can be used for edging, although they are dangerous from the flammability standpoint and are no longer inexpensive. Salt could be used, but it is so soluble that it leaches quickly and may wash into adjacent ground. Organic arsenicals (e.g., cacodylic acid formulations such as Phytar) have been available; they scorch green vegetation but they will not bother the bark of trees, and the chemical is immediately inactivated in the soil. Paraquat and glyphosate

Fig. 6-13 Chemical trimming about base of tree facilitates mowing. The tree will not be injured from spray hitting the bark. Cultivation, as here pictured, encourages weeds to sprout; it is better to leave the mat of dead grass as a mulch.

are even more efficient, requiring very little chemical; but as this is written they are not available as homeowner products. So applicability of chemical edging will depend largely upon whether or not you can get hold of "knock-down" chemicals.

Sometimes thin sheets of plastic, aluminum, or steel are driven into the ground as barriers along borders. If set low enough so that the mower rides over them easily, they will hardly prevent stems and leaves from growing over the top. They may, however, restrain the underground spread of rhizomes. Strongly rhizomatous grasses, such as weedy quackgrass in the North and bermuda and zoysia in the South, have a way of sending rhizomes deeply under an edging barrier. In such cases barriers are more effective if combined with a chemical sterilant.

LAWN SWEEPING AND LEAF "RAKING"

A lawn sweeper is a great convenience, especially when motorized (Fig. 6-14). Horizontal rotary brushes can be set as close to the ground as wished, to sweep detritus into a convenient hopper behind. Sweepers are ideal for quickly gathering clippings after mowing, for "raking" leaves in autumn, and for collecting debris kicked to the surface during dethatching.

Fig. 6-14 Motorized lawn sweeper, handy for gathering clippings, loose thatch, leaves, and other debris.

Other clean-up machines utilize air pressure. Some emit a strong stream of air that blows surface materials to the side in windrows of a sort. Others reverse the procedure and suck in air like a vacuum cleaner, collecting whatever solids are contained. Some manufacturers suggest that their rotary mower be used in this fashion with a special bag attachment. In fact, a powerful rotary mower will often fragment leaves sufficiently so that they can be left on the lawn as a relatively innocuous "mulch" that will mostly settle into the grass and gradually decompose.

TILLERS AND TRACTOR ATTACHMENTS

Rotary tillers are convenient for preparing a soilbed of limited extent, either for garden or lawn. The tiller should be powerful enough to cultivate a heavy soil, when damp, as deeply as is required. Direct drive allows you to devote full attention to guiding the tiller and maintaining depth of cultivation, but it does risk more serious damage than would a belt drive should an obstruction be encountered. Rotary tillage is not always so simple as it may seem; actually it may prove more cumbersome for cultivating small areas with precise boundaries than would spading. Tillers are destructive of structure, flailing the soil as they do; they are best used on crumbly-damp soil (if the ground is sticky-wet they will either bog down or form clods; if it is overly dry, tillers have difficulty cultivating deeply). Rotary tiller attachments are available for most home garden tractors having a power take-off.

Other occasionally useful attachments for the garden tractor are blades and snow blowers. Most garden tractors are so comparatively lightweight that they spin their wheels unless chains and wheel-weights are used to blade a sizable pile of soil or wet snow. But under favorable conditions a garden tractor can be quite helpful for leveling or dragging a soilbed. You will use them frequently to pull hauling carts, too. Snow blowers are available for tractors with a PTO; blowers are often more effective than a blade. Independently powered snow blowers justify their purchase in northerly locations where winter is long and repeated use justifies their capitalization.

LAWN ROLLING

Rolling the lawn was at one time a familiar spring ritual, the roller thought to be almost as necessary as a mower. We have since learned more about the undesirable soil compaction that rolling may cause. Very few lawns are rolled today. Where leveling is needed, it is better achieved by filling the low spots than by squeezing down high ground.

But where soilbeds are fluffy after cultivation, rolling may be useful for restoring capillarity. Occasionally rolling helps to firm partially heaved seedlings back into soft soil after spring thaw. Turfs needing very smooth surfaces, such as bowling greens or grass tennis courts, may require rolling even at the expense of some compaction. Normally watering is sufficient to settle soil as much as is required, with a new planting, rather than risking compaction through rolling. When rolling must be done, best that it be with a lightweight roller.

SPRAYING LAWNS

A good sprayer (Fig. 6-15) is almost a necessity around the house. Pesticide sprays that coat foliage are ordinarily more effective than would be granular materials; lower strengths of active ingredient suffice, and results are more certain. Particles roll off grass leaves easily and, unless they volatilize from the ground, are in large part wasted. Sprays, however, especially if "souped up" with a sticker-spreader (surfactant) cover foliage rather completely, and thus provide more intimate protection or opportunity for absorption.

As the lawn matures and weeds are eliminated season after season, spot treatments usually suffice to keep weeds under control (Fig. 6-16). Spot spraying is, of course, more economical than complete coverage, and it is environmentally more acceptable these days. A good pressure sprayer of about three-gallon capacity is great for spot treatment of dandelions and similar weeds, for edging drives, for chemical trimming around trees, and for dispersing whatever insecticides are needed. Larger knapsack and power units would be appropriate for larger properties, of course.

Many homeowners find it advantageous to have one sprayer for herbicides, another for insecticides and fungicides. Even slight residues of things like 2,4-D can injure sensitive trees or shrubs budding in spring. If one sprayer must serve all purposes, be sure that the spray tank is thoroughly rinsed out between uses. Ammonia water helps free the tank of phenoxy traces. Of course sprayers should be thoroughly cleaned to prevent corrosion and clogged nozzles. Trisodium phosphate helps with encrusted tanks, and vinegarized water may counteract hard-water deposits. Nozzles, strainers, and other metal parts may be soaked in kerosene to prevent corrosion. Movable parts should be oiled before storage.

Wheeled sprayers for the lawn are generally not as economical as the usual fertilizer spreaders. But one effective unit, the Meter Miser, is not costly. Made of molded plastic, it feeds out the spray solution by gravity from a rotating disc on the underside. Large drops coat the lawn with little or no drift such as often occurs under high pressure. As

Fig. 6-15 Sprayers familiar around the home.

Glossary of Terms for Sprayers and Dusters
(Approved 1961)

SPRAYER – COMPRESSED AIR

A Sprayer comprising a tank to contain the spray material; a manually operated air pump, or other source of air pressure, to compress air above liquid in tank; flexible discharge equipment through which spray material is forced by air pressure. Easily portable — carries over the shoulder, by hand, or mounted on a cart. Provides supply of spray material and energy for constant operation without need for continuous pumping.

SPRAYER – KNAPSACK
A Sprayer carried on the operator's back, knapsack style. Comprises a tank to contain unpressurized spray material; a manually operated pump which develops hydraulic pressure within the pump; flexible discharge equipment through which spray material is forced by hydraulic pressure. Generally provides larger supply of spray material and constant high pressure from pumping while spraying.

SPRAYER – FLAME
A Sprayer comprising a tank to contain flammable liquid; a manually operated air pump or other source of air pressure to compress air above liquid in tank; a generator-burner through which flammable liquid is forced by air pressure and burned. Carried over the shoulder or by hand. Provides supply of flammable material and energy for constant operation without need for continuous pumping.

SPRAYER – SLIDE, OR SLIDE PUMP
A manually operated hydraulic sprayer with telescoping plunger, operated by two hands. Draws spray material from attached or separate container and discharges it as a spray under pressure on either forward and back strokes of the plunger, or on forward stroke only. Provides higher pressures and greater spraying range.

PUMP – BUCKET OR BARREL

A manually operated hydraulic piston-type pump which may be held or mounted in a container holding the spray material. Draws spray material into the pump when plunger is operated and discharges it in a continuous spray through the discharge equipment. Provides flexibility in size and type of container and high pressures.

SPRAYER – WHEELBARROW
A manually operated hydraulic sprayer mounted on frame with wheelbarrow type handles and one or two wheels. Comprises a container holding spray material; a manually operated barrel pump mounted within which draws spray material into the pump when plunger is operated and discharges it as a continuous spray through the discharge equipment. Provides portability, large capacity and high pressures.

SPRAYER – HOSE END
An applicator attached to garden hose, operated by water pressure, which mixes liquid or solid spray materials in water stream and discharges the mixture.

SPRAYER – POWER, HYDRAULIC TYPE
A sprayer with hydraulic pump (piston, gear, roller, etc.) driven by gasoline engine, electric motor, PTO. Comprises a tank or other container for spray material; a power driven pump which draws spray material into the pump and discharges the spray material under pressure through the discharge system.

VALVE – SPRAY CONTROL A manually operated valve or cut-off located in the discharge line of a sprayer which permits one to start or stop the flow of spray material from a sprayer

DUSTER – CRANK A manually operated duster which comprises a hopper or container for the dust; an agitating device; a high velocity gear-driven fan driven by a hand-operated crank which develops a continuous current of air which carries the dust through the discharge equipment. Volume of dust discharged controlled by regulating device, and range of carry by speed of fan.

TUBE – SPRAY EXTENSION A hollow tube (lance, wand, extension rod) located in the discharge line of a sprayer beyond the spray control valve, at distal end of which is a spray nozzle.

DUSTER – KNAPSACK A manually operated duster designed to be carried on the operator's back, knapsack style. Comprises a hopper or container for the dust; an agitating device; a lever-actuated bellows which develops a current of air at each stroke which discharges the dust through the discharge equipment. Volume of dust discharged controlled by regulating device and range of carry by rapidity of actuating operating lever.

SPRAYER – CONTINUOUS A small, manually operated sprayer comprising a container for spray material; a pump which develops air under pressure to force the spray material through the liquid supply tube, and assist in atomizing the liquid at the nozzle as a continuous spray during the forward and backward strokes of the pump.

DUSTER – TRACTION A duster mounted on a frame with wheelbarrow type handles and one or two wheels. Comprises a hopper or container for dust; an agitating device; a high speed gear-driven fan, driven by traction power from the ground wheel, which develops an air current which picks up the dust and discharges it through the discharge equipment. The unit may be propelled by man, horse or tractor. Provides greater dust capacity and wider area of coverage.

SPRAYER – INTERMITTENT A small manually operated sprayer comprising a container for spray material; a pump which develops air under pressure, the air being passed over a siphon tube which draws spray material through the siphon tube from container and atomizes the liquid as it leaves the siphon tube. Spray is discharged only on forward stroke or pump.

DUSTER – KNAPSACK POWER An engine-powered duster designed to be carried on operator's back, knapsack style. Comprises a hopper or container for the dust; an agitating device; a high speed fan, driven by gasoline engine, which develops an air current which picks up the dust and discharges it continuously through the flexible discharge equipment. Provides complete portability and engine power instead of man power to operate.

DUSTER – PLUNGER A small manually operated duster comprising a container for the dust material; a plunger pump which develops a current of air at each forward stroke which picks up dust from the dust container and discharges it through the discharge equipment. Volume of dust discharged and range of carry controlled by size of pump and speed of stroking.

DUSTER – POWER A duster powered by a gasoline engine or PTO drive. Comprises a hopper or dust compartment; an agitating device; a high speed fan which may be engine or PTO driven and develops an air current which picks up the dust and discharges it continuously through the discharge equipment. Duster may be mounted on tractor, trailer, truck or other conveyance.

Fig. 6-16 Simple small pressure sprayer for spot treatment.

the mist from high-pressure spraying disperses widely in wind currents and can drift many feet to valuable ornamentals, be very careful when using herbicides such as 2,4-D upwind from susceptible species. Some pesticides volatilize; even their vapors are sufficient to cause damage downwind.

SHREDDERS

Powered garden shredders capable of grinding up sticks seldom play a very big part in lawn keeping. Shredded stems and leaves sometimes serve as a mulch for a new seeding. Of course shredded organic materials (preferably after composting) make valuable soil **141** amendments.

Managing the Lawn Community

Throughout the text measures designed to keep the lawn a vigorously growing, juvenile monoculture have been emphasized. This is not a stable ecological situation (i.e., not a climax community). No practice is more important for maintaining the lawn status quo than is mowing. A mowed lawn is a "dependent system" typical of urban areas and managed cropland ("independent systems" involve natural areas, sanctuaries, and wildernesses). Dependent systems are characterized by few species (but large populations) showing expansive growth. They're generally intensively used and require sizable labor and energy inputs. They tend to be productive, but they are poorly buffered (i.e., suffer change easily). They represent an unbalanced ecosystem needing constant attention.

If not mowed, the lawn would trend towards an "independent" ecology, with greater species diversity (i.e., weeds). Eventually it would reach a mature, rather steady state often dominated by trees. Productivity would be low, and thatch formation would be balanced by its decay. It would be even more of a sink for pollutants than is a highly managed lawn. Mowing is the chief means for imposing a dependent ecosystem upon what would otherwise turn into an independent one in which all sorts of plants would grow unrestrained. For esthetic reasons alone this can't be let happen, at least in populated communities.

Mowing may be something of a hallmark of today's suburban life style. But other labor-saving devices to ease homeowner burdens are ubiquitous, too. Some are helpful, others of dubious value. If you succumb to much temptation, you almost have to become a mechanic, serving rather than being served by your possessions. A list of grounds-care equipment preferred page by page in a single issue of one power equipment magazine follows. How insulated have we become from "sweat-of-the-brow" acquaintance with our immediate environment?

rubber tires	hauling carts	spare blades
clutch torque converters	earth drills	mufflers
compost shredders and chippers	power saw	sprayers, with parts
	powered log splitter	dead-man switch
lawn sweeper	drive belts	snow thrower
lawn vacuum	motorized cycles	recording device
rotary tiller	snowmobile	nylon rope
snow blower	hand rakes	trash gatherers
leaf-disposing rotary riding mowers	chain saw	crankshaft straighteners
	motorized plow	
reel mower	spiker-aerifier	lubrication products
power units	cultivator	windmill
self-propelled irrigation	roller	fuel additive
front end loader	tractor disc	blade balancer
mini-rake (for tractor towing)	leaf and litter blower	storage building
	replacement parts	magneto tester
earth-moving blade	trash disposer	edger-trimmer
high-wheel mowers	clamp-on lighting system	knapsack blower
grass catching devices		snow scoop
precision spreaders	luxury seating	[and so on]

Control of Pests Keeps the Lawn Shipshape

7

Control of pests is fraught these days with uncertainty and violent conflicts of opinion. At one extreme are those who advocate pesticide usage at the drop of a hat, to correct an immediate problem even though long-term consequences may not be clear. At the other extreme are those who find anything but natural control abhorrent and who resent the use of any pesticide because of possible environmental consequences.

Certain valid arguments can be advanced for either viewpoint. Pests have devastated huge areas and caused heavy crop loss, with tremendous financial consequences. Think of the inroads such pests as wheat rust and Hessian fly make on the wheat crop every year, and how some pests of trees have nearly wiped out certain species (e.g., chestnuts and American elms).

On the other hand, intensive pest control as practiced with crops such as cotton results in an increase rather than a diminution of problems over the years. Even with turf, dependence on pesticides can be self-defeating; their use sometimes results in a less self-reliant stand of grass. As was noted in Chapter One, introduction of pesticide molecules foreign to the ecosystem is frequently quite upsetting, particularly to a precariously balanced community of the dependent type (Chapter Six, boxed insert) characteristic of most lawns.

It is probably safest to follow procedures somewhere between the two extremes when practicing pest control. Pesticides certainly serve well for pestilential outbreaks and emergencies. But they should be carefully used, and only against target species for which there is no effective natural control. Remember, all chemicals are both poisonous and innocuous, depending upon dosage. Heavy concentrations of things like salt and aspirin are more dangerous than most pesticides at normal rates.

Even though we may be convinced in our own minds what is proper pest control, these days many practical difficulties and areas of confusion arise. Restrictions do make some highly useful pesticides unavailable, at least to a homeowner who has not passed certain test procedures to become a "licensed applicator." As this is being written, a final list of hazardous chemicals has not yet been confirmed by the Environmental Protection Agency. EPA enforcement is through the states, and some states already have pesticide laws more strict than the EPA regulations. California, for example, has a very comprehensive law. Almost certainly, a tightening up of what is available to the homeowner or even to a licensed applicator seems in the cards.

Thus some of the pest-control measures discussed in this chapter may be difficult to achieve for lack of pesticide availability. And fewer new pesticides are likely to be developed, simply because it has become so costly for a chemical company to go through all the developmental and testing procedures required for label clearance and permission to market the product. Many people feel this may be the most serious drawback resulting from stricter environmental controls; what will be at hand when presently useful pesticides "wear out," that is, when pest populations will have built up resistance to them? Experience has taught us that it is a continuing battle to stay one meager step ahead of the pests, not only those attacking turf but also those decimating food supplies and other vital agricultural products. The environmental benefits from restrictions must be weighed against the economic consequences, and eventually perhaps even the ability to provide adequate food and fiber, to say nothing of attractive surroundings!

Thus, with control of pests we are breaking new ground in an ecological sense, attempting to balance the benefits from control against possible degradation of the environment. Naturally, the latter assumes first importance: What good is the halting of a particular pest, if the overall environment is made uninhabitable? Much emphasis is therefore being placed upon the development of natural controls not likely to be upsetting to the ecosystem. Most appealing is the breeding of pest-resistant cultivars. As was noted in Chapter Two, great strides have been made in unearthing disease-resistant lawngrasses. The stage seems set, too, for developing others better able to fight weeds and insects. At the same time predators of some of our more serious pests are being introduced and dispersed, certainly a more convenient and economical way of putting a stop to the expansion of a harmful species than is constant spraying.

But there will always be need for emergency treatment where a pest outbreak threatens a limited ecosystem, such as your own front yard. The trend, however, is not to spray willy-nilly with a nontarget pesticide (like using an elephant gun to bring down a rabbit), but rather to pinpoint specific problems and to choose pesticides suited to them. Pesticides on the market today are generally biodegradable (i.e., they break down fairly quickly to harmless products after use and do not present a persistent hazard to the environment). Moreover, we are turning more of the pest-control tasks over to natural agents—birds, predator insects, and even competing microorganisms (a bacterium, *Bacillus thuringensis,* has already been licensed for use as an insecticide).

All of this makes sense, so much so that we shall not dwell in this chapter upon pest-control measures ordinarily beyond the capacity of a homeowner to carry out effectively. Particularly does this caution apply to preventive fungicidal spraying, complex even for the professional. It's almost impossible to identify diseases accurately, foretell their appearance in time to do something about them, compound the elixirs, and spray precisely enough with equipment ordinarily available around the home. We'd rather suggest preventing disease by planting disease-resistant cultivars. In fact, with restrictions on pesticide use increasing, it may be well for all of us to set our sights a bit lower and not expect to have a "spit-and-polish" lawn all of the time.

Many differing types of organisms can be pests on the lawn, even the neighborhood kids and pets (best handled through parental control or a stout fence). Of increasing concern are certain classes of organisms never before considered much of turf problem. Eelworms or nematodes, for example, are one such, particularly aggravating in the deep South but also thought by a Michigan pathologist to be the causal agent for spread of Fusarium disease. Arthropods other than insects may disturb lawns in certain places—crayfish burrowings, for example. Lots of lawns are bothered by mammal diggings (moles, mice, "gophers," and the like).

But the kinds of pests just mentioned are relatively unimportant compared to the three categories that are major lawn bothers—weeds, insects, and fungi (diseases). All are ubiquitous, though normally seasonal. The pesticides used to control these troublemakers are, of course, herbicides, insecticides, and fungicides respectively. Let's tackle these subject areas one by one, starting with weeds, perhaps the most persistent lawn affliction and the one for which the most responsive cures are available.

WEEDS AND WEED CONTROL

What is a weed? Actually, it is any plant that you don't want where it is growing. Weeds contrast badly with the attractive lawngrasses,

Fig. 7-1 Clumpy tall fescue, perhaps the "worst weed" of bluegrass lawns in the upper Midwest, but planted for turf in the border states.

generally being disruptively coarse. However, even the accepted lawngrasses can be "weeds." Bermudagrass is a pest when, unwanted, it invades bluegrass lawns; and it certainly is a weed in shrub beds and gardens. Bluegrass, although not quite so aggressive, can be considered a winter weed in southern lawns. Bentgrass is disliked when, not planted there, it makes patches in lawns of other species. Dichondra, in the morning-glory family, is widely planted for Los Angeles lawns; in the more humid eastern United States, where it suffers a lot of disease, it becomes a "weed." Clover can be a weed or a desirable component of a lawn, depending upon your outlook. Even species generally recognized as weeds, such as ground ivy (*Glechoma*), make attractive ground covers. Glechoma is frequently useful in the shade.

So, a lawn weed is simply some kind of plant that you don't want growing in your lawn. By and large lawn weeds contrast with and

146

disrupt the uniform carpetlike pattern of the grass. Blatantly discordant are such contrasting plants as dandelions, thistles, and dock. No one would hesitate to call these plants weeds. But grasses with a rough appearance can make unsightly patches in the lawn, too. "Haygrasses" are probably the worst lawn weeds, because getting rid of them is so difficult. We will see that it is easier to ease out species which are quite different from grass than it is to eliminate a weed grass without damaging the lawngrass.

Fig. 7-2 What a difference a herbicide can make! One treatment with a phenoxy weed killer did the job here!

Everyday experience tells us that nature abhors bare ground. Any bit of bare ground, given a little moisture, supports some vegetation. Even in the desert especially adapted plants sprout and complete their life cycle quickly after the occasional rains. If you don't have grass in your lawn, you will surely have weeds. Weed seeds abound everywhere. If they are not already abundant in your soil, they stand every chance of blowing or being tracked in from time to time.

Some weeds, such as crabgrass, have several "classes" of seeds, part sprouting one year, part the next, and still other parts later; perpetuation of these annuals is assured even if you do a good weeding job and prevent seeding for a year or two. Some seeds remain viable for many years; witness the sprouting of ancient seeds taken from Egyptian tombs thousands of years old. Most lawngrass seeds, however, lose their ability to sprout after two or three years in the ground. Annual ryegrass and Highland bentgrass are among the longest lived, viable in small measure even after as much as seven years' burial in Oregon soil.

Weeds are disliked not only because of their unsightliness in an old lawn but also because they are so competitive against new grass, too. A Tifway bermudagrass planting in Georgia covered only thirty-six percent of the lawn in one growing season where it was left unweeded, but the same planting produced ninety-six percent cover when well weeded (a pre-emergence chemical was first used, followed by arsonate–2,4-D sprayings). Investing as much as we do in lawns, certainly anything of aid to the grass has appeal.

Although various techniques can be called upon for assisting the grass, today we do have one advantage our forefathers lacked, excellent herbicides. It is no trick at all to get rid of dandelions and most other broadleaf weeds, these days (Fig. 7-3). In fact man and his

Fig. 7-3 Dandelion "on the way out" after treatment with 2,4-D spray.

herbicides have been a potent new ecological force, not only for lawns but also for agriculture. Annual weeds that were formerly very abundant and pernicious have proved rather easily and inexpensively controllable with herbicides. Unfortunately, their vacated role then seems to become filled by perennial weeds that spread vegetatively, a more difficult breed to handle. We seem, with our herbicides, to have tipped the balance in favor of the spreading perennials, the type of weed giving the most trouble these days. As was earlier noted, perennial grasses, sometimes introduced as crop in lawnseed (Chapter Four), have become the most difficult in lawns.

Many lawn weeds are hangovers from earlier times when the soils now used for lawns were agricultural fields. As with our better lawngrasses, these are highly successful species. Most of the "better" weeds in American lawns are introductions from foreign lands or at least globally spread species that are highly aggressive and just as adaptable as are the lawngrasses. They relish the disturbed habitat that goes with civilization. Weeds that flourish in lawns tend to be good seed producers (Table 7-1), have a low growth habit that helps escape mowing, and often show allelopathic tendencies (i.e., they secrete substances inhibitory to other vegetation).

Table 7-1 Seeds counted on a single plant of the weeds listed.

Weed	Seeds
Lambsquarters	72,500
Shepherd's purse	38,500
Plantain	36,000
Foxtail	34,000
Dock	29,500
Chickweed	15,000
Dandelion	12,000
Knotweed	6,400

WEED GROUPINGS

Weeds may be classified according to their growth cycle and grouped according to natural relationships. Weeds which complete their life cycle in a single year, often in just a short season, are *annuals*. Crabgrass, common chickweed, and crucifers like shepherd's purse are of this type. A few weeds troublesome in lawns are biennials, generally taking two years to complete their life cycle. Wild carrot and carder's teasel grow robustly the first year, produce seed-bearing stalks the next, then die. Of course *perennials* are plants that persist year after year; they include many of the weed grasses like quackgrass and nimblewill. One means of weed control depends upon the distinction between annual and perennial species, annuals being much easier to develop controls for because of their vulnerability in the seed and seedling stage.

The higher plants are broadly classified into *Monocotyledon* and *Dicotyledon* groups, the basis for selective weed control with phenoxy herbicides. The former include grasslike plants (also lilies, palms, and so on), with parallel veins, floral parts in threes, and of course a single seed cotyledon. Dicotyledons include broadleaf plants, their leaves generally having netlike veination, floral parts in fours and fives, and two seed cotyledons. As a group monocotyledonous plants withstand reasonable rates of 2,4-D and related chemicals quite well, while most dicotyledonous species are killed by the same concentrations.

GETTING AFTER THE WEEDS

Weed control is more efficient at certain stages of a weed's life cycle than at others, and at certain seasons of the year than at others. Of course various weeds differ greatly in their susceptibility to certain herbicides, and herbicides vary in effectiveness with the momentary physiological condition of the plant. Certainly weather conditions also have an influence.

On the whole weeds are more susceptible to herbicides when they are growing actively. That's why the pests succumb so well in the warm, humid weather of spring (warm-season weeds) and in early autumn

Fig. 7-4 An autumn-used fertilizer-herbicide combination is effective. Darker green rectangle of bluegrass lawn is where weed-and-feed fertilizer was applied October 12. Photo taken November 18.

(winter weeds). Weeds are more susceptible, too, when young and "thin-skinned" than when mature and physiologically played out. They pick up and translocate herbicide better when humidity is high. Plants having a less cutinized epidermis absorb herbicide better than those with a heavier waxy coating. Also, leaves covered with a fuzz of hairs are more likely to shed herbicide than are smooth ones.

As a rule plants growing where it is hot and dry develop a thicker waxy coating than do plants of humid environments. They also develop water-conserving features that often afford some protection against herbicide absorption. Weed control is more of a problem in the South than in the North, partly because warmer climates encourage intensified biological activity nearly year-around (new weeds start about as quickly as old ones die out) and because the floras become more diversified approaching the tropics (southern lawns generally contain more kinds of weeds than do northern ones, and seldom do all species respond to the same herbicide).

In a way we have been talking about weed control all through this book; —weeds are repressed by making the grass grow more vigorously. As we have seen, fertilizing at a favorable season, mowing, and watering properly all give the lawngrass some competitive advantage against the weeds. Keeping your lawn dense and vigorous is the best possible way to inhibit weeds; weeds stand little chance of invading ground that is thoroughly occupied by grass. So, weed control really begins with sensible lawn keeping. In most cases not a whole lot more is needed!

Mowing, as a facet of lawn keeping, deserves special attention for its influence in keeping weeds under control. We have seen how height of mowing exerts a direct bearing upon grass vigor and therefore of course, upon the frequency of weeds. But entirely aside from such niceties as mowing height, mowing puts the kibosh on certain kinds of weeds directly. Weeds which tend to grow tall won't produce a full complement of seeds under constant mowing. The main reason for not feeling overly upset by the huge assortment of weeds that usually shows up in a new seeding is because mowing will eventually prove repressive to most. The majority of agricultural weeds are not well adapted to mowing at lawn heights and gradually give way to the lawngrass.

Hand pulling of weeds is not to be overlooked for smaller properties and well-tended lawns. If the first few weeds gaining a toehold are pulled or dug, their spread can be prevented. It is sometimes less bother to yank up or cut out a few weeds than it is to mix up a sprayer full of herbicide. Sometimes deep raking will pull up trailing weeds such as Veronica, difficult to control with 2,4-D. And sometimes hand pulling is the only effective technique short of drastic non-selective kill as a means for getting rid of coarse grass clumps or pestiferous colonies of nimblewill and bentgrass (for which there is no good selective herbicide).

But on the whole mechanical measures for ridding the lawn of weeds have been made obsolete by the development of herbicides. Herbicides alone are not the answer, of course, but it is nice to know that a smidgen of 2,4-D can inexpensively rid the lawn of dandelions and plantains and would otherwise take hours of tedious hand digging. Combining occasional herbicidal treatments with choice cultivars that grow densely year-around is really all that is needed to keep a lawn pretty well free from weeds. Cooperative interplay between herbicide and cultivar has not yet received as much attention as it may merit, for it does seem reasonable that new cultivars can be bred which would be more tolerant of the "hotter" herbicides. In short, the breeding of new cultivars needs to consider tolerance to herbicides along with many other features for which new grasses traditionally have been screened. Incidentally, most herbicides are today combined with surfactants (surface-active or wetting agents), compounds which break down surface tension and enable herbicides to better coat the weed and penetrate its tissues.

THE WEED KILLERS

Soil sterilants are not much used by homeowners, and likely to be less used under the environmental restrictions shaping up. These are chemicals toxic to growing vegetation, most weed seeds in the soil, and various fungi and insects. They are used in soilbed preparation to give the newly seeded grass maximum opportunity. Degrees of soil sterilization have been achieved through the years, going back to calcium cyanamid. Cyanamid breaks down into usable nitrogen and calcium after a few weeks. Then the ground can be replanted. Large amounts of cyanamid are needed, however, and precise mixing of the material into the soilbed is required. Results are not always consistent.

More recently chemicals such as metham (Vapam), vorlex, and methyl bromide have been used for soil sterilization; these were discussed in Chapter Four. Many other materials can kill back surface vegetation—not exactly soil sterilization, but a method suited for eliminating competing vegetation. As we have seen, this technique is often used for renovation of an old turf without the bother of soil cultivation. The better chemicals for this, such as paraquat, glyphosate, and cacodylic acid (which are immediately inactivated by the soil, permitting seeding only a few hours wait) are difficult to procure and may be unavailable because of restrictions. Amitrol (which scorches almost all types of vegetation) and dalapon (more of a grass killer than for broadleaf plants) can be used to set back old lawns before reseeding; but these chemicals require weeks of dissipation (longer in cold-dry than warm-humid weather) before they have disappeared sufficiently to allow new grass to start safely.

Herbicides are *systemic* if they are absorbed by the weed and trans-located throughout the plant, presumably in the sapstream. Systemic herbicides are especially valuable because they are carried to under-ground parts of the weed difficult to reach otherwise, killing rhizomes and side shoots, for example, as well as the parts sprayed. In contrast, *contact* herbicides kill only the tissues they are sprayed upon and are little translocated. They depend upon direct toxicity, much like the "burn" of salt or gasoline. Some herbicides are both, of course, —systemic at low rates, immediately toxic to tissues at high rates. The most useful lawn herbicides tend to be systemic.

The feature of herbicides that makes them serviceable in an existing lawn is *selectivity*. A selective herbicide kills certain plants (the weeds) while not bothering the grass (at least when used at recommended rates). The 2,4-D group (phenoxies) is highly selective. Lawngrass is little if at all injured by things like 2,4-D, MCPP, and silvex, or even chemically different dicamba, though these herbicides have marked influence upon most broadleaf weeds (Dicotyledons). In the same way arsonates are seldom harmful to lawngrass, though they may cause it to yellow a bit in hot weather, or when overapplied; but they "do in" many annual grasses such as crabgrass, even nutsedge and certain broadleaf weeds.

Pre-emergence herbicides are widely used, too, especially as crab-grass preventers (Fig. 7-5). A number of chemicals have been proved

Fig. 7-5 Annual grass weed control. To the right a pre-emergence "preventer" was used (little *Poa annua*), to the left no preventer (much *Poa annua*). Bentgrass turf.

quite useful when spread to blanket the ground ahead of crabgrass seed sprouting (when soil temperature rises to about 60°F); they don't bother the growing grass, but knock out the newly germinated seedlings. One, siduron, is even selective enough that it kills crabgrass but will not bother bluegrass, fescue, ryegrass, and bentgrass. Others, such as bensulide, benefin, DCPA, and oxadiazon, are toxic to almost all sprouting grasses and even to many of the broadleaf weeds.

Fig. 7-6 Crabgrass, formerly "lawn enemy number one," now controllable with several preventers or mop-up herbicides.

Crabgrass prevention with pre-emergence chemicals has been well accepted, but the technique has negative as well as positive influences. Almost invariably some "depression" of the permanent grass occurs, often manifest in shallower rooting. Frequently the lawngrass will turn a bit coarser. In some cases the lawngrass may be slightly weakened, —just enough to make a disease attack more serious. Some of the older pre-emergence chemicals (viz., bandane) thinned bluegrass turf quite noticeably. The differential toxicity of pre-emergence chemicals is astounding: one ppm (part per million) of bensulide is sufficient to control barnyardgrass, while even one thousand times this strength is insufficient to stop wild carrot. Michigan researchers, after eight years of observation, concluded that some detrimental effects result from the use of almost all pre-emergence chemicals and that these are especially manifest in hot weather.

Herbicides may be applied as a spray or absorbed on granular materials which are then applied with a spreader. In previous discussions we have seen that, by and large, sprays are more efficient and more economical (requiring less active ingredient). Herbicides are sometimes impregnated on fertilizer to make the "weed and feed" products. Phenoxy weed killer on finely granular fertilizer (so that it adheres to the weed leaf) eliminates weeds while stimulating grass to fill the resulting voids. Not that fertilizer and herbicide might not be applied just as effectively separately, but there is a definite saving of labor with the combined materials.

Persistence of herbicides is a matter of environmental concern, as is their potentiality for leaching through the soil (perhaps affecting the deep-rooted ornamentals, even though used for surface weed control as may be the case with dicamba or picloram). Some herbicides remain toxic in the ground for many years, such as the chlorates used to keep down all vegetation under fences and guardrails. Even some of the selective materials, such as the triazines (atrazine, simazine) used for weed control in st. augustine turf, can be toxic to susceptible grass for a year or two. Most of the herbicides sold for weed control in lawns break down fairly readily in the soil and are totally gone in a matter of weeks, if not days. One test of silvex applied to a pond showed ninety percent disappearance within twenty-four hours, and no traces whatsoever in the sediment after a month.

Of course pre-emergence chemicals need to be of an intermediate nature; they must last long enough to cover the entire crabgrass sprouting season (usually two or three months), yet be gradually biodegradable so as not to be a problem later. Many seem to persist into a second season, so that booster applications need not be so heavy as the initial one. Longevity will vary with the individual products and with lawn conditions; label advice should be carefully followed whenever a herbicide is used. Bensulide may persist for several months, and the effective life of DCPA may not be a whole lot shorter; siduron has briefer influence, and of course none at all on most species other than crabgrass. Breakdown and dissipation of all pre-emergent chemicals is slower in the cool of early spring than in the warmth of late spring, when a bolstering treatment may be needed to control late-sprouting crabgrass.

WEEDING LAWNS

Of course differing lawns have different weeds, and certain herbicides will be appropriate only to certain lawngrasses. We have seen, for example, that the triazines can be used on st. augustine lawns, but not others. Both st. augustine and bentgrass are sensitive to certain of the phenoxy herbicides. Bermudagrass is not tolerant of siduron; nor are bahia, centipede, and st. augustine tolerant of the arsonates. Precautions about what herbicides are suitable for what weeds, on what lawns, are part of the product directions. Again the caution: *Follow label directions* carefully.

The phenoxy chemicals (the 2,4-D group) are actually plant hormones, a practical breakthrough from the "pure" study of plant growth regulators. They are weed control marvels, selectively eliminating some of the worst lawn pests with little chance of injury to grass (st. augustine being the exception). Only a pound or two per acre of active ingredient is required for effective weed control with 2,4-D. They are most efficient in spring, for reasons already advanced, but safest in autumn (when there is no risk to budding ornamentals). For most lawns the 2,4-D group is the backbone for lawn weeding. Its usefulness is extended by combining lesser amounts of silvex, MCPP, and dicamba with the more economical 2,4-D (amine forms are less volatile, so less hazardous; esters are more effective but also more volatile). One patented formulation called Trimec utilizes 2,4-D, MCPP, and dicamba in a precisely regulated ratio. The combination is synergistic, i.e., each component assists the others so that the trio is more broadly effective at lighter rates than would be the individual ingredients applied separately—a sort of $2 + 2 = 5$ situation. Other interactions show ammonium nitrate enhancing 2,4-D effectiveness, pinolene (from pine resin) doubling it, but copper and iron salts or chelates partially counteracting its effects.

The arsonates (organic arsenicals, the several salts designated as AMA, CMA, DSMA, MAMA) complement the phenoxies nicely. They

Fig. 7-7   Spot-killing tall fescue clump.

are mainly used to stop annual grasses, although they help with such broadleaf weeds as chickweed and have proven useful (with repeated application) in mopping up such "tough customers" as nutsedge. If crabgrass has escaped the pre-emergence treatment, two or three arsonate sprays should selectively eliminate it after it is up and growing. Certain cultivars, such as Touchdown and Nugget bluegrasses, have somewhat limited tolerance of the arsonates.

Of course nonselective weed killers for trimming and renovation and pre-emergence chemicals for prevention of annual grasses have a place in ordering up the lawn ecosystem to our tastes. Nonselective chemicals wipe out coarse perennial grasses for which there is no selective control. After treatment the vacated ground must be replanted.

THE LAWN WEEDS

The chief lawn weeds, nationwide, are cited in Table 7-2. Many of these are also illustrated. A "blacklisting" of the *Ten Most Troublesome Weeds in Turfgrass* was compiled in a survey undertaken by the Lawn and Turfgrass Division of the American Seed Trade Association (reflecting golf course perhaps more than home lawn interests). From worst to "less bad" the culprits were: annual bluegrass, quackgrass, tall fescue, nutsedge, nimblewill, bentgrass, crabgrass, bermudagrass, veronica, and orchardgrass. Many of these same species appear in a summary for *Horticulture* magazine ("A Baker's Dozen of the Worst Lawn Weeds"), a condensation from which appears as Table 7-3. It serves as something of a summary about lawn weeding.

Table 7-2 Commonplace lawn weeds (A, B, or P = annual, biennial, or perennial).

Broadleaf Weeds Predominantly of Northern Lawns

black medic (*Medicago lupulina*), A, B, P—yellow flowers, cloverlike leaves
carpetweed (*Mollugo verticillata*), A—whorls of leaves, prostrate
chickweed, common (*Stellaria media*), A—smooth leaves, white flowers
chickweed, mouse-ear (*Cerastium vulgatum*), A, P—hairy leaves, white flowers
dandelion (*Taraxacum officinale*), P—rosette with taproot
dock (*Rumex crispus*), P—broad leaves, taproot
ground-ivy (*Glechoma hederacea*), P—trailing, minty fragrance, blue flowers
hawkweeds (*Hieracium spp.*), P—rosettes of hairy leaves, runners
heal-all (*Prunella vulgaris*), P—purple flowers, square stem
henbit (*Lamium amplexicaule*), A—trailing square stems, purple flowers
knawel (*Scleranthus annuus*), A—harsh, spiny, dry situations
knotweed (*Polygonum aviculare*), A, P—silvery sheath where leaf joins
kochia (*Kochia scoparia*), A—bushy, narrow leaves, plains
lambsquarters (*Chenopodium album*), A—silvery mealiness
mallow or cheeses (*Malva rotundifolia*), B, P—umbrellalike leaves

peppergrass (*Lepidium virginicum*), A—rosette, round pods, new lawns
pigweed (*Amaranthus spp.*), A—new lawns, harsh
plantain, broad-leaved (*Plantago major*), P—rosette with taproot
plantain, buckhorn (*Plantago lanceolata*), P—narrower leaves than *P. major*
purslane (*Portulaca oleracea*), A—smooth, fleshy, watery
Russian thistle (*Salsola kali*), A—spiny leaves, dry plains
sheep sorrel (*Rumex acetosella*), P—rhizomes, acid soils
shepherd's purse (*Capsella bursapastoris*), A—rosette, heartshaped pods
speedwell (*Veronica persica*), A, P—trailing, small blue flowers
spurge, milky (*Euphorbia maculata*, etc.), A—milky juice, prostrate
thistles (*Cirsium spp.*), B, P—spiny leaves in rosette
winter cress, rocket (*Barbarea vulgaris*), B, P—yellow-flowered mustard
wood sorrel (*Oxalis stricta*), A, P—yellow flowers, shamrock leaf
yarrow, milfoil (*Achillea millefolium*), P—feathery, fragrant foliage

Fig. 7-8 Black medic—*Medicago lupulina.*

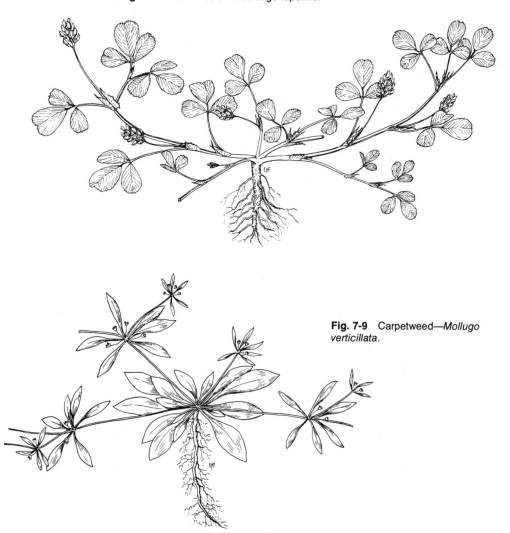

Fig. 7-9 Carpetweed—*Mollugo verticillata.*

Fig. 7-10 Common chickweed—*Stellaria media*.

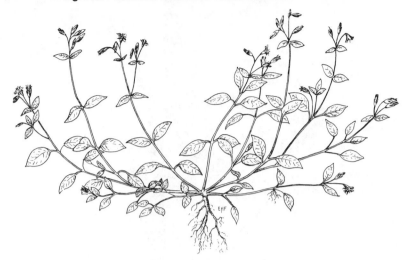

Fig. 7-11 Mouse-eared chickweed—
Cerastium vulgatum.

Fig. 7-12 Dandelion—*Taraxacum
officinale*.

159

Fig. 7-13 Dock—*Rumex crispus*.

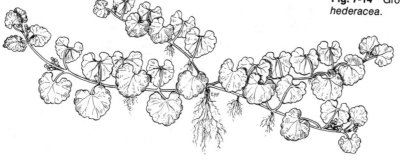

Fig. 7-14 Ground-ivy—*Glechoma hederacea*.

Fig. 7-15 Heal-all—*Prunella vulgaris*.

Fig. 7-16 Henbit—*Lamium amplexicaule.*

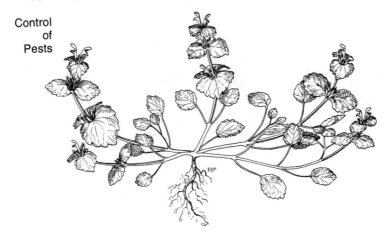

Fig. 7-17 Knawel—*Scleranthus annuus.*

Fig. 7-18 Knotweed—*Polygonum aviculare.*

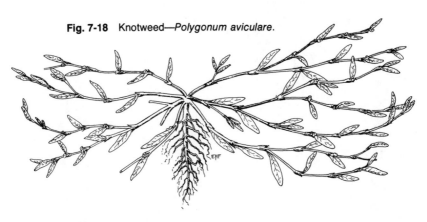

Fig. 7-19 Round-leaved mallow—*Malva rotundifolia*.

Fig. 7-20 Broad-leaved plantain—
Plantago major.

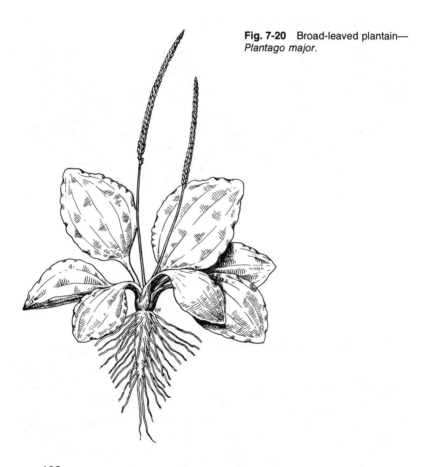

Fig. 7-21 Buckhorn plantain—*Plantago lanceolata.*

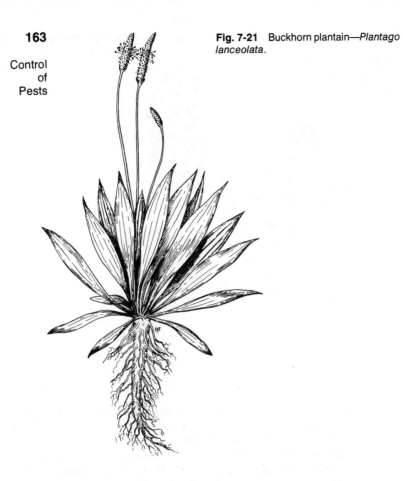

Fig. 7-22 Purslane—*Portulaca oleracea.*

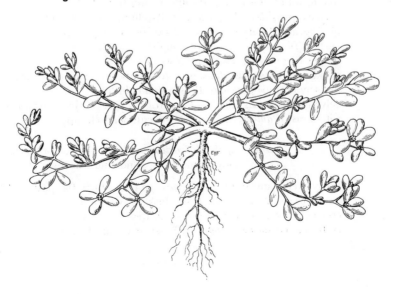

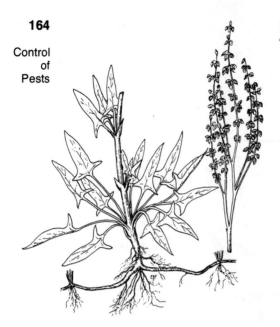

Fig. 7-23 Sheep sorrel—*Rumex acetosella.*

Grasslike Weeds Predominantly of Northern Lawns

barnyardgrass (*Echinochloa crus-galli*), A—coarse clumps, spiny seeds
crabgrass (*Digitaria spp.*), A—root at joints, "birdfoot" seedheads
foxtail (*Setaria spp.*), A—bunchgrasses, "bushy" seedheads
goosegrass (*Eleusine indica*), A—flat-stemmed, doesn't root at joints
nimblewill (*Muhlenbergia schreberi*), P—stems with knobby joints
nutsedge (*Cyperus esculentus*), P—deep tubers, three-ranked leaves
onion, wild (*Allium spp.*), P—ill-smelling tufts
orchardgrass (*Dactylis glomerata*), P—clumpy, leaves folded
quackgrass (*Agropyron repens*), P—difficult deep rhizomes
rushes (*Juncus spp.*), P—wiry, tough
sedges (*Cyperaceae*), P—three rows of leaves
stinkgrass (*Eragrostis cilianensis*), A—temporary, silvery seedheads
timothy (*Phleum pratense*), P—swollen culm base
velvetgrass (*Holcus lanatus*), P—soft gray foliage, dense seedheads
witchgrass (*Panicum* species), A—decumbent, clumpy

Broadleaf Weeds Predominantly of Southeastern Lawns
(additional to most northern listings)

beggarweed, sticktight (*Desmodium spp.*), P—sticky flat pods
buttonweed (*Diodea teres*), A—"whiskers" where leaves join
cresses, various (*Cruciferae*), A—rosettes
cudweed (*Gnaphalium spp.*), A, P—silvery-haired leaves

dichondra (*Dichondra repens*), P—heartshaped leaf
fogfruit (*Phyla spp.*), P—wedgeshaped leaves; button flower heads
hedge-nettle (*Stachys floridana*), P—underground stems
lespedeza (*Lespedeza spp.*), A—cloverlike leaves
pennywort (*Hydrocotyle rotundifolia*), P—umbrellalike leaves, moist habitat
richardia (*Richardia spp.*), P—similar to buttonweed
sida (*Sida spinosa*), A—mostly deep South
Spanish needles (*Bidens spp.*), A—white, daisylike flowers
vetch, hairy (*Vicia villosa*), A, B—trailing, purple flowers

Fig. 7-24 Speedwell—*Veronica persica.*

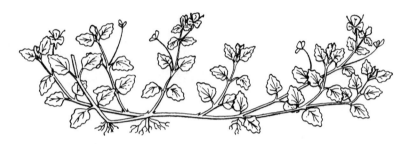

Fig. 7-25 Milky spurge—*Euphorbia maculata.*

Fig. 7-26 Canada thistle—*Cirsium arvense*.

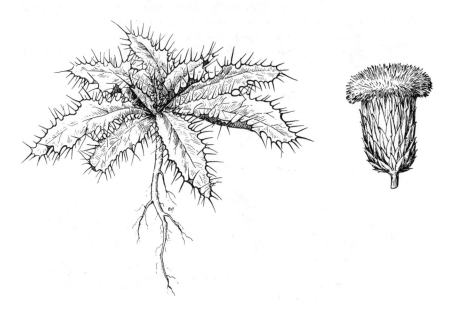

Fig. 7-27 Yarrow—*Achillea millefolium*.

166

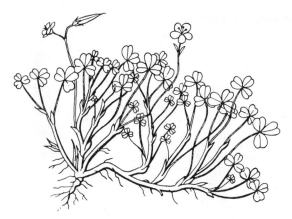

Fig. 7-28 Yellow wood sorrel—*Oxalis stricta.*

Fig. 7-29 Barnyard grass—*Echinochloa crusgalli.*

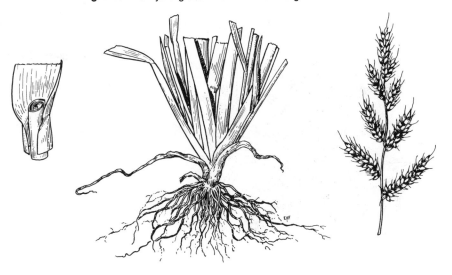

Fig. 7-30 Crabgrass—*Digitaria.*

Fig. 7-31 Green foxtail—*Setaria viridis*.

Fig. 7-32 Goosegrass—*Eleusine indica*.

Fig. 7-33 Nimblewill—*Muhlenbergia schreberi*.

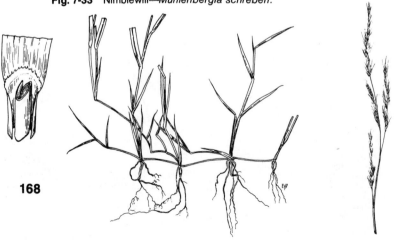

168

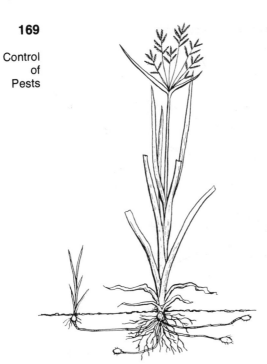

Fig. 7-34 Nutgrass—*Cyperus esculentus*.

Fig. 7-35 Orchardgrass—*Dactylis glomerata*.

Fig. 7-36 Quackgrass—*Agropyron repens.*

Fig. 7-37 Rush—*Juncus tenuis.*

170

Fig. 7-38 Stinkgrass—*Eragrostis cilianensis.*

Fig. 7-39 Velvetgrass—*Holcus lanatus.*

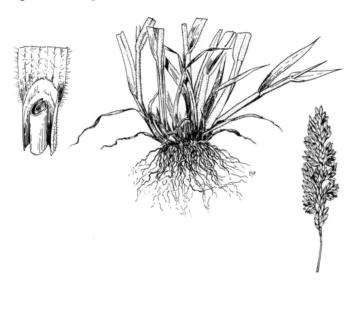

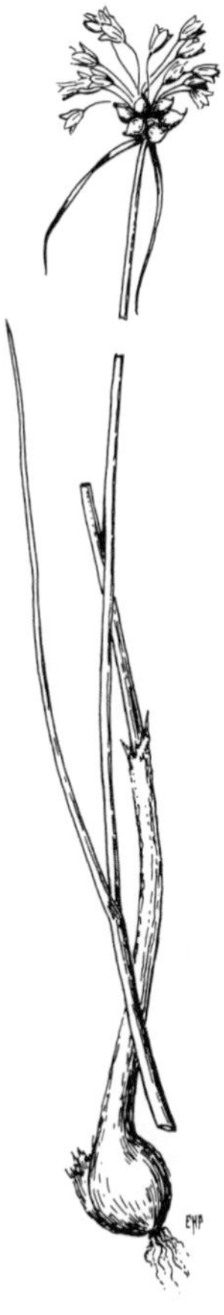

171

Fig. 7-40 Wild onion—*Allium vineale.*

barley, little (*Hordeum pusillum*, etc.), A—bushy seedheads, brown in summer
kikuyugrass (*Pennisetum clandestinum*), P—hard to eradicate, trailing
knotgrass (*Paspalum distichum*), P—creeping, hairy joints, moist soils
ripgut grass (*Bromus rigidus*), A—sharp, pointed seeds
soft cheese (*Bromus mollis*), A—velvety hairs

Broadleaf Weeds Predominantly of Southwestern Lawns
(additional to most northern listings)

baby tears (*Helxine soleirolii*), P—matted, mosslike
bur clover (*Medicago hispida*), A—yellow flowers, spiny fruit
buttercup (*Ranunculus muricatus*), A—damp areas, yellow flowers
cat's-ear (*Hypochoeris spp.*), P—stiff, wiry stems
cranesbill (*Geranium dissectum*), A—divided leaves, purplish flowers
drymaria (*Drymaria cordata*), P—Hawaii, like large chickweed
English daisy (*Bellis perennis*), P—rosette of hairy leaves
field madder (*Sherardia arvensis*), A—whorled leaves, square stem
filaree (*Erodium cicutarium*), A, B—prostrate, dissected leaves
petty spurge (*Euphorbia peplus*), A—leaves rounded, smooth
pineapple-weed (*Matricaria suaveolens*), A—leaves fragrant if crushed
puncture-vine (*Tribulus terrestris*), A—injurious spiny fruits
sandwort (*Arenaria serpyllifolia*), A—oval leaves, reversed hairs
scarlet pimperenel (*Anagallis arvensis*), A—low, matting, flowers red
spurry (*Spergula arvensis*), A—dense leaves, glandular hairs
verbena (*Verbena bracteosa*), A—much branched, flowers blue

Fig. 7-41 Buttonweed—*Diodea teres*.

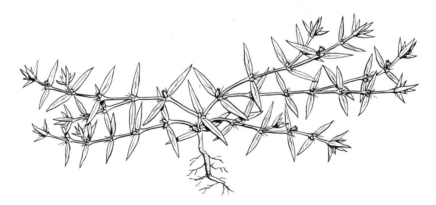

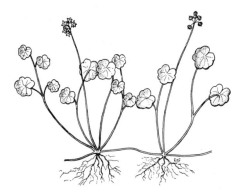

Fig. 7-42 Cress—*Lepidium campestre.*

Fig. 7-43 Pennywort—*Hydroctyle sibthorpioides.*

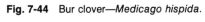

Fig. 7-44 Bur clover—*Medicago hispida.*

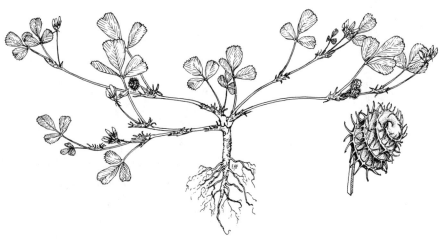

annual bluegrass (*Poa annua*), A—low seedheads
bullgrass (*Paspalum spp.*), A, P—broad, coarse blades
dallisgrass (*Paspalum dilatatum*), P—coarse, clumpy
sandbur (*Cenchrus spp.*), A—bunchgrass, spiny seeds
smutgrass (*Sporobolus poiretii*), P—mucilaginous seedhead gets black fungus

Fig. 7-45   Filaree—*Erodium cicutarium.*

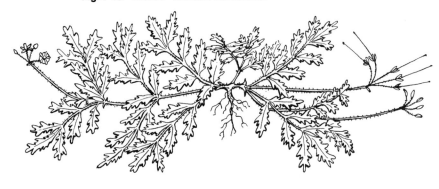

Fig. 7-46   Pineapple-weed—*Matricaria matricarioides.*

Fig. 7-47   Dallisgrass—*Paspalum dilatatum.*

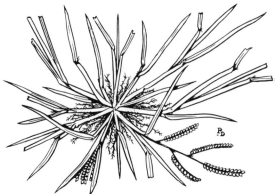

Table 7-3 "A Baker's Dozen of the Worst Lawn Weeds," as adapted from *Horticulture*.

Weed	Botanical Name (genus)	Problem	Can It Be Eliminated Selectively (no harm to grass)	Herbicide to Use	Usual Rate & Method (pounds active ingredient per acre are given; follow product directions)	Cautions and Hazards	Other Comment
Monocots: i.e., grass-like Crabgrass (and other annual weed grasses including barnyardgrass, foxtail, goosegrass, etc.)	Digitaria	discordant, spreading mats of different appearance; ugly seedheads later	yes	pre-emergence granulars (benefin bensulide, DCPA, siduron, terbutol, etc.)	2-12: spread granules uniformly	Sometimes reduce depth of grass rooting; chiefly for northern lawns (bluegrass, fescue, perennial ryegrass, fescue, bentgrass), and not always safe with southern lawngrasses; some may discolor bent or bermudagrass temporarily; siduron is toxic to bermudagrass	Apply early in the season before seeds sprout; blanket problem areas fully and uniformly; will prove mildly influential in checking the sprouting of all kinds of seed (but siduron is least effectual for species other than crabgrass, and is safe for use with lawn seedings).
				post-emergence sprays (arsonates:—DSMA, MAMA, CMA)	2-4: spray to coat foliage, best early in summer; repeat once or twice a week or 10 days	Perhaps some temporary discoloration of turf, especially in hot weather	Works best on young grass before seedheads form.
Quackgrass	Agropyron	crowds desirable grass; rather coarse	no	none selective; use general vegetation killer, then reseed; (methyl arsinic acid, etc.: dalapon or amitrol)	1-40: spray to coat	Dalapon and amitrol require waiting period of a few weeks before reseeding, to allow dissipation of chemical.	Paraquat or glyphosate may be available commercially in some states, but are not cleared for home use; as with arsinic acid little or no waiting is required before reseeding. Hand digging is seldom feasible because of vigorous spreading rhizomes underground, sections of which grow a new plant.
Tall fescue (and other perennial pasture species)	Festuca	rough, coarse clumps	no	as for quackgrass	as for quackgrass	as for quackgrass	Hand digging of clumps may prove feasible here, since this is a bunchgrass that does not spread vegetatively. Avoid in seed mixtures.
Nutsedge, yellow and purple	Cyperus	off-color colonies growing faster than grass	yes, with persistence	arsonates (DSMA, MAMA, CMA); 2,4-D, preferably in Trimec-type combinations; basagran when cleared for home use	1-5: spray liberally into crown of plants; repeat treatment during growing season	as for crabgrass, post-emergence	Because of corms ("bulbs") deep in the soil, requires persistence; chiefly a problem on wet ground, and often disappears if soil drys.
Wild onion and garlic	Allium	gangling tufts above the grass with undesirable odor	yes, with persistence	synergistic combinations of 2,4-D-dicamba	1-2: spray repeatedly spring and autumn	as noted below for *Dicots*	Seldom hardy in the far North, chiefly a mid-latitude pest.

Weed	Botanical Name (genus)	Problem	Can It Be Eliminated Selectively (no harm to grass)	Herbicide to Use	Usual Rate & Method (pounds active ingredient per acre are given: follow product directions)	Cautions and Hazards	Other Comment
Dicots: i.e., broadleaf families		most non-grass weeds	yes	2,4-D or its combinations as with silvex or Trimec (= 2,4-D + MCPP + dicamba); bromoxynil for newly sprouted lawns	1-2 generally, but follow product directions; best sprayed to coat foliage	Avoid drift onto susceptible garden plants; rinse sprayer thoroughly (as with ammonia water) before using for other purposes; don't use dicamba within dripline or over root-zone of ornamentals.	These hormonal sprays are one of the great breakthroughs in weed control, permitting excellent selectivity for taking most broadleaf (Dicot) weeds out of grass (Monocots) when used properly.
Chickweed (common and mouse-ear)	Stellaria, Cerastium	spreading patches that are unattractive	yes	Trimec-type or silvex	autumn, spring	"	Pre-emergence control in late summer (as for annual grasses) may work, and even arsonate post-emergence sprays.
Dandelion	Taraxacum	rosettes disrupting lawn texture; unattractive seedheads	yes	all are very effective	autumn—spring	"	Elimination before seed dispersal makes future control easier.
Dock (and related sheep's sorrel)	Rumex	very coarse rosettes or patches	yes	2,4-D is OK for dock but sheep's sorrel needs dicamba	when weeds show	"	Dock is very coarse but discrete; sheep's sorrel less obtrusive but spreads somewhat by runners
Ground-ivy	Glechoma	vines with contrasting foliage trailing through grass	yes	silvex or Trimec-type combinations	when weeds show	"	repeat treatments may be necessary.
Knotweed	Polygonum	tough, trailing plants that crowd grass	yes	dicamba or Trimec-type combinations	spring—summer	"	Characteristic of hard, compacted soil; aerification may help the grass.
Plantains (various species)	Plantago	coarse rosettes and unattractive seed stalks	yes	especially 2,4-D: dicamba not effective	autumn—spring—summer	"	Fall easily before 2,4-D.
Speedwell (Veronica spp.)	Veronica	hard-to-eliminate patches below mowing height	yes, with persistence	hard to control, suggest Trimec-type combinations or special formulations of endothal	spring—autumn	"	A "toughie," and no doubt repeat sprayings will be necessary.
Spurge, milky	Euphorbia	semi-prostrate colonies competing with grass	yes	silvex or Trimec-type combinations best	warm weather	"	Characteristic of hot locations with compact soil; aerification and soil improvement helps grass compete better; pre-emergence crabgrass treatments may help.

Control
of
Pests

Nothing seems to become out-of-date more quickly than recommendations for weed control. New chemicals are constantly developed that make older control methods obsolete. On the other hand, promising uses have a way of "fading," as wider experience shows some practices to be "not all that good." But I do want to mention a few special cases:

Nutsedge has always been a tough problem in damp locations. As was noted, the arsonates give fair control with repeated use, and cyperquat has proven even better. But most promising seems to be a selective chemical not yet labeled for home use as this is written, bentazon (Basagran). Reports suggest that this finally may be "the answer" for selective nutsedge control.

Pronamide (Kerb) has a good reputation for controlling annual grasses, particularly *Poa annua,* in bermudagrass. It is often used on southern golf greens dressed up for winter. Methazole and cisanilide, as well as phenoxy combinations, control broadleaf weeds well in dormant bermuda.

A green "scum" of algae or moss seems universally disliked. While herbicides, including copper sulphate (for algae), may temporarily restrain these lower plants, their presence is more the outgrowth of poor lawn ecology than a problem that can be cured with a spraying or two. Moss generally signifies that growing conditions are not good for the grass—usually compact soil with insufficient fertility. Shade intensifies the problem. Fertilization, better drainage, and perhaps aerification may be more appropriate responses than herbicidal treatment. Persistent moisture triggers algal growth; the answer here may be better drainage, aerification, and the other niceties of which a good lawn is deserving.

SAFETY WITH HERBICIDES

Before herbicides are permitted to be sold, they must be widely tested and proved reasonably safe. Where problems arise the difficulty generally stems from careless application and failure to follow label instructions. Of course well-designed spray apparatus is essential for safe and accurate application. If a herbicide can't be applied precisely, better not to use it at all. Invert emulsions and other foaming agents have been developed for better containing a herbicide, avoiding drift onto nontarget vegetation. Invert emulsions are especially used with herbicides applied by aircraft and along roadsides, although one foam applicator for home use has come onto the market.

Activated charcoal often serves to nullify a herbicide's effects if used quickly enough. Such charcoal, offered under brand names such as Gro-Safe, should be spread immediately where the herbicide was mis-applied. It goes a long way toward counteracting a mistaken treatment or an overapplication.

The possible toxicity of herbicides to human beings and animal pets is indicated by the "LD-50" rating (the strength at which fifty percent of the test animals die). Arsenites are the most dangerous of turf herbicides, with an LD-50 rating of only 10, which explains the disfavor they find with EPA! Paraquat, with a rating of 157, is moderately toxic. The organic arsenicals are only mildly toxic, both DSMA and 2,4-D rating about 600. The range extends upward from there to things that are hardly toxic at all, such as Azak (terbutol) at 34,600.

WHAT SOME EXPERTS RECOMMEND

Recommendations of *the Combined Extension Services, New England Universities.*

Problem	Herbicide	Rate/Acre Active Ingredient	Comments
I. Crabgrass *Preemergence*			Herbicides must be applied in April or the first part of May *prior to the time crabgrass seed starts to germinate,* usually at the end of forsythia bloom and before lilac bloom. If no rain occurs within a week of application, the applied material should be watered in. Some control of other annual grasses can be expected.
			The materials listed are available in a number of formulations and concentrations. Check with a dealer for details. Except for siduron do not use these materials on seedling grass or in soil where seed or sod will be used within 4 months.
	benefin (Balan*)	2 lb.	May cause injury to bentgrass. Only fair crabgrass control.
	bensulide (Betasan*)	10 lb.	Relatively safe on all turf species. May restrict rooting of transplanted sod.
	DCPA (Dacthal*)	10 lb.	May injure red fescue.
	siduron (Tupersan*)	12 lb.	Safe for use (1) at time of seeding turf grasses, (2) on seedling

Problem	Herbicide	Rate/Acre Active Ingredient	Comments
			turf and (3) on sod to be harvested and transplanted. Effective until crabgrass is in the 1-2 leaf stage.
Postemergence	DSMA, MAMA or MSMA	2-4 lb.	Two or three applications necessary. Some turf discoloration likely.
	PMA**		Used primarily on putting greens. Repeat applications needed. Also gives some disease control.
	siduron + DSMA (Tupersan*)	10 + 3 lb.	One application sufficient if applied before crabgrass reaches 5 leaf stage and/or 1 inch in height.
II. Annual Bluegrass *(Poa annua)*	bensulide (Betasan*)	15 lb.	Promising in preventing infestation of *Poa annua* from seed. Apply in early August. Use only in a turf where killing of *Poa annua* will not create bare areas. Several annual applications may be necessary before results are satisfactory. Follow label closely.
III. Established Broadleaf Weeds			Best time to treat is in early fall or mid-spring. These herbicides are available in a variety of formulations and trade named brands. Ask dealers for details.
	2,4-D combined with dicamba, mecoprop or silvex		Used for wide spectrum broadleaf weed control. Numerous commercial products containing mixtures of these are available. 2,4-D readily controls such weeds as dandelion and plantain while the other chemicals will control weeds resistant to 2,4-D such as chickweed and clover.
	2,4-D + dicamba (Banvel*)	1 + ⅛ lb.	Warning: If applied near trees or shrubs, root uptake may result in serious injury. Most injury has occurred from misuse of fertilizer mixtures containing dicamba.
	2,4-D + mecoprop (MCPP)	1 + 1 lb.	Relatively safe on all turf species.
	2,4-D + silvex (2,4,5-TP)	1 + ½ lb.	May cause some injury to bentgrass.

*Trade Name
**Use Extra Caution in Handling.

Recommendations of Dr. Duich, Pennsylvania, as reported in special
handbook on lawns, Brooklyn Botanic Garden.

	Herbicide Treatments for Seedbeds Prior to Planting		
Chemical	*Effect*	*Timing*	*Remarks*
cacodylic acid	contact herbicide; kills surface vegetation	5-7 days before seeding (or sodding)	spreader or spray; safe on tree roots; spot-kill of perennial grass weeds
paraquat	contact herbicide; kills surface vegetation	2 days before seeding	spray; safe on tree roots; spot-kill of perennial grass weeds
dazomet	fumigant; kills seeds, seedlings, soil diseases and nematodes	2-4 weeks before seeding	professional application only unless labeled for home garden use
metham	fumigant	1 week before seeding	"
vorlex	fumigant	4 weeks before seeding	"
methyl bromide	soil sterilant; kills plants, seeds, diseases and nematodes	1 week before seeding	"

	Herbicide Treatments for Newly Seeded Turf		
Chemical	*Effect*	*Timing*	*Remarks*
bromoxynil	kills broadleaf weed seedlings on contact	10 days after grasses emerge; until weeds have 3-5 leaves	spray; earliest herbicide on seedling turf for broadleaf weeds
siduron	kills crabgrass and other annual grasses as they emerge	during or immediately after seeding or re-seeding	spreader or spray; not on Bermuda grass and certain bents

	Herbicides for Controlling Annual Grass Weeds—Established Turf		
Chemical	*Effect*	*Timing*	*Remarks*
A. Preemergence treatment—apply before weeds germinate:			
bandane	crabgrass	early spring	for spreader; safe on young turf grasses
benefin	crabgrass & other annual grasses	early spring	for spreader; can injure fine fescue, bent, dichondra
bensulide	crabgrass & other annual grasses	early spring	for spreader or sprayer; can injure bermuda grass; safe on bent
DCPA	crabgrass & other annual grasses	early spring	for spreader or sprayer; may injure fine fescue & bent in drought
siduron	crabgrass	early spring to early summer	for spreader or sprayer; not on bermuda & certain bents
B. Postemergence treatment—apply after weeds germinate:			
AMA, CMA, DSMA,	annual grasses—crabgrass, dallis. Also	early to mid-summer	for spreader or sprayer; moist soil and less than

Herbicides for Controlling Annual Grass Weeds—Established Turf

Chemical	Effect	Timing	Remarks
MAMA, and MSMA	nutsedge and sandbur		80°F; repeat treatments at 10 days; not on st. augustine and centipede; may injure fine fescue

C. Spot treatment—kills annual and perennial grasses non-selectively:

amitrole and dalapon	kills all grasses	during active growth	spray; kills grasses in treated area; one month to reseed or sod

Recommendations of Dr. Bingham, Virginia, as reported in Virginia Protection Newsletter.

Herbicide and Broadleaf Weed Susceptibility

Weed	2,4-D	Silvex	Mecoprop	Dicamba
Bindweed	S	S-I	S-I	S
Bittercress	S	S-I	S-I	S
Black medic	R	S-I	I	S
Buttercup	S-I	I	I	S
Carpetweed	S	S	S	S
Chickweed, common	R	S	S-I	S
Mouseear	I-R	S	S-I	S
Chicory	S	S	S	S
Clover, crimson	S	S	S	S
Hop	I	S	S	S
White	I	S	S	S
Cranesbill	S	S-I	S-I	S
Daisy, oxeye	I	I	I	I
Dandelion	S	S	S	S
Dock	I	I-R	I-R	S
Dogfennel	I	S	I	S
Garlic, wild	S-I	R	R	S-I
Ground ivy	I-R	S-I	I	S-I
Hawkweed	S-I	R	R	S-I
Henbit	I	S	I	S
Knapweed, spotted	I	S-I	I	S
Knawel	R	S	I	S
Knotweed	R	I	I	S
Lambsquarter	S	S	S	S
Lespedeza	I-R	S	S	S
Mugwort	I	I-R	I-R	S-I
Mustards	S	S-I	I	S
Nutsedge	I	R	R	R
Onion, wild	I	R	R	S-I
Ornamental plants	S-I	S-I	S-I	S
Woodsorrel	R	S	R	I

Herbicide and Broadleaf Weed Susceptibility

Weed	2,4-D	Silvex	Mecoprop	Dicamba
Pennycress	S	S-I	I	S
Pepperweed	S	S-I	S-I	S
Pigweed	S	S	S	S
Plantains	S	I	I-R	I-R
Poison ivy	I	S	R	S-I
Pony foot	S	I	I	S-I
Prostrate spurge	I	I	I	S
Purslane	I	S-I	R	S
Red sorrel	R	I	R	S
Shepherdspurse	S	S	S-I	S
Speedwell	I-R	I-R	I-R	I-R
Spotted spurge	I-R	I	S-I	S-I
Thistle, musk, curl	S	I	I	S
Thistle, Canada	I	I	I	S
Vegetables	S	S	S	S
Wild carrot	S	S-I	S-I	S
Wild strawberry	R	I	R	S-I
Yarrow	I	I-R	I-R	S
Yellow rocket	S-I	I	I	S-I

S = weed susceptible; I = intermediate, good control at times with high rates, sometimes poor, usually require more than one treatment; R = resistant weeds in most instances.

Recommendations of Dr. Meggits, Michigan, in Extension Bulletin E-653.

CHEMICAL CONTROL OF LAWN WEEDS

Most broadleaf weeds can be effectively controlled by fall application of 2,4-D (1 lb./acre) mixed with silvex at ¾ lb./acre. For specific weed problems, use the control measures indicated below. All liquid formulations are 4 lbs. a.i. (active ingredient) per gallon unless otherwise indicated.

Weeds	Herbicide	How Used	Large Area Rate Lbs./Acre	Small Area Rate. Tsp. 1,000 sq. ft.	Remarks
BROADLEAVED WEEDS					
Black medic	silvex	Post-emergence	¾	3	Apply in fall or in spring before mid-May.
Burdock (a biennial)	2,4-D	Post-emergence	1	4	Spray in fall or early spring.
Common Chickweed	MCPP	Post-emergence	1	4	May be used in summer and on bent-grasses.
	silvex	Post-emergence	¾	3	Apply in fall, or in spring before mid-May. Turf injury may result at temperatures above 70°F.
Dandelion	2,4-D	Post-emergence	1	4	Fall treatment best. Spring treatment should be done before flowering.
Dog fennel	dicamba	Post-emergence	¼	1	Do not use within root zone of trees and shrubs.

Weeds	Herbicide	How Used	Large Area Rate Lbs./Acre	Small Area Rate. Tsp. 1,000 sq.ft.	Remarks
Ground ivy	MCPP	Post-emergence	1	4	May be used in summer and on bent-grasses.
	silvex	Post-emergence	¾	3	Repeat applications at 2-week intervals. Apply in fall or in spring before mid-May. Turf injury may result at temperatures above 70°F.
Henbit	silvex	Post-emergence	¾	3	Repeat application in 2 weeks. Apply in fall or spring before mid-May.
Hoary alyssum	2,4-D	Post-emergence	2	8	Spray in fall when in rosette stage.
Knotweed	dicamba	Post-emergence	⅜	1½	Do not use within root zone of trees and shrubs.
	MCPP	Post-emergence	1	4	May be used in summer and on bent-grasses.
Mossy stonecrop	2,4-D (Ester)	Post-emergence	2	8	Use spring or fall treatment. May require a second application the following season.
Mouse-eared chickweed	MCPP	Post-emergence	1	4	May be used in summer and on bent-grasses.
	silvex	Post-emergence	¾	3	Apply in fall or spring before mid-May. Turf injury may result at temperatures above 70°F.
Oxeye daisy	silvex	Post-emergence	¾	3	Apply in fall or early spring. Repeated applications may be necessary.
Plantains: Broadleaved Buckhorn	2,4-D	Post-emergence	1	4	Apply in fall or in spring before formation of flower spikes.
Prostrate spurge	dicamba	Post-emergence	⅜	1½	Do not use within root zone of trees and shrubs.
	silvex	Post-emergence	¾	3	Repeated applications may be necessary for complete eradication.
Purslane	MCPP	Post-emergence	1	4	May be used in summer and on bent-grasses.
	silvex	Post-emergence	¾	3	Apply in fall or early spring.
Red sorrel	dicamba	Post-emergence	⅜	1½	Do not use within root zone of trees and shrubs.
Roundleaved mallow	silvex	Post-emergence	3		Do not use on newly seeded lawns.
Sandbur	AMA	Post-emergence	3		Repeat once or twice at 7-day interval. May cause some discoloration of turf. Apply when 2 inches tall.
Shepherd's Purse	2,4-D	Post-emergence	1	4	Apply in mid-fall.
Speedwell	endothall (1.46 lb./gal.)	Post-emergence	1½	11	Apply in early spring or fall. May require a second application.
Thistles	2,4-D	Post-emergence	1	4	Spray in fall. Canada thistle will require several applications.
White clover	MCPP	Post-emergence	1	4	May be used in summer and on bent-grasses.
	silvex	Post-emergence	¾	3	Repeat applications at 2-week intervals; apply in fall or in spring before mid-May; turf injury may result at temperatures above 70°F.
Wild carrot	2,4-D	Post-emergence	1	4	Apply in fall or spring before mid-May.
Yellow rocket	2,4-D	Post-emergence	1	4	Spray in fall, use spring treatment for fall seeded turf.
Yellow woodsorrel	silvex	Post-emergence	¾	3	Apply in fall or spring before mid-May.
ANNUAL GRASSES Annual bluegrass	arsenate, lead and calcium	Pre-emergence	260	6 lbs.	Apply in early fall and again in early spring. After the second year, apply only in late summer and at one-half recommended rate to maintain arsenic toxicity in soil. High soil phosphorus levels can reduce herbicidal effectiveness.
	bensulide	Pre-emergence	12		Two applications per year, as with arsenate.

Weeds	Herbicide	How Used	Large Area Rate Lbs./Acre	Small Area Rate. Tsp. 1,000 sq.ft.	Remarks
Crabgrass	arsenates, lead and calcium	Pre-emergence	260	6 lbs.	Control is often achieved when an arsenate program is used against annual bluegrasses.
	azak	Pre-emergence	15		Variable results.
	benefin	Pre-emergence	2		Not recommended for use on bentgrass turf.
	bensulide	Pre-emergence	12		Safe on mature sod of all turfgrass species.
	DCPA	Pre-emergence	10		Safe for use on established bluegrass; may injure bentgrasses and fine fescues.
	siduron	Pre-emergence	10		Can be used simultaneously with seeding of lawn grasses.
	DSMA	Post-emergence	6		Apply when crabgrass is 2 to 3 inches tall. Repeat twice at 7-day intervals; may cause some discoloration of the turf.

Foxtail, barnyard grass and other annual grasses—see crabgrass

Silver crabgrass (Goose grass)—see crabgrass — Germinates 2-4 weeks after crabgrass. Very difficult to control when mature.

PERENNIAL GRASSES

Weeds	Herbicide	How Used	Large Area Rate Lbs./Acre	Small Area Rate. Tsp. 1,000 sq.ft.	Remarks
Bentgrasses	amitrol-T	Post-emergence	4	12/gal. water	Spot treat when actively growing, wait 4-5 weeks, then reseed.
	dalapon	Post-emergence	10	30/gal. water	Spot treat when actively growing, wait 8 weeks, then reseed.

NOTE: Dig out by hand and ensure removal of all underground plant parts.

Nimblewill—NOTE: No satisfactory selective chemical control (see bentgrasses).

Weeds	Herbicide	How Used	Large Area Rate Lbs./Acre	Small Area Rate. Tsp. 1,000 sq.ft.	Remarks
Nutsedge	DSMA	Post-emergence	6		Requires 2 or more applications at weekly intervals. Must treat within 2 months after emergence before nutlets form.

Quackgrass and tall fescue—see bentgrasses

MISCELLANEOUS

Weeds	Herbicide	How Used	Large Area Rate Lbs./Acre	Small Area Rate. Tsp. 1,000 sq.ft.	Remarks
Seedling broad-leaved weeds	bromoxynil	Post-emergence	⅜	1½	May be used safely in seedling turf.
Wild onion Wild garlic	2,4-D	Post-emergence	2	8	Will require several years to eradicate. Use spot treatment of isolated clumps.
	or				
	dicamba	Post-emergence	⅜	1½	Do not use within root zone of trees and shrubs.
Yarrow	dicamba	Post-emergence	¾	3	Apply in fall. Repeated applications may be necessary.
Vegetative desiccants	paraquat	Post-emergence	½		Use for chemical burn-off of annual grasses and broadleaved weeds.

Recommendations of Drs. Elmore and Gibeault, California, in California Turfgrass Culture.

A. Susceptibility of Broadleaf Weeds to Several Postemergence Herbicides

Plant Species	2,4-D w.s. amine	2,4-D o.s. amine	silvex	mecoprop	MCPA	dicamba	bromoxynil*
dandelion	S	S	S	MS	MS	MR	MR
English daisy	MR	MS	MS	MR	MR	S	—
broadleaf plantain	S	S	S	S	MS	MR	MR
buckhorn plantain	S	S	S	MS	S	MR	MR
common chickweed	MR	MR	MS	MS	MR	S	MR
mouseear chickweed	MS	MS	MS	S	—	MS	MR
soliva	MR	MR	MS	MS	—	MR	S
byzantine speedwell	R	R	—	—	—	—	—
white clover	MR	MR	S	S	MS	S	MS
burclover	MR	MR	S	S	MS	S	MS
yarrow	MR	MS	—	MR-MS	—	—	—
black medic	R	MR	S	MS	R	S	—

A. Susceptibility of Broadleaf Weeds to Several Postemergence Herbicides

Plant Species	2,4-D w.s. amine	2,4-D o.s. amine	silvex	mecoprop	MCPA	dicamba	bromoxynil*
knotweed	S*	S*	MS	MR	MR	S	S*
pearlwort	MR	MR	—	S	—	—	—
spotted spurge	MR	MS	MS	MR	MR	MS	S*

S = susceptible   R = resistant
MS = moderately susceptible   — = insufficient information
MR = moderately resistant   * = young weeds only

B. Safety to Grass Species with Broadleaf Herbicides

Herbicide	bentgrass*	Kentucky bluegrass	fine fescue	tall fescue	bermudagrass*	ryegrass
2,4-D w.s. amine	MS	R	MR	R	R	R
2,4-D o.s. amine	MS	MR	MR	R	R	R
2,4-D L.V. ester	S	MR	MR	R	R	—
dicamba	MR	R	MR	R	R	R
mecoprop	MR	R	R	R	R	R
MCPA	MR	R	R	R	R	R
silvex	S	MR	MR	R	MS	—
bromoxynil	MR	R	R	R	R	R

R = resistant to rates well above those needed for broadleaf weed control   S = sensitive
     * = known varietal response
MR = moderately resistant   — = insufficient information
MS = moderately sensitive—injury often results

C. Chemical Control of Grassy Weeds in Turf

Weed	Annual	Perennial	Germination Date	Preplant	Control Preemergence Bent	Control Preemergence Bermuda	Control Preemergence Kty. Blue	Control Preemergence Fescue	Control Postemergence
Crabgrass	X		Variable Jan.-May, June Depending on area	Methyl bromide Calcium cyanamide Metham Dazomet Amitrol Cacodylic acid Paraquat	Bensulide	Bensulide DCPA Terbutol Benefin	Bensulide DCPA Terbutol Benefin	Bensulide DCPA Benefin	DSMA AMA
Goosegrass	X		Variable Feb.-June Depending on area	Same as above	Bensulide	Bensulide	Bensulide	Bensulide	
Velvetgrass		X	—	Dalapon Dazomet Metham Methyl bromide	—	—	—	—	MSMA in bermuda, Kty. blue
Dallisgrass		X	—	Same as above	—	—	—	—	DSMA, MSMA
Kikuyugrass		X	—	Methyl bromide Metham					DSMA in Bent MSMA in bermuda, Kty. blue, fine fescue

INSECTS AND INSECTICIDES

Although insects are as ubiquitous as weeds, rather few are directly important in lawn upkeep. They get out of balance only infrequently, but their importance soars when it is *your* lawn that is attacked. Insects and insecticides have been very much the center of high drama recently, especially because of the controversy surrounding DDT. DDT has been banned for almost all uses in the United States, in deference to its adverse impact on ecosystems, and especially on birdlife. Restrictions have been imposed on many additional insecticides, too, some of which were widely used. Included are most of the chlorinated hydrocarbons: aldrin, BHC or benzene hexachloride, chlordane, dieldrin, endrin, heptachlor, toxaphene, and the like. Quickly biodegradable types are being substituted, not so persistent in the environment.

How the debate about insecticides in the environment will end is difficult to predict. Certainly mankind cannot risk marked ecological upset. Yet, one has misgivings about the high dudgeon over DDT. Finding DDT in remote localities and its being picked up in food chains everywhere seems open to some question. Some natural substances apparently provide the same chromatographic blips! In Wisconsin a soil sample collected before DDT had even been developed gave a positive reading, though continuously in storage since collection.

As with pests in general, the important thing is to keep insects in reasonable balance. In some cases insecticides are self-defeating. We've observed that many species, notably sod webworms with lawns, can become more troublesome where an insecticide such as chlordane has been persistently used. The webworms develop immunity to the insecticide, but their predators do not. Then, uncontrolled, a webworm population explosion occurs. On the whole, however, nature "absorbs the punch" of occasional insecticide application quite well. An ecological study in New Jersey, in which diazinon was sprayed over an abandoned field, showed only short-term changes in the micro-ecology; the ecosystem returned to "normal" (i.e., the microorganism population resembled those in unsprayed fields) within only a few months.

Many serious insect pests from foreign lands have been countered by the introduction of natural predators and diseases. Sex chemicals (pheromones) have been duplicated and used to lure males into traps. Hormonal compounds have been discovered which disrupt normal progression through larval and pupal stages, so that the insect does not mature in timely fashion. Males of certain species are sterilized in the laboratory, then released to mate with wild females, the union being progenyless (fertility regulation of insect populations parallels birth control with human beings). Many avenues exist for regulating insect populations without the use of persistent insecticides.

As for lawns, specifically, milkyspore disease (*Bacillus popilliae*) has been used to infect grubs of the Japanese beetle. The approach has been reasonably successful but does require a continuing light incidence of grubs to keep the disease "going" (many people are leery of a continuing low level of infection, would prefer to have a pest completely eliminated; of course this risks lack of protection as reinvasion occurs). Some lawn insects prey upon others, and large populations of anything tend to be brought under control by disease epidemics, termination of suitable weather, and so on. Birds provide quite an assist. Although urban birds such as starlings, sparrows, and grackles are ill thought-of by many people, an investigation in Connecticut showed that a flock of starlings reduced a Japanese beetle grub population by ninety-five percent and that Japanese beetle grubs constituted approximately sixty percent of the diet of grackles during a spring interval.

THE MOST TROUBLESOME PROBLEMS

Although insects have a way of erupting locally, outbreaks nationwide seem limited mainly to grubs, certain caterpillars, and chinchbugs. Many other insects—mosquitos, chiggers, ticks, and so on—may be a nuisance in the lawn, although they damage the grass very little. Lawn insects fall logically into three categories: (1) the underground root feeders, the "grubs"; (2) chewing insects that consume foliage; and (3) sucking insects such as the chinchbug.

1. The first group, the root feeders, is typified by the larvae of various beetles, primarily the Japanese beetles, June beetles, chafers, and recently a member of the dung beetle group, *Ataenius spretulus*, which doesn't even have a common name (Fig. 7-48). In the deep South

Fig. 7-48 Typical beetle grub found in the soil.

mole crickets, of which there are four species in Florida, behave in much the same way, burrowing into the soil consuming grass roots. Other than spreading milkyspore powders for the Japanese beetle, the standard measure for control is to soak long-lasting insecticides into the soil. No really good soil insecticide is available, what with current restrictions (especially on chlordane). Yet biodegradable chemicals can be useful even if not long-lasting (Table 7-4).

Table 7-4 Japanese beetle grub control trials. After Dr. L. M. Vasvary, Rutgers Turfgrass Proceedings, 1975.

Insecticide	Formulation	Rate/500 sq. ft.	Total Count
DYFONATE	4 EC	1½ fl. oz.	16
DYFONATE	4 EC	1 fl. oz.	10
FURADAN	4 lb/gal	2 fl. oz.	2
DIAZINON	AG500	4 fl. oz.	4
DASANIT	15% Granular	1½ lbs.	0
DURSBAN	2 E	2 fl. oz.	2
MOCAP	10% Granular	0.5 lb.	4
DASANIT	15% Granular	0.75 lb.	20
CHECK	—	—	93

Treatment Date: August 28, 1974.
Data Date: September 10, 1974

Grub infestations are not easily seen; protection comes a little late when sections of lawn dry out and lift up like a carpet because grass roots have been severed. If you live in a region where grubs are common, it may pay to dig up a small section of sod from time to time, looking for the culprits. If they are more frequent than two or three to the square foot, control is merited. Depending upon the species, a grub's life may last only a few months or for years (e.g., the "seventeen-year locust"). Damage occurs mostly in late spring or summer, the grubs burrowing deeply in winter. Grub presence is often indicated by bird, mole, or skunk activity; these creatures may tear into the turf in search of the insects.

2. The second group, the foliage consumers, is typified by caterpillars (larvae) of the armyworm, cutworm, sod webworm, billbugs, fiery skipper, and so on (Fig. 7-49). Sod webworms are probably the

Fig. 7-49 Foliage consuming caterpillars of the lawn.

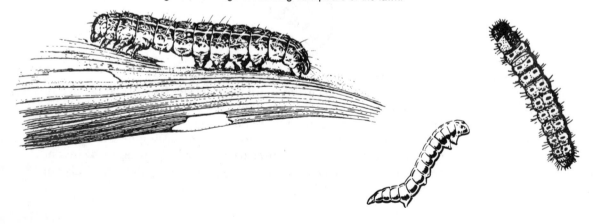

most troublesome of the group, both in the South and in the North (although different species are involved). Webworm moths are about an inch long, grayish, easily disturbed in the evening (they fly with a quick, short, jerky, zigzag trajectory). They will be laying eggs at random. The young caterpillars which hatch bury themselves deeply into the sod, where they build silk-lined "nests." They chew off grass foliage at its base at night. The brown patches of grass resulting may be confused with drought damage, since webworm activity reaches a crescendo during the hot dry weather of summer.

The caterpillars are light brown with dark spots, about an inch long when grown. They pupate in the lawn, and in favorable (warm) climates they create new generations on roughly a monthly cycle. Control is best achieved by applying an insecticide shortly after moths have been noted laying eggs, to stop the young caterpillars before they wreak too much havoc. Populations will probably not have built up enough to worry about until late June, after which monthly (bimonthly in northern states) applications of insecticide should keep the insects under control. Follow the directions for the particular formulation of insecticide used.

3. The third group contains sucking pests, primarily chinchbugs (species of which are active in all parts of the country), various scale insects (such as Ruth's and Rhodesgrass scales in Hawaii), groundpearl (primarily on centipedegrass), bermudagrass mites, and so on (Fig. 7-50). Chinchbugs, the worst of the lot, end hibernation in spring and

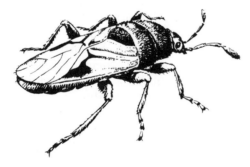

Fig. 7-50 Mature chinchbug typical of sucking insect pests of the lawn.

undergo at least two generations (more in more southerly climates) on about a five-week cycle. Adult chinchbugs are black-white, less than a quarter inch long; the immature bugs (nymphs) are wingless, perhaps only one sixteenth of an inch long, usually red-white. Chinchbugs are difficult to see, although "shaking" grass over a piece of stiff white paper inserted into the sod should show their presence. Flooding a small area with warm water (100 to 115°F) and covering it with a white cloth for about fifteen minutes generally results in the bugs climbing up the grass leaves onto the underside of the cloth.

Chinchbugs are most active in grass not yet showing any ill-effects, adjacent to patches that have turned brown due to prior feeding. The brown patches enlarge as the bugs work outward into the new grass. Insecticidal treatment in early June and again in early August usually results in good control for northern lawns, using any of the acceptable insecticides such as carbaryl (Sevin), chlorpyrifos (Dursban), diazinon (Spectracide), or trichlorfon (Aspon, Proxol), flushed deeply into the thatch.

Nuisance pests can be controlled with any of the acceptable home insecticides. Modern insecticides are effective upon contact and need not be consumed by the pests. Sprays cover the habitat better (certainly above ground), but granular insecticides are often longer-lasting (volatilization may occur from the granules). A number of acceptable insecticides are listed on pages 191–193; in addition, often useful around the home are the nontoxic natural plant products pyrethrum and rotenone and the toxic systemics (which spread through the plant in its sap), including carbophenothion (Trithion), dimethoate (Cygon), and phorate (Thimet). Synergism, in which a combination of substances is more effective than each would be applied separately, sometimes occurs with insecticides. Even atrazine, a herbicide, may enhance the effectiveness of certain insecticides.

SIMILAR OR RELATED NUISANCES

Moles are often troublesome in lawns, their tunnels making the surface uneven and drying out the grass. Moles are generally searching for grubs and other insects, their source of food; they will usually move on if soil insects are controlled by insecticidal drenches. Many methods for catching moles and gophers have their advocates, including various traps, poison baits, and "bombs" that release gases into their runs. All are probably effective under ideal conditions, although many people report that nothing works where moles are truly persistent.

Nematodes, small eelworms in the soil that burrow into grass roots, are of increasing concern. In Florida their damage is sometimes so severe that the turf thins greatly and seems on the verge of dying. Nematicides (most of which are highly toxic and may not be available to a homeowner) bring quick (but often temporary) relief. However, response to nematicides (such as Dasanit, Furadan, Nemacur, Vydate) is often poor on heavy soils in the North: Studies at Ohio State University show only modest reductions of the nematode populations. Fortunately, except in extreme cases such as Florida, nematodes are reasonably under natural control, and we have learned to live rather comfortably with them. Recall, however, that a Michigan pathologist believes that nematodes spread *Fusarium* disease.

Earthworms are on the whole beneficial to lawns, but they are sometimes unwanted. Most insecticides discourage earthworms, even if not killing them (the worms temporarily migrate deeply into the soil). Where earthworms disappear because of pre-emergence herbicides or insecticides, we have noted that thatch tends to mount.

Snails and slugs don't do a great deal of damage to lawns but are nasty to have around; their slimy trails can often be seen extending from turfed areas and other hideouts into the garden where they consume flowers, fruits, and vegetables. Metaldehyde baits or sprays are generally recommended for their control. Shallow containers of beer placed in the garden draw slugs to a glorious death by "drowning."

WHAT SOME EXPERTS RECOMMEND

Dr. Randell, Entomologist at the University of Illinois, recommends these procedures in the Proceedings of the 15th Illinois Turfgrass Conference.

Insects	Insecticide	Lb. of active ingredient per acre	Timing of application
Ants and soil-nesting wasps	diazinon spray	4	Apply when insects are present.
Aphids (greenbug)	malathion spray	1	Apply only when aphids are present.
	diazinon spray	1	
Armyworms and cutworms	carbaryl spray or granules	8	Treat when worms are present.
	trichlorfon spray or granules	5	
	diazinon spray or granules	4	
	chlorpyrifos spray or granules	1	
Chiggers	diazinon	1	Apply to grass area where chiggers have been a problem.
	malathion	1	
Chinch bugs	chlorpyrifos spray	1	Spray when bugs are numerous.
	trichlorfon spray	5	
	Aspon spray	10	
	diazinon	4	
Grubs, including true white, annual white, Japanese beetle, green June beetle	diazinon spray or granules	5	Treat damaged areas and where grubs are present in soil. Water-in very thoroughly.
	trichlorfon spray	8	
Leafhoppers and grasshoppers	carbaryl spray	4	Treatment not usually necessary unless hoppers are numerous.
Millipedes	carbaryl spray	8	Apply to turf where millipedes are migrating across area.
	diazinon spray	4	
Slugs	Mesurol bait		Apply by scattering in grass.
	Zectran bait		

Insects	Insecticide	Lb. of active ingredient per acre	Timing of application
Sod webworms	carbaryl spray or granules	8	Apply in late July or August when worms are present. Use 120 gallons of water per acre.
	diazinon spray or granules	4	
	chlorpyrifos spray or granules	1	
	trichlorfon spray	4	
	Aspon spray	10	

Insecticides: names and some commercial formulations

Common name	Trade names	Formulations
azinphosmethyl	Guthion	50% W. 5% G.
Bacillus thuringiensis	Biotrol, Dipel, Thuricide	
carbaryl[a]	Sevin	80% S. 50% W.
chlorpyrifos	Dursban	2 lb./gal. 1% G.
diazinon[b]	Spectracide	4 lb./gal. 25% E.C. 50% W. 14% G.
dicofol	Kelthane	18.5% E.C. 18.5% W.
dimethoate[c]	Cygon, De-Fend	2 lb./gal. 25% W.P.
endosulfan	Thiodan	2 lb./gal. E.C. 50% W.
malathion[d]	Cythion	50-57% E.C. 25% W.
superior oil	many brands	—
trichlorfon	Dylox, Proxol	80% W. 4 lb./gal.
	Aspon	13% E.C. 6 lb./gal.
	Imidan	50% W.

[a] Do not use on Boston ivy.
[b] Do not use on ferns or hibiscus.
[c] Do not use on chrysanthemums.
[d] Do not use on canaert red cedar.
Note: E.C. = emulsion concentrate; W. = wettable powder; G = granules; S. = sprayable powder.

Control
of
Pests

	Recommended Material	Suggested Formulation	Rate to Apply per 1000 ft²
Root Feeders			
White Grubs	chlordane	10% G.	2⅓ lbs.
Wireworms	chlordane	10% G.	2⅓ lbs.
Leaf Feeders			
Sod Webworms	chlorpyrifos (Dursban)	41% E.C.	¾ oz.
	diazinon	2% G.	5 lbs.
	trichlorfon (Dylox)	80% W.P.	3.2 oz.
	diazinon	25% E.C.	8 oz.
	zectran	22% E.C.	6 oz.
	Carbaryl (Sevin)	50% W.P.	½ lb.
Armyworms and Cutworms	Carbaryl (Sevin)	50% W.P.	2 oz.
		5% G.	1 lb.
	chlorpyrifos (Dursban)	41% E.C.	¾ oz.
Leafhoppers	Carbaryl (Sevin)	50% W.P.	2 oz.
	methoxychlor	25% E.C.	2 oz.
Others			
Ants	chlordane	45% E.C.	½ pt.
		10% G.	2½ lbs.
	diazinon	25% E.C.	6 oz.
		2% G.	5 lbs.
Earthworms	chlordane*	10% G.	2½ lbs.
Moles	Elimination of grubs and earthworms reduces mole problems.		
Wasps	chlordane*	45% E.C.	½ pt.
		10% G.	2½ lbs.
	diazinon	25% E.C.	6 oz.
		2% G.	5 lbs.

G = Granules, W.P. = Wettable Powder, and E.C. = Emulsifiable Concentrate
* Chlordane was banned for most uses by EPA order in early 1976.

DISEASES AND FUNGICIDES

Compared to weeds and insects, fungi (the chief cause of disease) have a highly involved ecology. Their behavior is so foreign to our everyday comprehension of things as to constitute an almost different world. It would be easy to devote a whole book to the myriad of diseases which at one time or another attack turfgrass, speculating about causes and cures. But we shan't accord them undue attention here, if for no other reason than that they represent something about which a homeowner is capable of doing very little.

Certainly, there are many fungicides reputed to stop various diseases; but even the expert has difficulty identifying diseases accurately and deciding what fungicide to apply when. A homeowner is likely to find "disease" confusing, specific fungicides hard to get, and precise application difficult (good spray apparatus and careful formulation of the fungicide are *de rigeur*). It is usually easier to hope for natural control—a change in weather, the interplay of ecological forces within the turf, physiological response that favors the grass, and the like. Even if some pretty bad lawn devastation may occur, in most cases the grass does snap back from rhizomes and crowns in the soil.

For a disease to break out, (1) the grass must be susceptible, (2) the fungus must be in an "aggressive" stage, (3) the season (weather) must be favorable, and (4) moisture must be ample. One or more of these conditions will surely turn to the disadvantage of the fungus, eventually, probably sooner rather than later. This is a blessing not always recognized.

One gets the impression that disease is more prevalent in lawns nowadays than ever before. Certainly new diseases do seem to be cropping up. This may be something of an illusion, however, as we pay more attention these days, searching out the diseases. Lawns are kept lusher, more prone to contract disease. Standards are higher, and diseased turfs stand out like a sore thumb. Introduction of grasses not native to the area (and thus not having evolved resistance to ambient diseases) hasn't helped, and insistence upon monocultures has given epidemics every opportunity. We really have been asking for trouble.

But measures have also been taken to counteract the pests. Breeding of disease resistance into new cultivars has been outstanding, much more accomplished than for insects or herbicides. The simplest, most effective measure for restraining lawn disease is to plant tolerant grass! Furthermore, disease abatement can often be accomplished through rather modest improvements in lawn keeping—better timing of fertilization, withholding of irrigation, and such like. Dr. Couch, Virginia Polytechnic Institute, has publicly said that he can make *any* cultivar either resistant to or susceptible to a particular disease, by altering its milieu!

While Couch is thinking in terms of laboratory control, Dr. Cole, Pennsylvania State University, declares that disease outdoors erupts only when "released" by "improper" management. "Improper" here is patently anything that doesn't work, but we can't deny that many environmental factors natural to grass become altered, such as avoiding drought by watering and fertilizing for greater than normal growth. Dr. Larsen, Ohio State University, mentions several lawn-keeping practices which he feels help to hold down disease. He recommends lowering humidity as much as possible (as by thinning trees, reducing shade, and the like), aerification and thatch removal (helping to restrict inoculum), improvement of drainage (thereby "drying out" the medium in which soil fungi such as Pythium thrive), keeping nutrients properly in balance, etc.; fungicides are a last resort.

Lawn disease philosophy has changed quite a bit from only a few years ago, when diseases appeared to be preventable only by consistent use of fungicides (similar to what is still practiced on golf greens). Dr. Endo, University of California, now views the fungi causing disease as weak competitors in the microbiological ecosystem; when biological activity is high, disease is depressed. Litter (clippings), warmth, and so on, encourage biological activity and therefore repress disease! In experiments, leafspot fungus spores scarcely germinated on moist debris typical of a lawn, but sprouted fully when such debris was washed and sterilized.

Dr. Jackson, University of Rhode Island, also views the fungus world as a system of checks and balances. Sometimes change of conditions tips the balance in favor of the disease; even fungicide applications may do so, such as when difolatan treatments result in more dollarspot, or benlate causes leafspot to erupt! Dr. Gould, Washington State University, notes that "take all" root rot has been highly infective on fumigated soil but that unsterilized soil can bring the disease under control. Dr. Colbaugh, University of California, has similarly experienced instances in which sterilization fails; unsterilized soil must be introduced to achieve the necessary ecological balance.

FUNGICIDES

Various compounds, a listing of which would fill many pages, can stall disease-causing fungi. Mostly they have been effective as contact agents, i.e., the chemical coats the grass foliage, forming a protective barrier that kills spores or fungal filaments seeking entrance into the leaf. Daconil, Dyrene, Fore, Thiram, and various dithiocarbamates such as Maneb and Zineb are of this type; for the most part they are the mainstays in disease prevention. Sprayed often enough to keep new growth covered, such fungicides are quite efficient.

More recently an exciting new class of fungicides has been developed, the systemics (benomyl, nurelle, thiophanates, thiabendazole, and so on). As with systemic insecticides, they are absorbed (usually through the roots) and spread throughout the plant in its sapstream. They are thus curative as well as preventive, and application can await appearance of the disease. Being internal in the plant they escape weathering loss. On the whole they are more selective than are contact fungicides. They are longer-lasting, requiring only infrequent application (differences of opinion do occur as to the length of time they are effective; Virginia pathologists claim only four or five week effectiveness in control of dollarspot, for example).

But systemics are relatively expensive; foliar diseases are often more economically controlled by contact fungicides. They work for only a limited range of diseases, primarily root infections that spread in the soil. They are often disruptive to ecosystems, being toxic to earthworms, for example (normally an undesirable end), and to nematodes (which may be a desirable outcome). The University of Rhode Island has noticed deterioration of turf quality with continued use of systemics. And in some cases they upset mite ecology, killing the mites (thereby eliminating sustenance for predators) causing a mite "explosion" when reintroduction occurs.

Systemics are supposedly not toxic to fungi until hydrolized within the plant. In an acid environment hydrolysis occurs quickly and may result in lack of persistence. Systemics are best used as a soil drench, for absorption by roots. The soil should be moist, and in most cases the treatment "watered-in" additionally (great success is claimed from application in the rain). Obviously ambient conditions, such as thatch, can have an influence on ability to suffuse the rootzone. It is generally agreed that systemics are not the answer of themselves but should be alternated with contact fungicides; otherwise diseases not controlled by the systemic may erupt and become worse than if no fungicide at all were used.

LAWN DISEASES

Accurate identification of a plant disease requires laboratory culture. But gross appearances are often characteristic enough to suggest what the disease is. Where colored illustrations are used, as is the case in many pathology manuals, reasonable identification becomes possible. Here we can provide only thumbnail sketches of a few of the many diseases which attack turf. A key patterned after that by Dr. M. B. Harrison, Cooperative Extension, New York State, does distinguish a few of the more commonplace diseases encountered on Long Island.

HARRISON TURF DISEASE KEY
(choose the appropriate alternatives)

1. Disease occurring in mid-winter
   or very early spring .... *Snowmold*
1. Disease occurring in spring, summer, or fall .... 2.
2. Grass dying in a circular ring or band (bands
   may overlap); mushrooms may be present ...... *Fairy Ring*
2. Grass not dying in a circular band .... 3.

3. Grass dying in patches outlined by gray ring,
usually in hot, humid weather .... *Brown Patch*
3. No gray ring around dying patch .... 4.
4. Leaves with outlined disease spots .... 5.
5. Leaf spot with purple-black border; most active
during cool, moist weather .... *Leaf Spot*
5. Leafspot straw color with brown border; most
active during hot weather .... *Dollar Spot*
4. Leaves with disease spots not outlined .... 6.
6. Fungus growth and spores easily seen
on grass blades .... 7.
7. Fungus covering leaves white; generally
in shaded areas .... *Mildew*
7. Fungus on leaves rust-red or black .... 8.
8. Fungus on leaves rust-red in color; often in
autumn, on low-fertility grass .... *Rust*
8. Fungus on leaves black, frequently on Merion
Kentucky bluegrass .... *Stripe Smut*
6. Fungus growth and spores not obvious
on grass blades .... 9.
9. Dead grass patch straw-yellow; leaf spot straw-
colored; active during hot weather .... *Fusarium Patch*
9. Dead grass patch reddish brown; leaf spot with
minute black scabs and minute spores .... *Anthracnose*

In the paragraphs that follow, brief comments are given on a number of the more prominent turf diseases, many of which attack both northern and southern lawngrasses. In general they can be restrained with fungicides if treatment is soon enough. In other words treatment is better preventive than curative. Often a disease has run its course by the time a homeowner becomes aware of it; a fungicide then may satisfy the urge to "do something," but it may also be a waste of effort. Golf courses generally have the skilled supervision and budgets necessary to anticipate disease and prevent its occurrence, while homeowners more often rely upon natural control such as a change in weather, drying, ecological correction, and so on.

BROWNPATCH, *Rhizoctonia solani,* is a major disease particularly of bentgrass, encouraged by high temperature and ample humidity. Blighted grass patches extend from a few inches to a few feet, first turning purplish-green, then fading rapidly to light brown as foliage withers. At times a purplish "smoke ring" develops at the extremities where fungus mycelium is active (visible in early morning). Control with systemic fungicides is dubious. Ample nitrogen, high humidity, and extremes in pH seem to encourage the disease. Weekly spraying with a contact fungicide is preventive.

CORTICIUM REDTHREAD, *Corticium fuciforme,* is a disease particularly on fescues and ryegrasses and in the Pacific Northwest. A pinkish web of hyphae covers small spots in the turf, the grass foliage becoming "water-soaked" and eventually brown. Chiefly it is a cold-weather disease, the grass usually recovering in spring even without application of fungicides.

DOLLARSPOT, *Sclerotinia homoeocarpa,* is a very prevalent disease on many species of grass during warm weather, resulting in small patches of dead foliage (about the size of a silver dollar, but often so close together as to merge). White, cobwebby hyphal growth is often noted in the early morning. Infection is generally within the temperature range of 60 to 86°F, and infections often become epidemic in late summer (particularly in wet weather). The disease is favored by low fertility, and while controllable with systemics tends to develop immune races. Some control has been noted from use of a sewerage sludge fertilizer.

FAIRY RINGS, caused by various fungi, are circles (or arcs) showing up in the lawn because of fungus (mycelium) activity in the soil (Fig. 7-51). Apparently there is little direct toxicity to the grass, but a cementing of the soil takes place, making it hard and dried out. Grass is often stimulated by nitrogen release after the ring moves outward to new soil. There is no good control short of complete soil replacement, though chloropicrin injections kill the mycelium in sandy soil. The usual technique is to fertilize the grass well so as to better obscure the

Fig. 7-51 A typical Fairy Ring, showing several mushrooms.

ring of stimulated growth. Poking holes into and drenching the ring may help. *Marasmius* is a frequent cause; *Tricholoma*, another, is stimulated by fertilization. Mushrooms appear from time to time, enabling identification of the fungus.

FUSARIUM BLIGHT, *Fusarium spp.*, usually causes damage in an irregular pattern, often with a clump of green turf remaining in the center of the browned patch (so-called "frog-eye"). Most grass species are attacked, severely in very warm weather, under high nitrogen fertility, and when calcium, phosphorus, and potassium are low. Warm-wet periods followed by drought cause grass stress that encourages disease, irrigation then helping (but often bringing in hydrophilic weeds). Fusarium is controllable with systemics, though resistant races do develop. Apparently it is sometimes transmitted by nematodes. *F. roseum* is often more severe on well-tended lawns than neglected ones. Bentgrasses, and Merion bluegrass, are quite susceptible. Preventive treatments during high temperature periods of July and August reduce damage.

LEAFSPOT and MELTINGOUT, caused by *Helminthosporium spp.*, are probably the most ubiquitous diseases of bluegrass lawns in the coolish weather of spring and autumn, with a meltingout phase in summer (life cycle diagram shown in Fig. 7-52). They are encouraged

Fig. 7-52 Life cycle of Helminthosporium fungi that cause leaf spot and meltingout.

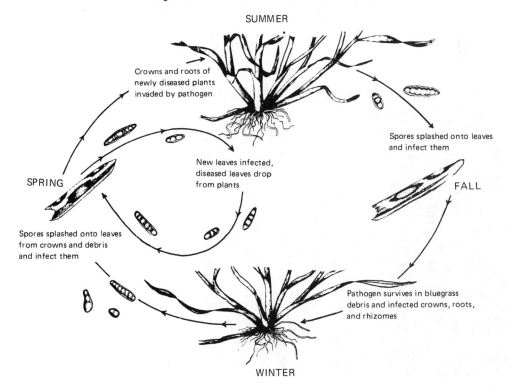

SUMMER

Crowns and roots of
newly diseased plants
invaded by pathogen

Spores splashed onto leaves
and infect them

New leaves infected,
diseased leaves drop
from plants

SPRING

FALL

Spores splashed onto leaves
from crowns and debris
and infect them

Pathogen survives in bluegrass
debris and infected crowns, roots,
and rhizomes

WINTER

by abundant nitrogen. Small "shothole" spots appear on the leaves, surrounded by a purple border, often enlarging to embrace almost the whole leaf and sometimes extending down to the crown (meltingout phase) with demise of the plant. Helminth is not controllable with systemics, and in fact systemic treatment results in greater incidence with Merion bluegrass. Contact fungicides such as Dyrene, though effective, are difficult to apply sufficiently often for continuous protection through the lengthy season. Leafspot is the prime disease for which new lawngrass cultivars are screened for resistance, perhaps the best approach to control.

OPHIOBOLUS PATCH, *Ophiobolus graminis,* is serious mainly in the Pacific Northwest, causing small dead patches of turf in late spring, primarily on bentgrass but also on other species. Black perithecia occur on the inside of leaf sheaths, a good identifying feature (see with a hand lens). Fungus flourishes under cool-moist conditions, but damage shows when weather turns hot-dry. Dead grass patches may expand for more than a season, reaching diameters of several feet. Since revival of grass is slow, damage is often repaired with sod. Sulfur is inhibitory, as are major fertility nutrients in balance. Chlordane, generally regarded as an insecticide, has helped.

POWDERY MILDEW, *Erysiphe graminis,* develops a gray-white coating on the surface of grass foliage, especially in the shade and in cool-damp weather. It is seldom lethal but debilitates the grass. Sprays such as Actidione-thiram are effective, but planting resistant cultivars or improving growing conditions (better air movement, less shade, occasional drying out) is more permanent.

PYTHIUM BLIGHTS, *Pythium spp.,* form a group of very destructive turfgrass diseases (Fig. 7-53), sometimes termed "grease spot,"

Fig. 7-53 To right of ruler: damage typical of Pythium.

"cottony blight," and so on. They can destroy entire stands of grass within a few hours under favorable epidemic conditions and often wipe out newly planted stands of wintergrass in the South. They are favored by warm, humid weather. Irregular patches with a "water-soaked" appearance fade to light brown, often merging to wipe out turf ten feet or more in extent. Damaged leaves may become "slimy" and mat together. Systemics give brief control, although nurelle is reportedly longer lasting. Continued use of systemics may increase blight. Dexon is a contact specific for *Pythium* on new seedings in the South. Ohio research indicates the presence of many previously un-recognized species of *Pythium* which may be more troublesome than the familiar ones.

RUST, *Puccinia spp.*, is named for the rust-colored pustules which develop on grass foliage on many grasses, both northern and southern, and seriously on Merion bluegrass and some ryegrasses in the North, on bermudagrass, st. augustine, and zoysias in the South. It is usually a summer and autumn disease in the North, a spring and summer disease in the South. Contact sprays such as the dithiocarbamates control rust, and the systemic Plantvax has been especially effective on perennial ryegrass. Seldom lethal (the grass usually snaps back), rust is nonetheless unsightly and disfiguring.

SAD (st. augustine decline), a virus, is a specialized disease of the deep South, starting in coastal Texas and spreading eastward. Grass foliage turns mottled and chlorotic, eventually yellows, the disease gradually extending to stolons causing retarded growth and dead patches of lawn. No effective fungicidal control, so plant SAD-resistant varieties such as Floratam.

SNOWMOLD, *Typhula* and *Fusarium,* are winter diseases most seri-ous on bentgrass but attacking all species; during cool, humid weather, as under snow, the fungus spreads over extensive areas, wiping out the turf, and is not noticed until spring thaw (Fig. 7-54). *Typhula* produces a

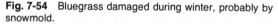

Fig. 7-54 Bluegrass damaged during winter, probably by snowmold.

characteristic black mass of sclerotia about the size of a pinhead in the soggy leaf tissue. It is not controllable with systemics, but treatment with such contact fungicides as Tersan SP and Triarimol have given excellent repression. Spraying is recommended just before the first expected snowfall, and again if a thaw exposes turf during winter.

STRIPESMUT, *Ustilago striiformis,* features longitudinal grayish-black stripes rupturing foliage, with release of sooty spores (often noted on footwear). It infects various northern grasses, being severe on some bluegrass cultivars while others are resistant; plant growth is slowed. It is most troublesome in cool, moist weather (spring and autumn) rather than during the heat of summer. The best control is with systemics applied in autumn, which can eradicate the fungus in and on the grass over winter. Some races resistant to benomyl have developed, and light rates of fungicide have even increased disease in Iowa; adequate phosphorus and potassium seem to help with control, but the best solution is to plant resistant cultivars.

WHAT SOME EXPERTS RECOMMEND

Because disease control is so involved it would be necessary to list innumerable remedies for each disease, which space does not permit. In most instances a wide selection of fungicides is not available to a homeowner, nor are there means for efficiently using them. When a fungicide seems called for, broad-spectrum ones can be procured at most garden centers (check the label for disease-control claims). Fungicide use is fraught with uncertainties, beginning with determination of what organism is actually causing the trouble; in some cases apparently a series of fungi work in concert on weakened grass. Included here are two condensed charts only, representative of Dr. Vargas', Michigan, generalized viewpoint, and Dr. Kurtz', California, specialized suggestions for shaded habitat.

Turfgrass diseases of Michigan and their control; J. M. Vargas, Jr., Assistant Professor, Department of Botany & Plant Pathology, Michigan State University

Disease and Causal Organism	Months	Grass*	Cultural	Chemical
Dollar spot (*Sclerotinia homeocarpa*)	May-Nov.	Bentgrass, Bluegrass and Fescue	(1) Increase nitrogen (2) Remove dew (Guttation)	(1) Daconil 2787 (2) Proturf DSB Fung. (3) Tersan 1991 (4) Acti-dione Thiram (5) Dyrene (6) Cleary-333 (7) Fungo (8) Spot-Kleen (9) Mertect 140
Brown patch (*Rhizoctonia solani*)	July-Aug.	Bentgrass, Bluegrass	(1) avoid high-nitrogen fertilizers (2) Increase air circulation	(1) Daconil 2787 (2) Dyrene (3) Acti-dione Thiram (4) Tersan LSR (5) Fore (6) Proturf Fung. III

Disease and Causal Organism	Months	Grass*	Cultural	Chemical
Meltingout Fading-out Leaf spot (*Helminthosporium spp.*)	April-Nov.	Bentgrass, Bluegrass and Fescue	(1) Remove clippings (2) Raise cutting height (3) Fertilize to maintain vigor (4) Resistant Kentucky Bluegrass cultivars: a. Merion b. Fylking c. Pennstar d. Nugget e. Baron f. Sodco g. A-34 h. Adelphi i. Galaxy j. Bonnieblue	(1) Fore (2) Daconil 2787 (3) Acti-dione (4) Dyrene (5) Tersan LSR (6) Terrachlor
Fusarium blight Nematodes (*Tylenchorhynchus dubius* + *Criconemoides spp.*) interacting with *Fusarium roseum* and *F. tricinctum*	May-Oct.	All grasses—most commonly found on Kentucky Bluegrass	Light frequent waterings during dry periods	(1) Tersan 1991 (2) Spot-Kleen
Stripe smut (*Ustilago Striiformis*)	April-June and Sept.-Nov.	Bluegrass & Kentucky Bluegrass (mostly merion.)	Blends of resistant cultivars	(1) Tersan 1991 (2) Spot Kleen (3) Fungo
Powdery mildew (*Erysiphe graminis*)	July-Nov.	Kentucky Bluegrass (shaded areas)	Reduce shade	(1) Tersan 1991
Fairy ring (Many *Basidiomycetes*)	April-Nov.	All turf areas	Removal of infested sod and soil and replacing with clean soil and re-seed or sod	Soil Fumigants (1) Methyl Bromide (2) Chloropicrin (3) Vapam (4) Vorlex
Pythium blight (*Pythium spp.*)	July and Aug.	Bentgrass, Bluegrass and Ryegrass	(1) Improve soil drainage (2) Increase air circulation	(1) Tersan SP (2) Koban (3) Proturf Fungicide II
Red thread (*Corticium fuciforme*)	Sept.-Nov.	All grasses but mostly Fescues & Manhattan ryegrass	Increased nitrogen	(1) Daconil 2787
Stem rust (*Puccinia spp.*)	July-Nov.	Kentucky bluegrass	Fertilize with nitrogen	———
Fusarium patch (Pink snow mold) (*Fusarium nivale*)	Sept.-May	Bentgrass, Bluegrass and Fescue	Avoid late fall fertilizings	(1) Tersan 1991 (2) Daconil 2787 (3) Fore (4) Fungo (5) Cleary's 3336 (6) Spot Kleen
Typhula blight (Gray snow mold) (*Typhula itoana*)	Under snow	Bentgrass, Bluegrass	Avoid late fall fertilizing	(1) Tersan SP (2) Proturf Fungicide II

*Unless specified Bluegrass refers to both annual bluegrass (*Poa annua*) and Kentucky bluegrass (*Poa pratensis*).

Major destructive disease fungi which commonly attack turfgrass species
in shade and the common name of a few fungicides used in their control.
After K. W. Kurtz, California Polytechnic State University, Pomona

Disease Fungi	Fungicides
Brown Patch (*Rhizoctonia solani*)	thiophanates, anilazine, benomyl, PCNB, TBZ, maneb + zinc ion, thiram, mercury compounds, chlorothalonil, cycloheximide
Fusarium Blight (*Fusarium roseum*)	benomyl, TBZ, thiophanates

Disease Fungi	*Fungicides*
Leaf Spot (*Helminthosporium spp.*)	anilazine, captan, chlorothalonil, cycloheximide, folpet, maneb, maneb and zinc ion, thiram
Powdery Mildew (*Erysiphe graminis*)	benomyl, cycloheximide, karathane, thiram
Pythium (*Pythium spp.*)	cadmium compounds, chloroneb, terrazole
Rust (*Puccinia spp.*)	anilazine, chlorothalanil, cycloheximide, maneb, maneb + zinc ion, oxycarboxin, thiram, zineb
Stripe Smut (*Ustilago striiformis*)	benomyl, thiophanate

Odds and Ends About Lawn Keeping

8

This final chapter is a mixed assortment of bits and pieces of information, some of which were touched upon in the earlier chapters, while others fit the format there not at all. They appear roughly according to the topic sequence of the book. A brief glossary ends the chapter, a reminder of the road we have traveled.

LAWNS IN SHADE

Lawn keeping in the shade is worthy of unified review. You will recall that grasses themselves differ in ability to endure shade. Bermudagrass, among southern species, is least tolerant of all; centipede, carpet, and bahia are fairly well adapted to shade; st. augustine and zoysia even more so. Among northern grasses differences are not so great. Fescues, *Poa trivialis,* and mildew-resistant bluegrass cultivars are a bit more tolerant of shade than are most bentgrasses, ryegrasses, and other bluegrasses. Physiological studies show red fescue to be more efficient under low light intensity than is bluegrass, its adaptively drawn-down respiration better balancing the inevitable reduction in photosynthesis in deep shade.

Shade may come from buildings or, more commonly, from trees. The latter is the more difficult for grass because, in addition to the loss of light, there is competition from the tree roots for soil moisture and nutrients. Undoubtedly there is a degree of "chemical warfare," too, in the repressive secretions from the tree (allelopathy). Lack of light is probably the chief limiting factor. A dense canopy of trees can screen out as much as ninety-eight percent of the incoming solar radiation. But even where considerable light penetrates to the ground, its quality may be reduced because the wavelengths best suited to photosynthesis have already been differentially absorbed.

Trees also intercept or deflect rain. They get first crack at circulating atmospheric carbon dioxide. Humidity is retained and wind movement restricted beneath a tree canopy, thereby providing conditions conducive to grass disease. Lawngrass growing beneath trees generally develops larger, thinner, more erect leaves (thus sacrificing much useful tissue to mowing). The plants become lanky, with fewer shoots, and have less well developed root systems, which creates a thinner, more succulent turf. No wonder a lawn under trees is less resistant to wear, to disease, and to other inadvertencies!

Obviously, no plant can grow where shade is very dense and persistent; a minimum of light is needed to keep a plant alive, although the exact amount varies with the species (Fig. 8-1). The trying circum-

Fig. 8-1 Partial shade allows ample light for grass growth if other factors are made favorable.

stances of shade can be mitigated by tall mowing; you might let the grass grow twice as tall in the shade as in the open. Fertilization should be adjusted to provide nutrients enough for both grass and trees but should not be excessive to the extent of forcing flabby grass growth. Generally fairly frequent but light feedings are appropriate, as is the use of long-lasting nitrogen sources. Irrigation that soaks deeply, and perhaps occasional aerification, may be in order. Try for greater breeziness and more light by pruning and shaping. Plant tolerant cultivars such as Nugget and Glade bluegrass; they resist powdery mildew, the worst disease of shade. Avoid excessive use; the grass will be weaker and wear less well in the shade than in the sun. When new trees are introduced, choose selections that root deeply rather than having mostly surface roots, and ones that will not cast exceptionally dense shade. Oaks, sycamore, tuliptrees, ginko, and various palms are generally less competitive with grass than are species like silver maple, beech, mulberry, sweetgum, and elm.

Lawn seeding mixtures designed for shade usually contain a high proportion of fine fescue, sometimes *Poa trivialis.* Fescues are tolerant of dry shade and poor soil, while *Poa trivialis* relishes damp shade. Though "Poa triv" is very attractive, unfortunately it wears poorly. Deciduous trees in leaf make an even denser shade than do most needle evergreens. However, they do shed their foliage seasonally, thus yielding a season of adequate light for grass growth, although other conditions may not be ideal at that time of year. Thus autumn may be occasion for planting fast-sprouting cultivars such as turf-type perennial ryegrasses just before tree leaf drop. Soil scarification, fertilization, and overseeding then could provide a reasonably satisfactory cover until the next summer (when shade stress will again thin the stand). If shade is so severe that keeping suitable grass under the trees is an unending battle, then one might turn to ground covers as grass substitutes, utilizing species such as periwinkle (*Vinca*), English ivy (*Hedera*), *Pachysandra,* bugleweed (*Ajuga*), and so on.

WINTERKILL

Although differing grasses exhibit degrees of hardiness, all northern species withstand reasonable cold if properly "conditioned." Both northern and southern turfs can be predisposed to winter injury if forced into a lot of "soft" growth late in the season, say from excessive nitrogen fertilization without balancing phosphorus and potassium. Even so, lack of hardiness stems less from absolute cold than from chilly snaps coming after the grass begins to ready itself for spring; it's much more susceptible to winterkill then.

Plants do process enormous quantities of air and strike a balance in the consumption and release of carbon dioxide. Carbon monoxide is apparently not greatly absorbed, but many other toxic substances are to a greater or lesser extent. In decreasing order these include: hydrogen fluoride, sulfur dioxide, chlorine, nitrogen dioxide, ozone, and nitrogen oxide. Considering the immense lawn acreage in the country, upward of fifteen million acres, turfgrass would seem capable of purifying a lot of air.

ADEPT DANDELIONS

The dandelion is a highly successful, global weed. It reproduces almost entirely by apomictic (non-sexual) seed. Dandelions from various parts of the world reveal populations that are much more aggressive than others; some "specialize" in early production of many seeds, while others produce fewer seeds later. In a lawn early production of abundant seed, and low rosette growth, would seem advantageous.

ENERGY USAGE

Cornell University has calculated that production of an acre of cabbage requires 76.7 gallons of gasoline (or its equivalent), probably more than twice what is required for maintaining the same acreage of lawn in the Ohio climate. In both cases the energy costs of making fertilizer, pesticides, and equipment for tending the crop are ignored. If these energy costs are added, almost a billion gallons of fuel (or its equivalent) might be required to maintain the nation's turf, about one eighth of what Cornell estimates is used for all farm production, and a small fraction of a percent of the national fuel requirements.

IDENTIFYING CULTIVARS

While seed technologists can clearly identify seed of different species under the microscope, it is not always easy to distinguish cultivars of the same grass species. Nor do the seedlings differ greatly. Experience has shown that seedlings behave in characteristic ways when treated in a particular fashion; peculiar colors develop under nitrogen deficiency, for example. Cultivars have even been "fingerprinted"—subjected to protein extraction, electrophoresis, and chromatographic analysis. Groups of cultivars show characteristic profiles.

Homeowners often experience invasion of white clover into blue-grass lawns. This is a partnership of long standing, for white clover and bluegrass together constituted the "English grass" of the early colonists. The combination has a lot of merit for pastures, providing balanced nutrition for grazing animals (the clover, because of root nodules, traps gaseous nitrogen and so improves fertility). Legumes such as clover are generally favored in competition with grasses by a high pH, ample rainfall, and limited nitrogen. Of course clover can be readily killed with phenoxy herbicides, but it often comes back again from "hard" (dormant) seed in the soil. Altering lawn keeping slightly to favor the grass may help restrain the clover.

TOTAL ENVIRONMENT INFLUENCES "TAKE" OF BERMUDAGRASS

We sometimes forget that cultivar response is tied to over-all conditions, not one factor. Bermudagrass, a hot-weather species, can be expected to root poorly in cooler (as compared to warmer) weather. But observations in Georgia show that light intensity and length of day are almost as controlling. Short days and low light intensity restrict formation of reserve carbohydrates.

GRASS PATHWAYS

Frequently grass will persist in pathways where it would otherwise disappear, if assisted with solid materials to help reduce compaction. Perforated concrete blocks have worked on parking lots, and in one experiment glass bottles were inverted into the soil so that only the bottoms appeared at path level. This proved effective, but the idea was abandoned for fear of glass breakage.

SIDE INFLUENCES OF PHOSPHORUS IN THE SOIL

Ample phosphorus in the soil counteracts the herbicidal influence of arsenic, as when arsenate crabgrass preventers are used. But it can have the opposite effect, too; high phosphorus levels increase phytotoxicity of amitrole and sometimes diuron.

It was once thought that sod should be selected from production areas having soil similar to that of the lawn which was to be sodded. Rooting was thought to be quicker and better. This is still suggested for patching athletic fields (i.e., sod grown on mineral rather than muck soil is chosen for patching a torn mineral-soil field). More recently no significant difference could be found in comparing mineral and muck sods. Sod rooting is almost entirely dependent upon development of new roots instead of continued growth of old ones. If sod is thinly cut (about half an inch rather than one or two inches), more than three times as many roots emerge in the early weeks. Thus thin sod "takes" more quickly. But it does require extra attention to keep it from drying out.

HURRYING ALONG SEED SPROUTING

Many lawnseeds must undergo a "curing" (maturing) process after harvest in order to germinate well. Apparently chemical substances within the seed or repressive compounds in the hulls put the brakes on sprouting and must be allowed to "mellow." When Kentucky bluegrass seed was gathered from Midwestern pastures, summer harvest was seldom fit for retail sale until the following spring. The full power of germination was slower to develop when bright, sunny weather rather than rainy spells prevailed at harvest time. Perhaps some soluble repressant is washed out of the hulls? Manhattan ryegrass has proven as much as ninety-four percent dormant at harvest; ryegrass germination seems greatly influenced by temperature during seed development.

Removal of seed hulls is often conducive to sprouting. Bermuda-grass seed that is dehulled germinates much better than that not dehulled, at least when the seed is fairly fresh. The same is often true of zoysia. In most other cases, however, special treatments are not worth the effort. Dampening seed, storing it at room temperature in a plastic bag for a few days, and sowing just as germination begins speeds things up. But this is a lot of trouble; and damp, sprouting seed doesn't distribute easily in a spreader, nor can the seed be kept viable many days once sprouted. A series of wetting-drying treatments leaving the seed dry enough to spread has sometimes hastened sprouting experimentally. Using a cool potassium nitrate solution for soaking has given best results. Sometimes growth regulators, such as gibberellins, enhance germination when conditions are marginal, as when moisture is barely adequate to trigger sprouting. Wetting agents dusted on the seed have encouraged sprouting, too. Scientists feel they are close to finding chemicals which "release" germination, presumably by nullifying catalase inhibition. Potassium azide has stimulated germination of certain grass seeds when applied to the soil in small amounts.

In the untypical climate that is Florida, lawn products often behave unconventionally. Florida agronomists report that all of the gradual-release fertilizers (sulfur-coated urea, IBDU, activated sewage sludge, and UF) do well under northern Florida conditions, compared to onerous weekly applications of ammonium nitrate. The sulfur coated urea is fine for summer fertilization but tends to "move" in the sod, providing an irregular pattern of response. IBDU experiences a lag before its full effectiveness is felt, but it performs well and rates best for turf stimulation in cold weather. Sewage sludge and UF are very similar, except that UF has greater residual influence. Nitrogen availability from IBDU is not so dependent upon temperature as is that from other sources, but its solubility varies appreciably with pH.

DEW

Dew has a surprisingly influential role in complementing irrigation. Dew is seasonally quite abundant in many climates and actually drips from foliage sufficiently to dampen the soil. But perhaps even more important, leaf stomata (the pores which admit carbon dioxide for foodmaking by photosynthesis) remain open as long as dew is present; until the dew has evaporated, maximum gas exchange continues, affording greater foodmaking potentiality.

NUTRITION AND DISEASE

Researchers in the "bentgrass country" of western Washington state have noticed considerable influence on pests from fertilizer nutrients. Abundant nitrogen increases *Fusarium, Corticium,* and *Helminthosporium* infections, but reduces *Ophiobolus.* Phosphorus and particularly potassium reduce *Fusarium, Ophiobolus,* and *Corticium.* Sulfur improves the color of grass independently of other treatments; it eliminates or reduces *Ophiobolus* and *Fusarium,* controls algae, represses earthworms, and keeps the turf free from *Poa annua* (provided phosphorus is held low).

WASTE WATER FOR IRRIGATION

Conservation efforts have been launched to utilize waste water for crop and turf irrigation. Many problems exist, including such economic ones as matching availability with times of need (most northern installations can use irrigation only for a month or two in summer;

it's hardly worth the effort to lay pipe, say to a golf course, for disposal over so limited a time). The quality of waste water varies greatly, depending upon its source and processing. Seldom is anything detrimental to grass found in household sewage, but industrial wastes (which contain heavy metals) may prove toxic when used persistently. Homeowners often wonder whether water from the swimming pool or similar treated sources is suited for the lawn. Almost invariably it is; if water is fit for a human being, it is not likely to be too heavily salted or chlorinated for plants. Persistent watering with tap water may alter pH; water from municipal facilities is often quite alkaline.

SALT FOR ICE CONTROL

Grass adjacent to walks, driveways, and roadways often suffers damage from salty meltwater. In one study (Rochester, New York) the ecology of a lake bay was disrupted by salty road runoff. Conventional lawngrasses seldom survive if the salt concentration even approaches one percent. However, the salt-tolerant species *Puccinellia distans* has survived a two-percent salt concentration; both it and species of *Distichlis* have "moved in" on freeways in the Chicago area where the planted vegetation has been killed because of winter salting. Around the home consider utilizing fertilizer in place of salt for melting ice, in locations where runoff is apt to affect the turf.

NITROGEN FIXATION CHANGES WITH TIME

As a grass stand ages and thatch becomes more voluminous, nitrogen fixing microorganisms seem to thin out. Perhaps they diminish because of tannin accumulation. The implication is that older, "tired" lawns may need proportionally more nitrogen than do immature swards!

Fig. 8-2 Dog urine spots on a badly underfertilized lawn.

For reasons that are not always clear, weed preventers can have both "good" and "bad" years. Most certainly weather must be involved. Some years early application proves best, other years late is best. Siduron reportedly experiences occasional brief periods of weak performance.

SYSTEMIC AND NONSYSTEMIC PESTICIDES

Contact pesticides often act like meat cleavers compared to the surgeon's scalpel of a systemic pesticide. Contacts are broadly toxic to almost any pest encountered, constituting a protective film coating the vegetation. Systemic pesticides, on the other hand, usually interfere with but a single reaction (such as nullifying an enzyme function). A pest can more easily overcome the latter by point mutation, thus developing a resistant race, than it can cope with a non-specific preventive barrier.

INCREASING SEVERITY OF DISEASE

Some pathologists believe that the increasing incidence of troubles such as summer leafspot is caused by the intensive growing of modern lawns that are watered and fertilized so much that disease is favored. More virulent strains of disease may be evolving, too. Sometimes a custodian starts out to control a few dandelions and does so successfully, but ends up altering the ecology sufficiently to make the grass a pushover. Experts seem to feel that the least possible manipulation of the lawn environment needed to achieve the desired results is the best route. Of course, many times things beyond the control of the custodian, like air pollution, may make a turf prone to disease. One examination showed that sulfur dioxide (a frequent air contaminant) favored annual weed grasses such as foxtail over the perennial lawn species.

HERBICIDE RESIDUES IN THE SOIL

In Oklahoma degradation of familiar herbicides often used on lawns was found to be: (measured as the average half-life) 2,4-D, four days; silvex, seventeen days; 2,4,5-T, twenty days; dicamba, twenty-five days; picloram, one hundred or more days. Interestingly, degradation was more rapid where grass was growing than under trees. We hear from Virginia that 2,4-D persists in the soil for three or four weeks, dicamba for two to three months, silvex for five or six months, and a "hot" pre-emergence chemical (terbutol) for twelve months or more. All such herbicides must be reapplied periodically to retain effective strength in the soil, because there is a gradual loss of potency with time (i.e., in each step of the biological chain).

Glossary

Although throughout the book the context has been relied upon to make terms understandable, a brief glossary may nonetheless prove helpful.

Acidity   Having a pH less than 7, not alkaline; technically, having an excess of hydrogen ions.

Adapted (adaptation)   Suited to particular situations; ability to survive and flourish in an environment.

Adventive   Introduced by chance; not native.

Aerification   With lawns, the "cultivation" or loosening of sod and topsoil for improved gas exchange; punching holes into the lawn.

Aerobic   Having access to air (oxygen).

Alkalinity   With a pH higher than 7, not acid; technically, having an excess of hydroxyl ions.

Allelopathy   A repressive influence by one plant upon another because of secretions or chemical influence rather than crowding or competition.

Analysis   With fertilizer, a percentage listing of the major nutrients, always in the order of nitrogen—phosphorus—potassium: for example, 20–5–10.

Apomictic   Seed formation without sexual fertilization, such as with bluegrass and dandelions; heredity solely from the mother plant.

Biodegradable   Susceptible to breaking down and disappearing under natural conditions (mainly because of attack by microorganisms).

Biomass   The total organic accumulation derived from and including living organisms.

Capillarity   Rise of a liquid in a narrow-pore system because of liquid adhesion and surface tension; rise of moisture in fine pores of soil.

Carbohydrate   A class of organic compounds consisting of carbon, hydrogen, and oxygen in roughly a 1–2–1 ratio; an elementary food resulting from photosynthesis.

Chelate   A mineral element linked to an organic molecule that "protects" it from quick loss in the soil; a source of minor nutrients.

Chlorosis   A blanching of vegetation due to the absence of the normal green chlorophyll, often caused by an imbalance of nutrients (particularly the minor element iron, which may become unavailable to plants on alkaline soils).

Clone   A group of plants originating vegetatively from the same parental source, all alike genetically.

Compost   Well-decomposed organic materials turned mostly to humus; usually made by mounding (and dishing) organic wastes.

Cool-season grass   "Northern" species adapted to cooler climates, as opposed to species adapted to the tropics and subtropics.

Culm   The upright, leafy stem or "shoot" of a grass plant.

Cultivar   A horticultural *variety*; a selection or "strain" that can be perpetuated without loss of identity.

Dicot (Dicotyledonae)   One of two great divisions of flowering plants, the so-called "broadleaf" group: having two cotyledons, net veination, and flower parts in fours and fives.

Dormant   Temporarily inactive though alive; seeds and plants withstand unfavorable growing conditions by turning dormant.

Drift   The movement of small particles or vapors in air currents, from locus of spraying to surrounding habitat.

Ecology   The relationship of living things to their environment.

Ecological niche   A particular location (or set of conditions) suited to an organism, where it can survive even if not adapted elsewhere.

Ecotype   A group of organisms distinguished by their ability to colonize a particular ecological niche.

Endemic   Native to or natural, as opposed to adventive.

Evapotranspiration   The combined loss of moisture (as from leaves) due to transpiration ("breathing") and evaporation.

Fungicide   A pesticide used to control disease; lethal to fungi.

Genome   The hereditary complement distinguishing an organism, consisting of a characteristic set of chromosomes.

Genus   A classification unit of higher rank than species, typically including several species; the first of the Latin names by which species are identified, such as *"Poa"* of *Poa pratensis.*

Germination   Initiating growth or sprouting, as when referring to seeds or spores.

Growth regulator   A "master" compound, usually hormonal in nature, capable of profoundly altering growth habits and physiology in a very small quantity.

Habitat   The environment or locale inhabited by living organisms.

Herbicide   A vegetation-killing compound or weed killer.

Hybrid   An organism produced by the crossing of two dissimilar parents.

Infiltration   Insoak, as when water passes into the pore system of a soil.

Insecticide   A pesticide used for controlling insects and related organisms.

Ion   An electrically charged atom from salts that are disassociated in solution.

Key (for identification)   Logical presentation of alternatives which if progressively followed serve to identify a particular entity; a series of eliminations leading to identification.

Ligneous   Literally containing lignin; hard or "woody."

Major elements   The fertilizer nutrients most important for plant growth, namely nitrogen, phosphorus, and potassium.

Microclimate   The "climate" of a limited environs, such as within the sod; may be quite different from the readings normal to man-sized weather observation.

Micronutrient   Fertilizer nutrients needed only in small quantity (trace elements), such as magnesium, manganese, iron, and zinc.

Microorganism A small, scarcely visible organism (such as a bacterium or "microbe"), important for decay and similar biological activity in sod and soil.

Minor elements Micronutrients.

Monocot (Monocotyledonae) One of two great divisions of flowering plants, including the grasses and related families: having one cotyledon, parallel veination, flower parts in threes.

Monoculture Planting in which all plants are genetically alike.

Mulch Any loose, inert, protective material such as is used to cover new seedings: straw, woven netting, chopped vegetation, and so on.

Natural selection Survival of the fittest in the competition for habitat.

Nitrification The changing of reduced forms of nitrogen to nitrate.

Nitrogen fixation organisms Microorganisms capable of changing gaseous nitrogen into forms usable by higher plants.

Nutrients (fertilizer) Elements typically picked up through the root system having fertility value; fertilizer components useful to plant growth.

Organic Derived from living organisms, the molecular structure based upon carbon linkages; cf. biomass, compost, humus.

Oxygenation Provided with oxygen; "aired."

Pathologist A student of pathology, the cause and cure of disease.

Pesticide A compound employed to kill or control pests: herbicides, fungicides, insecticides, nematicides, and the like.

pH Indication of acidity or alkalinity, 7 being neutral; readings above 7 are alkaline, below 7 acid.

Photosynthesis The process whereby plants combine carbon dioxide and water under the auspices of chlorophyll (green pigment of plants), to build carbohydrates and other foods.

Plug A biscuit of sod used for transplanting grasses vegetatively.

Pollination The fusion of the male reproductive cell of a plant (pollen) with egg-bearing tissues (in the pistil).

Porosity Pore space; with soil, the ability to accept infiltration, allow percolation, and determine density.

Post-emergence Application (as of a herbicide) after the crop (grass seedlings) are growing.

Pre-emergence Application (as of a herbicide) before the crop (grass plantlets) have sprouted and emerged.

Rhizome (rhizomatous) An underground stem by which many grasses (and other plants) spread.

Rogueing Removal of off-type plants in a monoculture (as a seed field).

Saline (salinity)   Salty.

Scalping   With lawns, mowing so low as to remove most of the green foliage.

Scarification   Scratching, as when slicing into the soil; making striations in which seed might lodge during lawn renovation.

Selective   With pesticides, use of a compound that will affect the unwanted pests but not prove detrimental to other organisms.

Sink   Absorbing or withdrawing, as opposed to being a source or emitting; a particular habitat may serve as a sink for phosphorus, for example.

Soluble   Dissolving in a liquid, typically water.

Seed blend   A seed conglomeration containing cultivars of the same species.

Seed mixture   A seed conglomeration containing differing species.

Species   The unit of classification for living organisms; a grouping of individuals having common characteristics, isolated from other species either genetically, spatially, or ecologically.

Sprig   A stem fragment used to propagate grasses vegetatively, especially bermudagrass and zoysia.

Sterilization   A treatment to eliminate offending organisms, such as chemical sterilization of a soilbed with methyl bromide (kills disease organisms, weed seeds, living plants).

Stolons (stoloniferous)   Spreading stems of grasses that run above ground, rooting at the nodes; "runners."

Succession   The progressive replacement of organisms in an ecological sequence until the permanent ("climax") complement is attained.

Systemic   Absorbed and carried throughout the organism, as in the sapstream of growing plants.

Succulent   Watery, fleshy, "soft."

Transpiration   Loss of moisture from foliage through the stomata; plant "breathing."

Vegetative   Characterized by nonreproductive asexual parts, such as vegetative propagation (separations like plugs, sprigs, and clones).

Volatilization   Change to a gaseous form, such as when nitrogen may be lost from ammoniacal fertilizer particles on alkaline soil.

Warm-season grass   Species adapted to tropical and subtropical environments; southern lawngrasses as contrasted to northern ones.

Wetting agent   A chemical compound designed to break down surface tension, thus making solutions more absorptive and better able to coat surfaces to which they are applied; surfactant.

Index

anions, 101
annual, 150
annual bluegrass, 179
annual ryegrass, 19
annuals, 149
antitranspirants, 98
ants, 4
aphids, 4
apomixis, 29, 45
Aqua-Gro, 58
Arboretum, 30, 44
Argentine bahiagrass, 40
Arista, 30
armyworm, 188
arsenate, 183, 184
arsenicals, 178
arsenite, 178
arsinic acid, 175
arsonate, 88, 156, 177
arthropods, 145
artificial turf, 22
asphalt mulching, 80
Aspon, 190, 192
Astoria, 45
Astroturf, 22
Ataenius spretulus, 187
athletic turf, 22
atrazine, 155, 190
auricle, **41**
autumn planting, 78
Axonopus, 19, **21**
Azak, 178, 184
azinphosmethyl, 192

B

Bacillus popilliae, 187
Bacillus thuringensis, 145, 192
bacterial nitrogen fixation, 73
bahiagrass, **18,** 40
bahiagrass, discussion of, 40
Balan, 178
balance, destruction of, 3
balance, ecological, 3
bandane, 154, 180
Banvel, 179
barnyardgrass, 88, **167,** 175
Baron, 30
barriers, for borders, 135
Basagran, 177
basal growth, 13
battery-powered tractor, 122
beachgrass, 21
beech-maple climax, 24

beetles, 4, 187
benefin, 154, 175, 178, 180, 184, 185
benlate, 195
benomyl, 195, 202, 203
bensulide, 154, 155, 175, 178, 179, 180, 184, 185
bentazon, 177
bentgrass, 33, 45, 96, 151
bentgrass, Colonial **16**
bentgrasses, discussion of, 33
benzene hexachloride, 186
bermudagrass, **17,** 24, 36
bermudagrass, discussion of, 36
bermudagrass mites, 189
Betasan, 178, 179
BHC 186
biennial, 149
billbug, 38, 188
biodegradable, 155
biodegradable pesticides, 145
Biotrol, 192
birds, control of insects, 187
Bitter Blue, 39
black medic, **158**
blend, 26, 76
bluegrass, annual, 179
bluegrass-fescue interaction, 33
bluegrass, Kentucky—see Kentucky bluegrass
Bonnieblue, 22, 31
borders, 133
broadleaf weed control, 180
broadleaf weeds, 153, 176, 179
broadleaf weeds, susceptibility of, 181, 184
Bromacil, 25
bromoxynil, 184
brownpatch, 197
Buchloë dactyloides, 19, **20**
buffalograss, 19, **20**
bugleweed, 207
bunchgrass, 22, **41**
bur clover, **173**
burlap mulch, 80
buttonweed, **172**

C

cacodylic acid, 88, 135, 152, 180, 185
cadmium compounds, 204
calcium, 108
calcium carbonate, 112
calcium cyanamide, 185
California plant climate zones, **6**
capillary pores, 94
capillary water, 50, **54**
captan, 204

Cythion, 192

D

Daconil, 195, 202, 203
Dacthal, 178
Dactylis glomerata, **169**
dalapon, 88, 152, 175, 181, 184–185
dallisgrass, **174**
dandelion, **158**
Dasanit, 190
Dawson, 32, 33
dazomet, 180, 185
DCPA, 154–155, 175, 178, 180, 184–185
DDT, 9, 11, 186
debris collection, 136
decomposition, 11
De-Fend, 192
defoliation, 13, 125
degradation of herbicides, 213
denitrification, 105
dependent ecosystem, 142
Derby, 36
detritus, 69
dew, 211
Dexon, 201
diazinon, 186, 188, 190–193
dicamba, 155–156, 175–176, 179, 182–183,
    213–214
dichondra, 12, 21, 146
dicofol, 192
dicots, 176
Dicotyledons, 153
Dicotyledon weeds, 150
dieldrin, 186
difolatan, 195
Digitaria, **167,** 175
dimethoate, 190, 192
Diodea teres, **172**
Dipel, 192
Diplomat, 36
discing, 69
disease, 193
disease control, 202
disease fungi, 203
disease, increasing severity of, 213
disease, key to, 196
disease, related to nutrition, 211
disease repression, 195
disease-resistant cultivars, 194
diseases, causes, 194
dissipation, of soil sterilants, 152
Distichlis, 212
dithiocarbamates, 195, 201

diuron, 209
dock, **158,** 176
dollarspot, 195, 196, 198
dolomitic limestone, 108, 112
domestic species, 21
dragging the seedbed, 69, 74
drainage, 65, 66
drench, 196
drift, 141, 177
drought, 95
DSMA, 156, 178–179, 180, 184–185
dung beetle, 187
Dursban, 188, 190, 192–193
dusters, 139
dye, for turf, 98
Dyfonate, 188
Dylox, 192–193
Dyrene, 195, 200, 202–203

E

earthworm ecology, 58
earthworms, 4, 130, 191, 196
earthworms, soil aerification, 57
Echinochloa crus-galli, **167**
ecology, 1, 9
ecology, of the lawn, 3, 142
ecology, pests, 144
ecosystem, 4, 9–10, 64
ecotypes, 46
edging lawns, 133
eelworms, 4, 145
electric mower, 121–122
electrophoresis, 208
Eleusine indica, **168**
Emerald, 22, 39
endosulfan, 192
endothall, 183
endrin, 186
energy, 8, 9
energy crisis, 101
energy, for ecosystem, 5, 7
energy reserves, of grass, 124
energy usage, 208
English grass, 209
English ivy, 207
environment, 208
environmental considerations, pesticides, 144
environmental influences, 209
Environmental Protection Agency (EPA), 144
EPA regulations, 144
epidemics, of disease, 194
equipment, 116
equipment, for grounds-care, 142

granulars, 175
grass, artificial, 22
grass characteristics in shade, 206
grass, cool-season, 13
grass family, 12
grass, in shade, 207
grass, natural compared to artificial, 23
grass pests, 145
grass plant, parts identified, **29**
grass retardation, 132
grass, structure, **41**
grass, warm-season, 13
grass wear, 127
grasses, 12
grasses, northern, 14, 15, 26
grasses, southern, 14, 15, 36
grasses that thatch, 128
grasslands, natural, 5
gravitational water, 94
gravitational water, in soil, **54**
grazed grasslands, 13
green manure, 56
ground ivy, 146, **158,** 176
groundpearl, 189
ground water, 8
grounds, preparation for lawn, 65
Gro-Safe, 178
growth cycle, northern vs. southern, 28
growth retardants, 132
grubs, 4, 187, 188
Guthion, 192
gypsum, 56, 72, 109

H

habitat, alteration, 7
habitat, forest, 7
habitat, lawn, 4, 25
hammerknife mower, 119
hand pulling of weeds, 151
hard fescue, 19
hardiness, 207
harrowing, 69
haygrasses, 147
hazardous materials, 9
heal-all, **158**
heat islands, 8
heat, plastic grass, 23
heavy soil, 52
Hedera, 207
Helminthosporium, 199
henbit, **158**
heptachlor, 186
herbicide absorption, 151

herbicide, conditions for best performance, 151
herbicide degradation, 213
herbicide leaching, 155
herbicide longevity, 155
herbicide persistence, 213
herbicide recommendations, 178
herbicide residues, 213
herbicide safety, 177
herbicide selectivity, 153
herbicide toxicity in the ground, 155
herbicide, weed and feed, 155
herbicides, 152, 213
herbicides, contact, 153
herbicides, nonselective, 157
herbicides, persistence of, 155
herbicides, phenoxy, 156
herbicides, pre-emergence, 153
herbicides, susceptibility to, 150
herbicides, systemic, 153
Hieracium, **160**
Highland, 22, 34, 45
Highlight, 32, 33
Holcus lanatus, **171**
hormonal herbicides, 156
humus, of soil, 52
hybridization, of bluegrass, 45
hydrated lime, 114
Hydrocotyle, 96, **173**
hydrogen fluoride, 208
hydrophobic soil, 58
hygroscopic water, **54**

I

IBDU, 105, 106, 211
ice control, 212
identification of diseases, by key, 196
identification of lawngrasses, by key, 42
Imidan, 192
inbreeding, 30
independent ecosystems, 142
inorganic fertilizer, 105
insect control, 193
insect control, by birds, 187
insecticides, 11, 186, 190, 192
insecticides, systemic, 190
insect pests, controls for, 191
insects, 186
insects, foliage consumers, 187
insects, root feeders, 187
insects, sucking types, 187
insoak, of water, 58
integrated control, 10
interface, of lawn, 11

nurelle, 195
nutrient balance, 101
nutrient, charge in runoff, 8
nutrient content, grass foliage, 102
nutrient diffusion, 103
nutrient imbalances, 101
nutrient insufficiency, 99
nutrient interdependence, 101
nutrient ions, 101
nutrient minimums, 102
nutrient solubility, related to pH, 112
nutrient toxicity, 101
nutrients, contaminating, 8
nutrients, essential, 99
nutrients, fertility, 99
nutrients, in clippings, 127
nutrients, in thatch, 130
nutrients, natural sources of, 102
nutrients, trace, 100
nutsedge, 96, **169,** 175, 177, 181

O

oak-hickory climax, 24
Oaklawn, 40
Old World lawngrasses, 21
onion, wild, **171,** 175
Ophiobolus graminis, 200
ophiobolus patch, 200
orchardgrass, **169**
organic arsenicals, 135
organic content, of soil, 52
organic fertilizer, 105
organic residues, of soil, 52
organics, as soil additives, 65
overseeding, 91
overwatering, 68
oxadiazon, 154
Oxalis stricta, **167**
oxycarboxin, 204
ozone, 208

P

Pachysandra, 207
Paraguay bahiagrass, 40
paraquat, 88, 135, 152, 175, 178, 180, 184, 185
parent rock, 58
Park, 44
Paspalum dilatatum, **174**
Paspalum notatum, 18
pathways, 209
PCNB, 203
penetration, of rainfall, 57

Penncross, 34, 44
Pennfine, 36
Pennlawn, 33
Pennstar, 31
pennywort, 96, **173**
Pensacola bahiagrass, 40
percolation, of water in soil, 54
perennial, 150
perennial ryegrass, **16,** 207
perennial ryegrass, discussion of, 35
periwinkle, 207
pesticide, dosage, 144
pesticide sprays, 138
pesticides, 8, 143
pest outbreak, 145
pest resistance, 145
pH, 55, 72, 111
pH, and nutrient solubility, 112
phenoxy herbicides, 153, 156
pheromones, 186
Phleum nodosum, 21
phorate, 190
phosphatic fertilization, 72
phosphorus, 107
phosphorus diffusion, 107
phosphorus fixation, 72, 107
phosphorus, in foliage, 102
phosphorus in the soil, 209
phosphorus, need in soilbed, 72
phosphorus requirements, 107
Phytar, 135
picloram, 155
pineapple-weed, **174**
planning the lawn, 64
Plantago, 176
Plantago lanceolata, **163**
Plantago major, **162**
plantain, **162**
plantain, buckhorn, **163**
plantains, **176**
Plantvax, 201
plowing the soilbed, 69
plugging, 84
plugs, 82
Plush, 31
PMA, 177
Poa annua, 96, 177, 179
Poa nemoralis, 21
Poa pratensis, **15**
Poa trivialis, 19, **20,** 96, 207
pollution, 7, 11
polycross, 46
polycross seed, 44
polyethylene mulch, 81

starlings, 187
starting the lawn, 78
st. augustinegrass, **17**
st. augustine, discussion of, 39
Stellaria, 176
Stellaria media, **159**
Stenotaphrum secundatum, **17**
sterilants, soil, 152
sterilization failure, for disease, 195
sterilization, of soil, 70
sterilized insects, 186
stinkgrass, **171**
stolon, 22, **41**
stolonizing, 87
"stolons," 82
stoma (stomata), 93, 211
straw mulch, 79
stress, 96
strip-mining, 57
stripesmut, 202
structure, of soil, 52, 69
structures of grass, **29**
subsoil, 52
succession, direction of, 23
succession, ecological, 10
succession, in the lawn, 23
succession, stages of, 24
successional pathways, 24
sulfur, 108, 109, 200, 211
sulfur-coated urea, 106, 211
sulfur dioxide, 208, 213
Sunturf, 38
surfactant, 138, 152
survival value, 10
sweeping lawns, 136
sweet soil, 56
Sydsport, 31
synergism, 190
synergistic herbicides, 156
synthetic-organic fertilizer, 105
systemic fungicides, 195, 196
systemic herbicides, 153
systemic insecticides, 190
systemic pesticides, mode of action, 213

T

take-all root rot, 195
tall fescue, **18,** 175
tannin, 212
Taraxacum officinale, 159
Tartanturf, 22
TBZ, 203
temperature comparisons, 8

terbutol, 175, 178, 185, 214
terrazole, 204
Tersan, 202, 203
texture, of soil, 50, 51
texture, of soilbed, 69
Texturf, 38
thatch, 11, 22, 58, 127, 128
thatch accumulation, 130
thatch and earthworms, 130
thatch behavior, 129
thatch, decomposition, 130
thatch, features of, 129
thatch, fertility value, 130
thatch forming, 128
thatch, mechanical removal, 130
thiabendazole, 195
Thimet, 190
Thiodan, 192
thiophanates, 195, 203, 204
thiram, 195, 203, 204
thistle, **166**
Thuricide, 192
ticks, 187
Tifdwarf, 36, 38
Tifgreen, 38
Tiflawn, 38
Tifway, 38
tiles, for drainage, 67
tiller, 29, 137
timothy, dwarf, 21
tobacco stems, for mulch, 81
tools, garden, 133
topdressing, 82, 84, 87, 130
topsoil, 52
Touchdown, 31, 157
toxaphene, 186
toxicity, 178
toxic substances, 208
trace elements, 100, 109
tractor attachments, 137
transpiration, 93
trees, care of in lawn making, 66
tree succession, 24
Triarimol, 202
triazines, 155
Tricholoma, 199
trichlorfon, 190, 191, 192, 193
Trifolium, 96
Trimec, 156, 175, 176
Trithion, 190
Tufcote, 38
Tupersan, 178, 179
turf, artificial, 22
turf community, juvenile, 24

turf, natural compared to artificial, 23
turf pests, 145
turf retardation, 132
turf wear, 127
turfgrass cultivars, origin, 44
turfgrass diseases, 202
turfgrass habits, 24
2,4-D, 150, 153, 156, 176, 178–179, 182–184
2,4,5-T, 213
2,4,5 TP, 179
Typhula, 201

U

U-3, 38
UF (ureaformaldehyde), 105, 106
UF efficiency, 106
underground irrigation, 68
urea, 105
ureaform, 105

V

Vapam, 70, 152, 203
vapor, in soil, **54**
vegetation, native, 58
vegetative propagation, 81
velvet bentgrass, 34
velvetgrass, **171**
Veronica, 151
Veronica, 176
Veronica persica, **165**
vetch, 21
Vinca, 207
vorlex, 152, 180, 203
Vydate, 190

W

warm-season grass, 13
wasps, 4
waste water, for irrigation, 211
water, 94
water, amount used by lawn, 92
water deficit, **95**
water-holding capacity of soils, 94
water infiltration, 58
water insoak, soil, 50
water pressure, 68
water quality, 212
water surplus, **95**
watering, 92
watering apparatus, 97
watering checklist, 115
watering new seedings, 78

waterlogging, 105
wear, of turf, 127
webworm, 186, 188
webworm, moths of, 189
webworm, pupation, 189
weed competition in lawn, 148
weed control, 146, 150
weed control, annual grasses, 180
weed control, broadleaf, 180
weed control, geographical, 151
weed control, mechanical, 152
weed control recommendations, 178
weed habits, 149
weed killers, 152
weed killers, nonselective, 157
weed life cycle, 149
weed repression, 151
weed seeds, 147
weed seeds, abundance, 149
weed susceptibility, 151, 181
weeds, 10, 78, 146, 157
weeds, annual, 149
weeds, broadleaf, 153
weeds, broadleaf, susceptibility to herbicides, 184
weeds, chemical control of, 182
weeds, perennial, 149
weeds, susceptibility to herbicides, 150
weeds, worst in lawn, 175
weed-and-feed, 155
weeding lawns, 155
wetting agent, 58, 152, 210
wheatgrass, 19
wild garlic, 175
wild onion, 175
Wilmington bahiagrass, 40
winter color, 22
Wintergreen, 33
winterkill, 207
winter salting, 212
woods bluegrass, 21
wood sorrel, **167**

Y

yarrow, **166**
York rake, 69
Yorktown, 36

Z

zectran, 191, 193
zineb, 204
zoysiagrass, **17**
zoysia, discussion of, 38